TREKKING THE TAMANG HERITAGE TRAIL OF NEPAL

INCLUDES LANGTANG, HELAMBU AND GOSAINKUNDA

Alonzo Lucius Lyons

A.L.L.

ISBN-10: 1463718004

ISBN-13: 978-1463718008

LOOK FOR THESE OTHER TITLES BY ALONZO LYONS:

THE GUERRILLA TREK, *AKA, THE SHANGRILA TREK*

ANNAPURNA, SANCTUARY AND CIRCUIT

THE CHITWAN CHEPANG HILLS TRAIL

THE KATHMANDU VALLEY RIM AND BEYOND

THE INDIGENOUS PEOPLES TRAIL

THE GURUNG HERITAGE TRAIL

TREKKING NEPAL, (WITH STEPHEN BEZRUCHKA, 8TH EDITION,
   THE MOUNTAINEERS PUBLISHERS)

People, places, things and events are in constant flux in Nepal and the greater world. Therefore, the author cannot guarantee the accuracy of the information in this book. As with any activity in a foreign country, both seen and unseen risks abound. Although every effort has been made to provide valid material, safety is the reader's responsibility.

A NOTE FROM THE AUTHOR

Although changing swiftly along with the rest of the world, trekking in Nepal continues to be an experience of a lifetime. In most rural areas away from popular trails, there are few tourists, enabling more personal encounters with local residents. However, there are occasional reports of serious harm to tourists. Visitors can check with respective embassies to keep up with the latest travel precautions and advisories.

Nepal experienced an internal conflict from 1996-2006, and a peace accord was signed in 2006. Despite recent global economic upheaval, tourist arrivals are growing. The Nepal Tourism Board has initiated a **Visit Lumbini** (**birthplace** of **Prince Siddhartha Gautama** of the Shakya Clan, later known by the title of **Buddha**) **2012** campaign with the ambition of doubling the 500,000-plus annual visitors.

CONTENTS

COUNTRY BACKGROUND

Nepal is a landlocked republic that stretches from the **Mahakali River** in the west to the **Mechi River** in the east with 1050 mi (1690 km) of open border with India to the south, east and west. To the north, the mighty Himalaya serve as a buffer with China-controlled Tibet. The altitudinal range of this country is extreme, ranging from almost sea level at **Kanchan Kalan** (230 feet, 70 m) to the highest point on Earth, **Mount Everest** (29,029 feet, 8848 m).

Initially, the name Nepal denoted only the Kathmandu Valley and was associated with its original inhabitants, the Newar. *'Ne'* is derived from Tibeto-Burman meaning **livestock** and *'pala'*, Sanskrit for **guardian**. (Another suggestion is 'Ne' was a yogi who lived in the valley in ancient times.)

Nepal's three major tributary systems are fed by Himalayan snows and glaciers: the **Koshi** (east), **Kali Gandaki** (central; this river runs through the world's deepest gorge), and **Karnali** (west). The economy is based on subsistence agriculture. **Overseas remittances** are the biggest source of foreign income followed by **tourism** and **exports** (chiefly carpets, pashmina and garments).

POPULATION AND GEOGRAPHY

Nepal's population was less than **9 million** in **1950** and the 2011 census estimate is nearly **27 million** (the world's **forty-sixth** largest), with an annual growth rate of over **1.4 percent**. The country shape on a map is essentially trapezoidal, roughly 500 by 120 miles (800 by 192 km). At **58,826 mi² (147,181 km²)**, it is the world's **ninety-fifth** by area and larger than Greece but smaller than Tunisia and about the size of the state of Iowa, USA. The geography is roughly **15% mountains, 68% hills and valleys, and 17% plains** sandwiched together in three distinctive belts running lengthwise.

The northernmost belt is the Himalaya region with over 240 peaks above 6,000 m (19,685 ft), and eight of the following ten highest peaks in the world (listed highest first, **bold** indicates wholly or partially in Nepal): **Everest**, K2, **Kangchenjunga, Lhotse, Makalu, Cho-Oyu, Dhaulagiri, Manaslu**, Nanga Parbhat, **Annapurna**. The mountain region is sparsely settled by people who mostly practice Tibetan Buddhism.

The southern belt, a broad, fertile strip of jungle and farmland called the ***tarai*** *(for pronunciation of Nepali words, please see the Nepali language section)*, is an extension of the Gangetic plain of northern India, and contrasts markedly with the alpine region to the north. **50%** of Nepal's population resides in the *tarai* and they mainly practice Hinduism. Between the lowlands and alpine heights is the broad middle belt, the ***pahaaD***, with hills and fertile valleys. The *pahaaD* serves as an interface to the two extremes and inhabitants generally practice Hinduism with Buddhist, animist, and shamanic influences.

Nepal is divided into **14 zones** or *anchal*. Two are religiously named and lie in the *tarai*; Lumbini Zone is named after the birthplace of **Buddha** and Janakpur is considered to be Hindu deity Sita's birthplace and named after her father **Janak**. Two zones are named for mountains, **Sagarmatha (the Nepali word for Everest) and Dhaulagiri (a massif that includes the world's seventh highest peak)**. The remaining ten zones are named after the following rivers (listed generally from west to east): **Mahakali** (western border), **Seti, Karnali, Beri, Rapti, Gandaki, Narayanti** (formed by the joining of the Marsyangdi and Trishuli rivers near the town of Mugling), **Bagmati** (Kathmandu's zone), **Koshi** and **Mechi**. The Zones are comprised of **75 districts**. There is a strong push by certain political factions for boundaries to be re-drawn, given new names, and administered locally, rather than centrally, under a federal system of government.

BRIEF HISTORICAL SKETCH

A dense **malarial jungle** to the south and the **snowy Himalaya** to the north served as natural barriers that protected Nepal's mid-hills and valleys from invaders. Although the land's history before the 4th century remains largely undocumented, it is known that the Kathmandu Valley was ruled by the **Licchavi Dynasty** from the 4th to 9th centuries, a time when art and sculpture flourished. The next period from the 9th to 12th centuries saw a notable expansion in **Vajrayana Buddhism** but is otherwise unremarkable from a historical perspective. Hinduism became fortified as the predominant religion during the subsequent **Malla Dynasty** that ruled the valley for approximately 600 years from the 12th century to the 18th. **Western Nepal** was dominated at that time by the **Khas** people whose realm of influence extended into what are now the hill provinces of Kumaon and Garhwal in northwest India.

The area of modern day Nepal was controlled by **minor principalities** before unification in the late 18th century. The valley's Mallas, due to internecine rivalry and lack of unity, were overthrown by **Prithvi Narayan Shah**, ruler of a sovereignty in central Nepal named **Gorkha**. Shah is considered the **Father of the Nation** for politically unifying the country in the late 1760s.

A war with China from 1787-1792 began after Nepal encroached on Tibet and Sikkim and subsequently led to a defeat and an end to expansion to the north and northwest. Skirmishes with the British East India Company from 1814-1816 resulted in Nepal ceding nearly 30% of the territory held at the time (including the Garwhal, Kumaon, and Darjeeling hills regions and large areas of the *tarai*) to British-controlled India. Some of the previously held land was regained for supporting Britain during the 'Indian Mutiny' in 1857).

> **"Jai Mahakali, Ayo Gorkhali!" ("Glory to the Goddess of War, here come the Gurkhas!")** -Gurkha War Cry

The British command was so impressed with Nepalese fighting skills (led by Gorkha hills men) during clashes in the early 1880's, that they actively recruited them into their own troops. Nowadays, Nepalese make up the Brigade of Gurkhas in the British Army as well as the Gurkha Regiments of the Indian Army and serve in the Singapore Police Force as well as a special force in Brunei (additionally, the Nepalese Army has two battalions of Gurkhas).

Around 200,000 Gurkha fought for Britain during World Wars I and II, and more than 45,000 Nepalese have died in British uniform. Presently, over 3,400 Nepalese are serving in Britain's army (and 40,000 in the Indian Army).

During yearly recruiting season nearly 20,000 Nepali applicants are pared down to around 300 invitees to join the esteemed Brigade of Gurkhas. The first cut is the most challenging, a written test that reduces those eligible to under 1000. The remaining candidates are put through rigorous physical tests and medical examinations. The Maoist Party considers service by Nepalese in foreign armies as mercenary and degrading and has vowed to end recruitment. Nepal's Army has 5,000 soldiers deployed on UN peacekeeping missions.

AUTOCRATIC LEADERS

From 1846 until 1951, the country was authoritatively ruled by a succession of hereditary prime ministers of the Rana family who overmastered the monarchy. In 1854, Jang Bahadur Rana wrote the *Muluki Ain*, or legal statute that codified and thereby entrenched caste discrimination by outlining different rights and privileges according to ethnicity. During the self-serving Rana dynasty, Nepal shut itself off from outside influence with the exception of a British diplomatic residence in Kathmandu. The tyrannical oligarchy was finally overthrown in 1951 and a re-instated King Tribhuvan opened Nepal's borders to the world.

Nepal made international headlines on **May 29, 1953**, when **Tenzing Norgay** and **Edmund Hillary** become the first men to reach the summit of Mount Everest (**Junko Tabei** of Japan was the first female to summit in **1975**; Nepal's first female, **Pasang Lhamu Sherpa**, achieved the feat in 1993). The Dalai and Panchen Lamas attended the ceremony for the accession to the throne of King Mahendra in 1955 and a brief attempt at democracy followed until 1960. The new system was not to the king's liking and he dissolved the nascent government and outlawed political parties; subsequently, parties went underground while the country was ruled by a hierarchical system of *Panchayat*, or local councils, with absolute power vested in the king and a coterie of royalists including the king's personally appointed prime minister.

A *Nayaa* **(New)** *Muluki Ain* was written in **1964** that stated that **superiority cannot be claimed based on race, creed or caste**, but the statute did little to nothing to change actual circumstances. To this day, there is roughly a 40% difference in literacy between the Brahmins and the so-called 'lowest' caste as well as a lifespan difference that favors Brahmins by 10 years. In fact, it wasn't until the year 2000 that the *kamaiya* system of bonded labor was formally banned, officially ending slavery for many, although bonded labor largely continues with exploited children. According to a National Labor Survey report in 2008 by Nepal's Ministry of Labor and Transport, there are **2.14 million child laborers** in Nepal. Nearly **28%** of these children are **5-9 years old** and **51%** are **10-14**.

Nepal held a national referendum in 1980 following student protests in 1979; the vote was to ascertain a consensus on continuing with the *Panchayat* system (with needed reforms), or introducing a multi-party system. The *Panchayat* system won by a slim margin amidst charges of vote rigging. However, in early 1990, there was again a widespread outcry for democracy, and a massive *Jana Andolan*, 'people's movement', with protests, demonstrations and marches led to the relatively peaceful overthrow of royal primacy. Political parties re-emerged and a new constitution was set forth with a constitutional monarch and power vested in a popularly elected parliament. The newly formed system was rife with political maneuvering and corruption. Since then, there has not been a government that has survived more than two years.

Among the political parties that re-surfaced after the *Jana Andolan* were several variations of communism. One of these groups, the **Maoists**, was barred by a court ruling from the electoral process. In response, they rebelled against the electoral system as well as ruling class and police harassment, especially in Rolpa and Rukum districts, and declared a People's War in 1996. The Maoists managed to gain local support in the west, and the insurrection spread throughout the country.

The circumstances of the insurgency took a dramatic change following the **Royal Massacre** of June of **2001** when King Birendra and 12 members of his family were killed. The poly-regicide at the palace was not without intrigue. Dubiously, the crown-prince perpetrated the slaughter singlehandedly. Suspicions abound that the king's nephew, present at the scene but unharmed and his father, the king's younger brother, were involved. With a pathway to the throne cleared, the slain king's brother was enthroned.

The new crowned king authorized the Royal Nepal Army to pursue the Maoists, a move that his brother had shunned as the royalists and the Maoists shared a implicit truce and common opposition to the ruling government. King Gyanendra's decision changed the political landscape and the Maoists in turn began targeting the army. The unpopularity of the new monarch only served to strengthen his opponents, and their position with the disenfranchised population was fortified.

In late 2005, the Maoists came to the table and joined a coalition of seven leading parties to oppose the king after he attempted to re-assert royal rule by dissolving parliament. Widespread protests began in early 2006. During this second people's movement, *Jana Andolan II*, hundreds of thousands of people marched in Kathmandu defying martial law. The king capitulated, which eventually led to a formal **dismantling of the 239 year old monarchy and an end to the ten-year civil war.**

Nationwide elections were held at the beginning of 2008. The Maoists unexpectedly won the highest number of parliamentary seats. The new government formally declared Nepal a secular, federal, democratic republic in May 2008 with none other than the leader of the Maoists, Pushpa Kamal Dahal, a former schoolteacher, nicknamed *Prachanda* "fierce" (*Prachanda* has a double connotation and can mean "shining", depending on context; ***Prachanda Path***, is comparable to Peru's ***Sendero Luminoso*** or **Shining Path** movement from which the Maoists draw inspiration), as the first Prime Minister and leader of the republic. Since that brief period of extraordinary cooperation, the political camps quickly regressed to spiteful bickering and soliciting of adversaries for power swaps. *Prachanda* resigned in May 2009 following a disagreement with the president over control of the military, and a tenuous coalition government was formed with the Maoists in opposition and stalemate ensued.

Stagnation has resulted despite a mandate for the constituent assembly, elected in 2008, to complete a peace process that had been agreed to by the coalition including a decision on integration of 19,000 Maoist soldiers stationed in UN-supervised cantonments. After 7 months under caretaker government, on February 3rd, 2011, a new prime minister was elected through a joint power sharing deal between the Maoists and the United Marxist-Leninists (UML), seemingly giving Nepal's communist government a second wind. The new administration received little support from other parties, including the Nepali Congress, which ranks second in amount of parliamentary seats (110 out of 601). The Nepali Congress decided to sit in opposition to the communist coalition until they were invited into the power sharing rotation.

The assembly was to write the republic's constitution within a two-year deadline but failed, leading to a last-hour extension on May 28, 2010, of the assembly's term by a year and the deadline has since been extended three times. Although in the spring of 2008, the birth of the republic was celebrated across the land. Since then, jubilation has turned into a four-year, post-partum hangover as the public has waited in vain for a charter constitution with the final deadline, May 27th, 2012, come and gone.

As political feuding continues to inhibit progress, easy solutions are not availing themselves. In much of the country outside of Kathmandu, particularly in the *tarai*, systemic corruption and the prolonged weakness and even absence of government has led to deterioration of the rule of law. A new constitution may set the agenda for a more functional government and prosperous Nepal, notwithstanding a historical track record that suggests otherwise. All the while, tourists continue to arrive to enjoy the natural splendor of the Himalaya and a heartfelt reception from the people of Nepal.

NEPALI DIASPORA

The decade-long conflict, endemic political turmoil, and a dearth of jobs have compelled many Nepalese to take great risks to venture abroad in search of employment. Formerly, India was the destination of choice. Nowadays, Nepalese are traveling farther afield, and over 2 million Nepalese work in over forty foreign countries other than India. Nearly 300,000 Nepali workers left home for foreign employment in 2010. Qatar, Malaysia, the United Arab Emirates (UAE) and Saudi Arabia receive more than 90 percent of Nepal's migrant workers. (Alarmingly, Qatar, Malaysia and Saudi Arabia had the lowest designation in the U.S. State Department's 2009 report on human trafficking and are among countries that do not follow even minimum standards for opposing trafficking. The United Arab Emirates fared only slightly better. 2011's report had Saudia Arabia stagnating in the lowest tier but saw improvements for the other three although Qatar and Malaysia are on a watchlist for severe violations.

Many jobs are fraught with danger and involve hard physical labor at factories and construction sites or as domestic help. With a weak home government and virtually no representation, Nepalis are exploited, and this starts with recruiting agencies back home. Stories abound of people mortgaging family property against exorbitant recruiting fees, only to find on arrival to a foreign land that conditions are entirely different than promised. Passports are sometimes held captive as workers endure inhumane, long hours in stressful jobs with low wages and little to no rights. **Amnesty International's "False Promises: Exploitation and Forced Labor of Nepali Migrant Workers"** reports that 90% of interviewed returnees and prospective migrant workers felt deceived by recruitment agencies and brokers on basic fundamentals of their contract.

Recruiting agencies typically take 100,000 NRS in fees from each applicant, three times the average annual income for Nepal in 2010. It might take years of labor just to pay back placement companies. In 2001 it was estimated that twelve Nepalese were dying every month in Middle Eastern countries due to poor work conditions and mistreatment. In 2012, Nepal's Ministry of Foreign Affairs estimated that 25-30 Nepalies die every month in Saudi Arabia alone, most deaths attributed to workplace accidents, exposure to an extreme climate, suicide and murder. Seventy-five percent of the recruiting agencies in Kathmandu were damaged in riots in 2004 following the deaths of twelve Nepalese migrant workers in Iraq. In Malaysia, industrial accidents killed fifty-two Nepalese in 2005, fifty-eight in 2006, and fifty-nine in 2007, and work-site injuries harmed many more; recourse in compensation is not available to widowed families or injured workers. It is estimated that a third of migrant workers are women, many unregistered and thus, even more susceptible to mistreatment.

Nevertheless, Nepalese are eager to work abroad due to the dismal employment scene in Nepal. Until recently, most of these workers sent remittances home via the age-old *hawala* or *hundi* system of money brokers that was time-consuming, charged a high commission, and relied on honor rather than receipts. Nowadays, bank-to-bank transfers and remittance companies are making life at least a little easier for some of the Nepali diaspora. However, unskilled workers are still, by and large, sending money home through unofficial channels.

In 2004, after a steady rise, **overseas remittances** surpassed both **tourism** and **exports combined** as Nepal's biggest source of foreign income. A Nepalese network, **www.helpnepal.net** , has been set up to help connect those living abroad, and together this group has been donating funds for Nepal-based development projects.

The Desert Eats Us is a documentary film by Kesang Tseten about Nepali migrant workers in the Gulf. π

CHALLENGES OF THE FUTURE

The environmental challenges facing the world are magnified in developing nations and Nepal is no exception. An abundance of glaciers, rivers, and forests make the region particularly susceptible to distortions in climate, and although far from clear, some data indicate that the Himalaya might be warming at a pronounced rate. The fertile Indo-Gangetic plain, from areas of Pakistan in the west across southern Nepal and northern India to Bangladesh, is a densely populated area and home to one-ninth of the world's population. Residents of this plain and the Tibetan plateau rely on Himalayan runoff for survival. Obviously, weather imbalances can have dire consequences for subsistence farmers; recently, the **earth's thermostat seems to have lost its bearings** and the region has seen disruption in critical monsoon timings and a marked retreat of some glaciers. With the majority of the Nepal's people farming, decreasing food security is a concern, particularly in the far west due to the former insurgency and prolonged drought and unusual rainfall patterns that have disturbed growing seasons.

CORRUPTION

As well as environmental challenges, mercurial political changes in the last fifteen years add to the complexity. With rich resources of willing, able, and talented people, Nepal is ascending the development summit for which it is aiming. At the same time, it has a long way to go. Although improving on many fronts, Nepal ranked a miserable **154**[th] in the watchdog group **Transparency International's 2010 Corruption Perception Index** (on par with **Zimbabwe**, yet outranked by the likes of **Syria**, 129th, and **Pakistan**, 134th) and poor governance has and continues to severely impede development. Leaders typically give patronage to their stooges rather than qualified candidates and these coveted positions in government are then exploited for profit.

Political cliques spend valuable time and effort currying favor for personal advantage, and venality stifles most areas of progress and taints the inordinate amount of financial 'aid' that pours in every year. (The World Bank committed a monstrous $782 million to Nepal for 2010 and 2011, with nearly 45 percent grants and the rest loans.) **Despite little to show for the money and effort and even negative consequences, foreign 'aid' agencies somehow justify continued, massive funding while resources evaporate from under their noses.** (However, in this day and age of widespread availability and sharing of information, it is perhaps becoming more difficult to conceal misdeeds. Technological advances might help to expose deficiencies in governance and hopefully open up the system to transparency and improvements.)

NGOS, INGOS AND GIVING

A glut of non-government organizations (NGOs), and international non-government organizations (INGOs) operate in **aid-ridden** Nepal. 27,000 NGOs and 223 INGOs were registered in 2010 (with an equal number of unregistered NGOs). With droves of agencies and legions of manpower devoted to development, you might imagine there would be vibrant evidence of it happening. In actuality, the deluge and subsequent leakage of money with a despairing lack of something to show for it, along with conspicuous, petrol-guzzling, decaled vehicles and plush offices, fosters an unhealthy resentment in much of the population. The following sobering assessment, *Victims of Kindness*, is provided by Declan Murphy, a grassroots social worker and is based on longtime interactions with Kathmandu's street kids. His organization, **www.just-one.org**, helps abused and disadvantaged children to rehabilitate and access educational opportunities. His discernment of the unexpected effects of even the best of intentions provides telling insight into the nature of the donor business in Nepal and its consequences. Extrapolate the problems mentioned below to the foreign 'assistance' paradigm for an idea of the mixed effects of hundreds of millions of dollars of annual funds and mismanaged projects and the donor mentality it foments.

VICTIMS OF KINDNESS
by Declan Murphy, Founder, www.just-one.org

Initially, it may be difficult to comprehend, but the last thing street children need are more "random-acts-of-kindness" by well-meaning individuals. These acts have unwittingly contributed to children choosing to remain on the street in vulnerable circumstances. For anyone wishing to truly help them, the solution is simple yet incredibly difficult to properly explain or practice: "Do nothing!" Unfortunately, this advice is all too often ignored, as it goes against the grain of human nature.

At first look, doing nothing does little to ease feelings of helplessness when witnessing firsthand the inequality and injustice of crushing poverty, and herein lies the biggest problem. The primary beneficiary of the gift-giving (be it a few rupees, a piece of fruit, an unfinished sandwich, or even a moment of friendship) is generally the donor, whose guilt is assuaged. These acts of compassion turn out to be problematic as the child's persistent attempts are rewarded and he or she is further encouraged to continue begging rather than seek the widely accessible assistance of numerous local organizations which exist to provide longer-term support to these children. The casual donor's short-term gifts only compete with these organizations' long-term solutions. In a young mind, the organizations' facilities and care program pale in comparison to the boundless excitement of the streets including gifts, especially money which is often distressingly used to procure glue that is inhaled for intoxicating effects.

The child's guardians too, can become insidiously aware of the child's earning potential and often promote what becomes a lucrative street-side drama performed for an ever-revolving audience of tourists. More worrying is that these children also learn the benefits of being friendly with strangers—the dangers of which often only become apparent to some of the children when it's already too late.

The desire to help is understandable and truly commendable, but the reality of the situation is such that, more often than not, it's more helpful to do nothing and simply enjoy your time in a troubled yet amazingly beautiful county of contrasts. It should never be forgotten that by being a tourist in Nepal, you already contribute in a real and meaningful way to one of the country's most valuable sources of income, tourism. An almost endless list of service providers, both seen and unseen, *will* benefit directly from your time in Nepal. So, please, take a moment to contemplate what you *are* already doing just by being in Nepal, and consider the result of attempting to satisfy that nagging feeling of needing to do more.π

If the desire to donate is irresistible, the following from **The Center for Responsible Travel www.responsibletravel.org** provides valuable guidelines for those wishing to make a difference while traveling:

> **Travelers' desire to help, interact, and learn from those they meet during their holiday is clearly positive. However, there are sometimes unintended consequences from these good intentions. Misguided contributions can perpetuate cycles of dependency, cause corruption, burden communities with unwanted or inappropriate donations, and require recipients to spend time and resources to handle 'gifts' they didn't request or cannot use...when, how, and what to contribute needs to be decided by the host community, not the tourist or the tourism company.**

PRACTICALITIES

TIME, DATE AND ELECTRICITY

Nepal is **five and three-quarters hours** ahead of Greenwich Mean Time (**GMT**) and Coordinated Universal Time (UCT) whereas New York City, Eastern Standard Time (EST) is five hours behind GMT (four hours during Daylight Savings Time, ie, from the second Sunday in March until the first Sunday of November). If it is **12:45 PM in Nepal**, then on the **East Coast of the United States it is 2 AM** (3 AM during Daylight Savings Time), **7 AM in London**, and **6 PM in Tokyo**.

Nepal follows **two calendars**, both the **solar-based Gregorian** calendar and the **lunisolar Bikram Samvat** (BS) calendar which is roughly fifty-six years, eight months, and fifteen days ahead of the Gregorian calendar. For example, the year 2012 CE corresponds to 2068– 69 BS (CE or Common Era, is a secular designation identical in numbering of years to AD, Anno Domini. CE can also be thought of as "Current Era" or "Christian Era". BCE refers to Before the Common Era and is identical to BC in the Anno Domini form). The Bikram Samvat calendar begins at the start of the solar new year in mid-April. The advent of this calendar is said to mark the victory of an emperor in India over invaders in 56 BCE and was initiated then as the beginning of a new era. Nepal adopted this calendar during the reign of the Rana family dynasty, domineering oligarchs who ran the country from the mid-1800s until 1951.

Electricity averages **220 volts/50 cycles** in Nepal and most sockets are fitted for two or three-pronged, rounded pins. Rural Nepal is becoming increasingly electirifed by localized hydropower and small solar panels.

VISA

15, 30 and **90 day visas** are issued on arrival at entry points to Nepal. The costs are amended frequently; as of February 2012 a fifteen-day visa was $25 USD payable in Nepalese rupees, U.S. dollars, or other convertible currency; $40 USD for a thirty-day visa; and $100 USD for a ninety-day visa. Visas can also be obtained from one of the Nepali Embassies and Consular Services in thirty-seven countries throughout the world. A passport-sized photograph is necessary, and travelers should bring a dozen for use in formalities including permits to trekking areas. Passport photos can be obtained at shops in Kathmandu.

Indians do not need a visa, and a thirty-day *gratis* visa is available for citizens of the other South Asian Association for Regional Cooperation (SAARC) bloc countries of Bangladesh, Bhutan, the Maldives, Pakistan, and Sri Lanka, excepting Afghanistan. Nationals of the following countries are not granted visas on arrival: Afghanistan, Cameroon, Ethiopia, Ghana, Iraq, Liberia, Nigeria, Palestine, Somalia, Swaziland and Zimbabwe.

VISA EXTENSIONS

Although the initial entry visa is valid for 15, 30, or 90 days, extensions of 15 days to two months are granted at the Central Immigration Office of the Home Ministry (www.immi.gov.np), in **Kalikastan, Kathmandu** (north of the compound that houses parliament, Singha Durbar). To get to the Immigration Department, head east along Pradarshaan Marg (also known as Exhibition Road), just down (south) from Ratna Park and the Old Bus Park (also known as City Bus Park) and east of the large parade ground and open space known as Tundikhel. Follow Pradarshaan Marg (Exhibition Road) for .3 miles (.5 km) or just over five minutes to Ram Shah Path (passing Kathmandu Fun Park on the right hand side along the way). Cross Ram Shah Path and head right or south (to the left or north is **Putali Sadak, well-known computer arcade and site of Nepal's bourse**). In less than a minute, head left (east) at the first road that you come to, Tankaprasad Gumti Sadak (also known as Anam Nagar Road). Cross New Plaza Marg road and in two minutes from Ram Shah Path, head left at a roundabout on a street named Adhikaari Galli. The Immigration Department is less than two minutes up on the right side. The cost is **$2 USD per day** with a **minimum** of **15 days** ($30 USD). Hovering touts will usually solicit you, often subtly, and as if authorized staff.

Sometimes officials require U.S. dollars and sometimes rupees, usually depending on which is stronger at the time, and do not expect a good exchange rate. Visa extensions are also granted at the Immigration Department office in Pokhara near Ratna Chowk in the southern area of town, west of the airport.

The Immigration Department and other government offices are closed on Saturdays (however, during high season, they might be open to process visas from 11 AM to 1 PM on Saturdays) and sometimes Sundays and on other frequent holidays. Otherwise, hours are 10 AM to 4 PM (Friday, 10 AM to 3 PM) but not strictly followed. Applications are processed the same day and can be submitted until 3 PM (1 PM on Friday) and picked up before closing. During less busy times, you may be able to get everything processed in a single visit, that is, without having to return later in the day; sometimes (unofficial) extra fees are requested to 'expedite' processing. Border crossings are open seven days a week and applications are processed relatively quickly, overstays notwithstanding.

The **maximum limit** for a stay in Nepal on a tourist visa is **150 days per calendar year**; however, the last 30-day extension (that is, from days 120 to 150) might require presenting an airline ticket with a confirmed departure date within the 150-day time limit. There are fines and penalties for overstaying a visa, roughly $30 USD (equivalent to a 15 day visa, the minimum visa) plus an additional penalty fee of $3 USD per day of overstay and sometimes a discretionary fine as well) for overstays up to two weeks. That is, overstays of two weeks or less can be processed at the airport or land exit point upon emigration. Overstays longer than 15 days risk detention and fees of $5 USD per day of overstay and up to a 50,000 NRS penalty (most foreigners at Kathmandu Central Jail are incarcerated for drug or visa violations).

ENTRY POINTS

The common **eight entry points** are (1) Kathmandu, for those arriving by air; (2) Kodari, along the Nepal–Tibet border; (3) **Birgunj** across from **Raxaul**, India, along the main road from India to Kathmandu; and (4) **Belahia** across from **Sunauli**, India, near the town of Bhairawa on the route from India to Pokhara and close to **Lumbini, birthplace of Buddha)**. Other border points with India, less used by tourists, are (5) Kakarbhitta on the far eastern border with India, (6) Nepalganj and (7) DhangaDi in the far west, and (8) Gaddachauki (Mahendranagar) along the far western border with India. Bus service is available on the main roads linking the entry points.

CUSTOMS

Travelers coming by private vehicle need a *carnet de passage*. Otherwise, a daily fee is charged with a maximum of one month allowed in-country for foreign-registered (including India) motorcycles and other vehicles.

Bringing extensive electronic equipment through customs in Nepal can be precarious if discovered, especially if you have more than one item per category. You may be asked to pay fees and to give assurance that you will take the items with you on departure.

Indian Embassy www.indianembassy.org.np

Many tourists may need to avail themselves of the visa services of the Indian Embassy. It is located on Kapurdhara Marg road in the Lainchaur area of Kathmandu, just down from the British Embassy and the CIWEC Travel Medicine and Dental Center. The Indian Embassy Service Centre is adjacent to the Indian Embassy itself and has service hours of 9:30 AM to 12:00 PM.

Embassy of the People's Republic of China http://np.chineseembassy.org/eng/

The consular section of the Chinese embassy is located in Hattisar, Kathmandu. Applications for a visa can be made from 9:30 AM to 11:30 AM Monday, Wednesday and Friday. Fee payment and collection of visa is from 2:30 PM to 4:30 PM Monday, Wednesday and Friday. Telephone, (01) 4440286, (01) 4425520, or (01) 4411740.

EMBASSY REGISTRATION

It is advisable to register with your country's embassy or consulate when you arrive in Nepal to provide contacts for both emergencies in Nepal and emergencies at home. Let the embassy officers know your dates and itinerary, and a contact should they need to follow up. Often registration can be done online and also for free at the Kathmandu Environmental Education Project office (KEEP) in the Kesar Mahal section of Thamel, as well as the Himalayan Rescue Association (HRA). HRA has a second-floor office in the Sagarmatha Bazaar complex in the center of Thamel along Mandala Street, one of Nepal's few "walking streets" (no vehicles allowed). Additionally, a lecture on altitude is available at HRA. The branch in Thamel is often closed during the slow season.

MONEY

Individual trekkers should take small denominations on the trails for convenience, including 10-, 20-, 50- and 100-rupee (*rupiyAA*) notes. Rural shopkeepers may not be readily capable of handling large notes. The Nepalese Rupee (NRS) is pegged to the Indian Rupee (INR): 100 INR equals 160 NRS. The exchange rate in June 2012 for other major currencies is 84 NRS per 1 US Dollar (USD), 130 NRS per British Pound (GBP), 103 NRS per Euro and 97 NRS per 100 Japanese Yen.

There are many ATMs and foreign exchange stalls in Kathmandu and Pokhara, however, they often limit the amount of cash retrievable to 10,000 NRS (under $150 USD), and therefore it might be comparably better to have cash to avoid successive ATM charges. There are now even cash dispensers along the popular routes in remote places such as Jomsom and Namche Bazaar, but do not rely on it as machines are often out of service. You can get advances on credit cards, too, for an exorbitant fee.

While banks have branches in most of the district centers and a few other towns, exchanging foreign currency at rural locales will be time-consuming and doubtful. Hard currency is necessary for purchasing air tickets, as well as for paying for trekking permits to certain areas. U.S. dollars may be handy if your trekking route is near an airstrip and you decide to fly out unexpectedly. Bring at least some cash and traveler's checks to Nepal, especially if not trekking with a foreign-based agency. Even if everything has been arranged by a prepaid trekking company, hard currency might be needed for tips to porters, kitchen staff, and guides.

COMMUNICATIONS

Nepal's country telephone code is 977, with city codes of 01 for Kathmandu and 061 for Pokhara (you might have to eliminate the zero depending on from where you are calling). When calling home, keep in mind that Nepal is five-and-three-quarters hours ahead of GMT/UCT. Internet cafes abound in Kathmandu and Pokhara for sending and receiving electronic mail.

Mobile Phones Mobile phones in Nepal use a Subscriber Identity Module (SIM) card. The SIM card is basically a memory chip inserted into a phone and can be transferred between phones. SIM cards may be purchased at the sales offices of service providers and require an original passport as well as a photocopy of both the passport and visa for Nepal. A company is now offering SIM cards at the international airport arrival area. The Global System for Mobile Communication (GSM) network and the Code Division Multiple Access (CDMA) network are both in operation in Nepal. The best coverage for remote areas may be the CDMA network.

Internet Internet access is available for laptops from mobile phone service providers via pen drive-sized data card devices. The devices operate through a USB port and fees depend on MB of usage. Internet cafes abound in Kathmandu and Pokhara for sending and receiving electronic mail. Occasionally, internet shops are encountered along trekking routes, although connections in remote places can be tortuously slow and unreliable.

Post Office Kathmandu's main post office is in Sundhara, to the west and across the road from Tundikhel Parade Ground near Bhimsen Tower (also known as *Dharahara*). Hours are 10 AM–4 PM, closed Saturday. For receiving mail, you might try the following general address (keep in mind that an import duty will likely be assessed and there are occasional reports of pilfering):

Post Restante, Kathmandu General Post Office, Kathmandu, Nepal

Postage rates from Nepal are calculated according to the following regions: **1)** SAARC countries (Afghanistan, Bangladesh, Bhutan, India, the Maldives, Pakistan, and Sri Lanka), **2)** Asia (not including SAARC countries, South Korea and Japan), **3)** Europe, South Korea and Japan, **4)** the Americas, Australia and New Zealand. As of February 2012, Postcard and letter (up to .7 ounces or 20 grams) rates by region are respectively the following:

1) 15 NRS/18 NRS, **2)** 22 NRS/30 NRS, **3)** 25 NRS/35 NRS,
4) 30 NRS/40 NRS

TRANSPORTATION

BUSES, TRUCKS, AND CARS

Vehicle transportation outside of Kathmandu valley is usually time-consuming and might entail most of a day. Consider hiring a **private vehicle** for greater comfort and speed. Trekking agencies can help with arrangements and provide pickup services, too. **Tourist Bus tickets** can be purchased from travel and trekking agencies, and the buses often leave from Kantipath Road, five minutes down (south) from Thamel's Tridevi Marg road and other convenient sites. To find public buses, go to the following bus parks in Kathmandu: the Old Bus Park (also known as City Bus Park or Ratna Bus Park) for Sundarijal, Jiri and Dhunge, and Balaju Bus Park (aka, *Nayaa Bas Park* or New Bus Park) for Dhunche, Hugdi Bazaar, Syabrubensi, Dumre and Pokhara.

Purchase the ticket a day or more early, but often seats can be had on the same day, too. By purchasing a ticket early, you can have a better selection of seats. Toward the front of the vehicle is usually preferred for a smoother ride. On the day of departure, arrive early enough to find the correct bus and be prepared for contingencies. Same day buses and mini-vans can also be found at an intersection or *chowk* along the west side of Kathmandu's Ring Road named Kalanki. **Kalanki Chowk** is at a crossroads for vehicles departing the valley via the Thangkot escarpment; all transport vehicles heading out of the Kathmandu valley to the east, west, and south use this west exit route except those going north, eg, to Tibet at Kodari and Jiri in the Everest area. This may change with construction of highways heading directly south and east from Kathmandu, and the one to eastern Nepal is nearing completion.

Mini-vans are more expensive and faster. People prone to motion sickness are advised to use a bus rather than mini-van because the larger buses usually give a *relatively* smoother ride compared to the stop-and-go lurching of mini-vans, although both can be challenging. Local buses are crammed with people, often smoking is allowed and goats, chickens, and luggage sometimes share the limited space. Riding on top of buses is currently prohibited within the Kathmandu Valley and when approaching police check posts and can be particularly dangerous due to low hanging electric wires and tree branches. Night travel in general is not recommended for safety and comfort. Bring ear plugs for blaring stereos.

At all times keep your arms and head inside the vehicle and not hanging out a window. Roads are narrow and the passing of other vehicles and objects can be harrowingly close. While traveling, be aware that packs and luggage left unattended such as on tops of buses might be targeted by thieves. Locks are useful and it is best to keep easily removed items deep inside a bag. During a bus stop, it is safest to bring carry-on items with you, out of the vehicle. Make copies of your passport and visa and other valuable documents should you have the displeasure of needing replacements.

AIR TRAVEL

Flights are arranged in Kathmandu through travel agents or offices of the airlines operating in Nepal. Trekking and travel agencies in Kathmandu can take care of domestic and international flights. Checked baggage allowance is usually limited to 15 kg (33 pounds) per person with about half of that for carry on items. Sometimes everything, including carry-on luggage, is weighed, especially on flights to high-altitude areas.

USEFUL WEBSITES

The following sites may be useful for general as well as trekking information: **www.welcomenepal.com, www.trekinfo.com , www.info-nepal.com, www.nepal.panda.org, www.yetizone.com, www.nepalmountaineering.org, www.taan.org.np, www.ChangingNepal.org.np, www.himalayanmentor.com, www.trailrunningnepal.org, www.annapurna100.com, www.oceannepal.org, www.activenepal.wordpress.com.**

Himalayanists may find interest in the website of *Himalaya, the Journal of the Association for Nepal and Himalayan Studies,* at **http://digitalcommons.macalester.edu/himalaya/** .

Additionally, a remarkable aerial view of the Himalayan Range has been mapped out as a *Himalaya Atlas of Aerial Panoramas, Volume I,* available at **http://130.166.124.2/himalaya_atlas1/**.

RELIGION AND FESTIVALS

Religion is an integral part of Nepali customs and lifestyle. Religious practices include an extensive range of beliefs and rituals with considerable influence on daily routine. Hinduism prevails from the southern plains, home to 50% of the population, up through the mid hills where it blends with Buddhism and both are interwoven with animism and shamanism. As elevation is gained, Vajarayana Buddhism becomes predominant. Only a small percentage of Nepalese are **Muslim, or Musalmaan**, and most live in the lowland *tarai*. Even fewer are **Christians** although inroads have recently been made by proselytizing missionaries and the number of converts is rising.

Kathmandu defies classification with a hearty fusion of Hinduism, Tantric Buddhism and animism, often inseparably intertwined. Occasionally, the same icon at a temple might have different names according to visitors' convictions.

HINDUISM

Hinduism distinguished itself from Vedic rites and rituals around the **6th Century BCE** when followers started to question the meaning behind priestly ceremonies. The theme began shifting away from formalities, sacrificial offerings and incantations towards **inquiry, ethics** and **personal experience.**

Hindus generally believe in the existence of *atma* or **soul** with an aim to manifest or realize the divine nature of the soul. This occurs through *moksha,* or liberation, from *Samsara*, striven for in many ways. *Samsara* is the relentless flow of change exemplified by birth, death and rebirth. An integral component of this continual rotation is *karma* (action), simply, current circumstances are conditioned by previous actions. Rather than a higher being meting out punishment and reward, *karma* might be considered a universal principle likened to Newton's 3rd Law of Motion, "To every action there is always an equal and opposite reaction".

The perpetuation of the karmic cycle is caused by ignorance which imbues *Maya*, **the world of illusion,** with unending variation. Liberation is founded on the realization that the soul's core (*atma*) and Ultimate Truth (*Brahma*) are not different from each other and their essence is absolute or immutable. The wisdom that leads to this understanding is gained through various disciplines and devotion to personal gods, representations of the divine.

The fundamental texts of Hinduism include the ancient Vedas and the Upanishads as well as two beloved epics: the *Ramayana* which has **Rama**, an avatar of **Vishnu**, as the hero, and the *Mahabharata* which includes the *Bhagavad Gita* ("Song of God") where **Krishna**, another avatar of **Vishnu**, is the protagonist. The myriad divinities (Shiva alone has 1,008 manifestations) are said to be archetypal mirrors of the intricacies of human behavior and psychology.

HINDUISM IN NEPAL

Temples and shrines are common in Nepal in rural villages and at nearly every turn in urban areas. Most dwellings across the land have household shrines dedicated to a personal deity that receive daily attention. Nonetheless, the majority of Nepal's Hindus do not adhere to formal dogma or a systematic set of beliefs.

Although practices are diverse, devotion to deities usually plays a large role for most practitioners. In general, most Hindus believe that a person's current circumstances are preconditioned by former lives. People who perform well the prescribed duties of this life pave the way for favorable circumstances of a next incarnation. With regard to caste, an individual who aspires to rebirth in a higher caste must live a proper life in his or her present caste.

There was a time when caste was not designated by birth. Social assignment was according to tendencies and talents a person developed through choice and predilection. Persons were then grouped according to the path that a person selected. However, that era is far gone and the domain of caste has long since been determined by a person's pedigree.

Caste protocol was codified as law in Nepal in the ***Muluki Ain*** of 1854. Although this law has been repealed, it still influences behavior. Moreover, the view that a person's circumstances are pre-determined and ineluctable is cited as an impediment to development. In other words, because of a belief in pre-destiny, people are more inclined to accept unfavorable circumstances rather than strive to improve them.

HINDU FESTIVALS OF NEPAL

The observances listed below follow the **lunar cycle** and therefore, have **no fixed yearly date** but are determined by monthly phases of the moon.

Magh Sankranti (official government holiday)
mid-January, the first day of the Nepali month of Magh

Winter's ending is heralded and the sun is honored as it continues approaching northward from the southern hemisphere. Sankranti means '**sacred transition**' and people celebrate by taking ritual baths in rivers throughout the country. **Devghat,** just north of the city of Naryanghat where the Kali Gandaki and Narayani rivers flow together, sees some of the largest crowds. Patan's **Sankhamulghat**, along the banks of the Bagmati River is Kathmandu Valley's focal point for ablutions. Due to pollution of the Bagmati, most participants nowadays sprinkle a little water on themselves rather than fully submerging.

Sweets made of sesame and ***jaggari*** (unrefined brown sugar) are popular on this day, as is a dish named ***kichari*** (rice and lentil mixture) and foods with **ghee**, **molasses**, and **yam**.

17

Tharu people celebrate this day as their new year with feasts, traditional attire, song and dance.

Basanta (Shree) Panchami
January/Feburary

The birthday of **Saraswati, Goddess of Education and Wisdom**. This day is especially celebrated by students; they make a point to bathe, wear new clothes and pay respect at a Saraswati Temple. Parents will escort toddlers to a shrine to have them write requests in chalk on temple walls requesting Saraswati's blessings. On this day, spring's arrival is foretold at Kathmandu's Hanuman Dhoka (and Vajrayana Buddhists take occasion to honor Manjushri, Slayer of Ignorance).

Shiva Ratri
New moon in February/March

A night consecrated to Shiva and celebrated the **night before and day of the new moon in February/March** with activities a few days before as well. All-night vigils with sacred bonfires are held at Shiva shrines, and the largest take place at the **World Heritage Site of Pashupatinath Temple**, which lies along the banks of the **Bagmati River** in eastern Kathmandu. **Pashupati** is actually another manifestation of **Shiva** considered the **"protector of animals"**. Shaivites and onlookers crowd into the Pashupatinath grounds where a hearty mix of Brahman priests, ash-smeared yogis, wandering ascetics, beggars, vendors, and sightseers mingle. *Rudraaksha* **(seeds of *Eleocarpus ganitrus*)**, worn by many followers, are a sign of respect to Shiva.

Ardent Hindus consider it auspicious to visit Pashupatinath Temple at some point during the festival, and pilgrims travel from afar to take place in the rituals, which include fasting, singing, tabla and sitar music, praying, chanting, reciting of holy text, and meditating, (along with conspicuous consumption of *bhang*, aka, cannabis, which is overlooked during this devotional time).

Although **Pashupatinath** is the focal point in Kathmandu, celebrations take place throughout the valley and country. Devotees around Nepal and India enjoy *prasad*, an offering of food that has been blessed and pay homage to Shiva by building sacred bonfires and holding vigils on this night.

*Holi (*also known as *Fagun Purnimaa)*
February/March

Countrywide trench warfare with water balloons. The festival heralds the arrival of spring and legendary defeat of demoness Holika by Vishnu. Happy Holi or holy hell? Be thee fairly warned, exuberant groups of young people take over and roam about throwing water and brightly colored powder on everybody and bucketfuls of water and water balloons are launched from balconies above the streets.

Being feted with water and colored powder is meant to be an honor. Enjoy the fun or hideaway indoors until it's over. If you join the raucous free-for-all, wear clothes that can be ruined by color stains and leave valuables in your room or cover them in plastic to keep them from being soaked. The commotion lasts only a day, whereas India undergoes a merciless multi-day event.

GhoRe Jatra
March/April

Originally a Newari event centered around Kathmandu's Bhadrakali and Kankeshwari temples, it now showcases a military pageant with horse racing at Tundikhel Parade Ground. According to legend, the pounding of hooves keep the demonic fiend Gurumpa hidden underground for another year. Other activities at Tundikhel include mounted mock warfare and acrobatics on horseback.

Chaite Dasai
March/April

Dasai is celebrated biannually. This much smaller version of the 10-day fall affair features a public ceremony at Kathmandu's Durbar Square where goats and water buffalo are ceremonially decapitated by the Nepal Army. The rites begin around 8 am and end a few hours later when military banners are doused with sacrificial blood.

Rato(Red) Machhindranath
April/May, first day of the Nepali month of Baisakh

Rato Machhindranath is considered a God of Rain and Crops and has ties to Tantric Buddhism. The idol is ritually bathed and put on a chariot and honored as it is pulled by manpower throughout the city of Patan. The chariot is three stories high and tremendously heavy, requiring up to a hundred or more people to move it. Music with drums and cymbals accompany the chariot which stops overnight at four symbolic locations. People offer plates of food to the icon, signifying gratefulness for harvest blessings. The festival is a vibrant jamboree with feasts and merrymaking. Kathmandu has a similar chariot procession, **Seto (White) *Machhindranath*,** presided over by Kumari, the living goddess who resides in Durbar Square.

Ghantakarna
July/August

Mostly a Newari festival for boys. Ancient in origin, it commemorates the victory over **Ghantakarna**, a demon that was vanquished by the natives of Kathmandu Valley. On this day, effigies of Ghantakarna are erected along walkways and roadsides and groups of boys take a toll from passersby for the demon's mock funeral. In the evening, the figure is beaten and dragged to a river where it is burned and thrown into the water whereupon the boys sing and celebrate the victory on the way home.

Janai Purnimaa
Full moon of July/August

The name refers to a sacred thread worn by higher castes (Brahmin and Chhetri). A fresh thread is put on at this time, representing renewal and cleansing of body and mind. The cord is three-ply, with separate strands representing energies of **Brahma (creative), Vishnu (preservative),** and **Shiva (destructive).** People also wrap thread around a wrist as protection from harm until **Laxmi Puja** (the third day of *Tihaar*, see below), when it is removed and, if possible, tied to the tail of a cow for good fortune. Thread was traditionally soaked overnight in 108 herbs by a priest. Nowadays, turmeric is used which turns the cord golden and has antiseptic properties.

At this time, many people take part in the celebrations and not just the high caste. Devotees make a pilgrimage to a sacred location, often a high altitude lake such as **Gosainkunda** (4,381 m, 14,374 ft) where one form of piety is to take a plunge in the chilly waters.

Gai Jatra
New moon of July/August

Usually falls on the **first two days of the new moon of July/August** and is marked by a procession from the palace squares of Kathmandu, Patan and Bhaktapur. 'Gai' means 'cow' and 'Jatra' means 'journey'. Gai Jatra is a celebration of cows (which represent the deity **Laxmi**) leading a procession to heaven for the deceased to follow. Entertainers paint their faces and join parades to amuse onlookers with satire, drama and comedy. Some of the performers are hired by relatives of recently deceased people. They are joined by accomplices in masks wearing unusual garments who represent departed souls in need of guidance by the celestial cows.

Krishna Janmastami (also known as *Krishna Ashtami*)
August/September

A celebration of the birth of Krishna, a hero of the classic ***Mahabharata***, and regarded as an avatar of **Vishnu**. He is often depicted with blue-hued skin, a reminder to followers that he is as unending as the blue sky above. Devotees celebrate by flocking to Patan's Krishna Temple in Durbar Square (as well as Krishna temples across the nation) and sing hymns.

Teej (transliteration, *tij*) (also known as *Hari Talika*)
August/September

According to legend, **Parvat Raj, Lord of the Himalaya** decreed that his daughter **Parvati** would join **Vishnu** in matrimony. Parvati's heart was elsewhere and the night before her nuptials, friends spirited her away to a forest where Shiva was abiding. Shiva became enamored with her but only after trials to verify that the love was mutual.

Single women fast on this day in the hopes of being blessed with a suitable husband while married women also fast and wear red (the color of matrimony) *saris*. They pray and perform rites for marital harmony and the well-being of their families. Pashupatinath and other Shiva temples are especially crowded on *Teej*.

It has become a modern tradition for female friends to get together and celebrate with each other just prior to *Teej*.

Ganesh Chauthi or Chatha
August/September

Celebrated as the birthday **of Ganesh ("the elephant god"), son of Shiva and Parvati**. Ganesh is beloved as a divinity auguring good luck and removing obstacles.

Indra Jatra
September/October

The **King of the Gods, Indra**, is celebrated by the raising of a victory banner in his honor (this happens in Kathmandu at Hanuman Dhoka temple). Among other duties, Indra is also considered the controller of rain and harvests and is especially important to people whose livelihood depends on a successful growing season. Indra is known to have gathered flowers in Kathmandu Valley for his mother and is a slayer of demons which represent natural disasters. The festival lasts eight days highlighted by appearances from the **Living Goddess Kumari**. The massive idol of **Bhairav, a form of Shiva**, in Kathmandu's Durbar Square, also figures prominently in the proceedings which involve chariot processions, singing and masked dancing.

Dasai
late September/October

Dasai is a Hindu festival that commemorates the legendary victory of the goddess **Durga (Kali)** over the demon-buffalo, **Mahisashur** and symbolizes the **triumph of Good over Evil**. This is Nepal's grandest festival and generally coincides with the end of monsoon and is a time of family reunions. The holiday pervades the nation and lasts for **ten days** beginning in late **September or early October** depending on the lunar cycle. Schools, shops and government offices are closed for up to two weeks during *Dasai*, and all transportation is overcrowded and difficult to book. There is much feasting as friends and families unite, gifts are exchanged and blessings imparted. Bamboo swings are set up around the country and city skies are filled with kites.

The festival begins with *Ghatasthapana*, the ceremonial setting of a jar of water in a place of worship in one's house, and symbolizes *Shakti*, **the primordial force of femininity or Universal Mother**. A prominent feature of *Dasai* is the ritual decapitating of buffaloes at the *koT* (fort) near Kathmandu's Hanuman Dhoka in Durbar Square on the ninth day of the festival. Throughout the nation, goats and sheep are sacrificed and festive banquets are held. The tenth day, called *Vijaya Dasami*, celebrates Durga's victory, and *Tikaa* is given (a vermilion mark of religious as well as decorative significance placed on the forehead during the festival and generally at religious ceremonies and other occasions; giving someone *Tikaa* express good wishes, friendship and honor). In rural areas, village leaders administer *Tikaa* to the public. On this occasion, before the monarchy was dismantled in 2008, the former King and Queen received citizens at the royal palace.

Tihaar (aka, *Diwali, Deepawali, Bhai Tikaa*, and *Lakshmi Pujaa*)
October/November

Tihaar is a five-day **'festival of lights'** in late **October or November**. The lights represent **Knowledge** and its victory over **Ignorance**. During the five days of *Tihaar* special rites are performed and during days one to four, certain animals receive worship and positive attention with special offerings of food and sometimes flower garlands and *Tikaa*.

Day 1: crows, messengers of **Yama Raj, King of the Dead**
Day 2: dogs, general protectors and especially guardians of homes; also the vehicle of **Bhairav**, an emanation of **Shiva** revered by the Valley's Newars
Day 3: cows, divine representations of **Laxmi**
Day 4: bulls, sacred animals for many reasons in Hinduism, chiefly as **Nandi**, Shiva's transport and foremost devotee. Nandi is also guardian at Shiva and Parvati's abode.
Day 5: The final day, ***Bhaai Tikaa***. Sisters ceremonially give younger brothers *Tikaa* and wish them prosperity and long life, and brothers offer a gift in return, usually money or clothing.

The **third day** of this festival is also known as ***Laxmi Pujaa***, dedicated to **Laxmi, goddess of wealth**. Houses and shops are given a thorough cleaning. Buildings are trimmed with marigold flowers, and hundreds of tiny oil lamps and candles light up Kathmandu as dusk falls with the hopes that **Laxmi** herself will visit the cleanest and brightest homes.

During *Tihaar*, public gambling is condoned, and crowds gather around groups of *juwaa* (cowry shell) players, or card players. **Among the Newar community, *Tihaar* marks the beginning of the New Year.**

Kirat Parba (Udhouli Parba)
November/December

This festival is celebrated by **Limbu and Rai ethnic groups**, mainly in eastern Nepal to express gratefulness for harvest blessings. The term ***Udhouli*** means a migration of birds between climes, and *Udhouli* is also celebrated during the planting season in May/April.

Yomari Punhi
Full moon in December

Yomari is a Newari delicacy and the word simply means "pastry that is liked". On this event, the delicious confection is prepared with rice flour and the standard filling is **khuwa, a milk product, brown sugar and sesame seeds**. The dumpling is steamed and an offering is made to the goddess of harvests.

Additionally, *yomari* are important in Newari culture on the birthday of youngsters. A garland is made with the number of *yomari* in the necklet representing the child's age, especially important for the second birthday.

BUDDHISM

"I am concerned only with suffering and the release of suffering"
-Buddha, *The Anuradha Sutta*

The historical figure of **Siddhartha Gautama** of the Shakya Clan was born in Lumbini in Nepal's *tarai* circa 623 BC. He came to be known by the title of **Buddha, "the awakened"**. Hindus consider him to be an **avatar of the Hindu deity Vishnu** and frequent Buddhist temples and are accepting of Buddhists at Hindu shrines.

Nowadays, there are diverse traditions of Buddhism with wide-ranging practices depending on what they consider the Buddha taught with varied interpretations of those teachings. The traditions include **Theravada (also known as Hinayana), Mahayana and Vajrayana (Tibetan) Buddhism** with disparate beliefs and practices.

Buddhism is often considered more of a philosophy or even a therapeutic discipline than a religion, and this may have been true of the earliest versions of Buddhism. In this day and age, some practitioners see the Buddha as a deity and petition to him as such. Additionally, **Mahayana and Vajrayana Buddhists** ascribe supra-human characteristics to *bodhisattvas* (beings that lead others to enlightenment), as well as to some current and former *lamas* and intercessory entities. Ritual observances and the entreating of and devotion to divine beings give this type of belief and practice religious attributes.

PRECEPTS

A number of people consider the Buddha as a pathfinder above all else, and he is said to have not proscribed behavior for monks and nuns until he saw a need for it. Eventually hundreds of regulations were promulgated. These precepts lay a moral foundation considered necessary for successful spiritual endeavor. The following are the **primary five moral teachings** (precepts are stricter for monastics than for laity):

1. No killing (in other words, **non-injury to living beings**, including oneself). Meat consumption is a contentious issue; some Buddhists do not consider it a dilemma if the animal was not killed specifically for the consumer, whereas others assert that an animal killed for meat eaters is part of the chain of supply and demand; accepting any meat increases demand and the eater thereby shares a responsibility in the animal's death

2. Not taking that which hasn't been freely given, in other words, no stealing

3. Not misrepresenting the truth, in other words, no lying

4. No sensual (often represented as 'sexual') misconduct, or more precisely, no one is hurt in fulfilling one's sense-pleasure desires; interpretations vary as to what this implies

5. Not becoming intoxicated (another variation is not taking intoxicants whatsoever) as intoxication is said to reduce one's will to practice *dhamma*, ie, teachings, responsibilities and practices

The list goes on and **not touching money** is actually in the first ten original precepts but now widely disregarded by all but the most orthodox Theravada monks and nuns.

The Buddha is said to have advised, **"Strive for your own liberation with diligence...Do not simply consider truth what is persistently repeated, or is tradition, or scripture, or because of a person's apparent ability, or because 'He is our teacher', but only when you yourselves recognize: This is good; this is not faulty; this is commended by the sensible; tried and perceived, these things lead to benefit and happiness. Thereupon, live up to it."**

MAHAYANA AND VAJRAYANA

May you be safe from inner and outer harm.
May you be free from guilt, shame and hatred.
May you enjoy physical and mental well-being.
May you live with the ease of an open heart.
May you go beyond your inner darkness and awaken to your radiant true nature as boundless love. –Anam Thubten

Compassion and devotional practice are emphasized in **Mahayana and Vajrayana Buddhism** along with the notion of non-dualism and *shunyata* (emptiness). These concepts explain that all phenomena arise from other phenomena and, consequently, have identity only by originating from and relating to other phenomena. Conversely, **ultimate reality** is beyond relative association and empty of comparison; ultimate reality is likened to the quintessence of beings and matter before incarnation and manifestation, in other words, before identification.

Mahayana and Vajrayana followers believe in a separate canon that was vouchsafed by the Buddha and concealed until the time was right and the world was ready. As well as emphasizing **compassion**, their path or vehicle is claimed to be the most effective and swiftest to realize enlightenment, efficiently cutting through all obstacles. Buddha is deified and capable of performing miracles and considered eternal rather than a transient, historical person. Many aspirants believe in the possibility of the transfer of merit from teachers and *bodhisattvas* to laypeople.

May you have happiness that is free from suffering. May you have love that is beyond suffering. –Mahayana Blessing

MEDITATION

Meditative practices are a primary component for many Buddhists. According to some, there are two broad categories of meditation, **sammatha** or concentration meditation which brings stability to the mind and is considered a prerequisite for **vipassana**, or insight meditation. *Vipassana* means 'to see clearly' and may beg the question, 'to see what clearly?' Through the practice of *vipassana*, insight into what are known as the **three characteristics of existence** is said to be developed. These three characteristics are **anicca** (nothing is stable, all things change, and therefore, true comfort cannot be taken in any phenomenon, as it, too, is changing), **anatta** (non-self, there is no independent self; all phenomena are interdependent) and **dukkha** (unsatisfactoriness or suffering is inherent to a conditioned or interdependent existence continually in flux).

The above facile rendition of the three characteristics is undoubtedly incomplete when years of meditative practice may not reveal the import and meaning of any one of them. On the other hand, according to some theorists, understanding can also happen in a flash, without even a moment of formal practice.

The Buddha is said to have preached **'the middle way'** which is thought to pertain to a balance between self-denial and self-indulgence realized by the **Noble Eightfold Path**. Interpretations include the idea that the body should not be neglected as it is the means for spiritual development. In this regard, the Buddha's practice was extremely austere by modern standards, for example, he had but a single meal daily taken before midday, ie, noon.

Upon stealing away from his royal palace for the last time, Siddhartha Gautama is believed to have informed the attendant at the gate, **"For countless ages I have enjoyed sensual objects of sight, sound, taste and touch in all their variety and they have not satisfied me. Realizing this, I will embark on the raft of dhamma."**

BUDDHIST FESTIVALS OF NEPAL

Losar, aka, Gyalpo Losar (and Monlam)
February

The New Year celebration of people of Tibetan descent together with Monlam, "the great prayer festival" last for two weeks with activity at monasteries across the nation. This is a time for family reunions, new clothes and jewelry, exchanging gifts, replacing tattered prayer flags, *pujaa*, feasting and drinking spirits. The Baudhnath Stupa area is particularly lively with large processions, singing, dancing, praying, and at a certain auspicious time, *tsampa*, roasted barley flour, is thrown into the air.

Buddha Purnimaa (also known as *Buddha Jayanti*, and *Saga Dawa* or simply Buddha's Birthday)
Usually the full moon in May

The birth of **Siddhartha Gautama Shakyamuni** took place in **Lumbini, Nepal**, during the **full moon**, and is celebrated as ***Buddha Purnima***. The commemoration usually occurs **in May on the full moon, but sometimes as early as April or as late as June** depending on the lunar schedule The day is also the anniversary of his attainment of **liberation** in **Bodh Gaya, India**, as well as **death** (referred to as *Mahaparinirvana*) in **Kushinagar, India**. That is, all three events occurred on the same full moon day of the yearly lunar cycle. Observances are held in Lumbini and in Buddhist temples and monasteries throughout the land. Kathmandu's **Baudhnath Stupa** is especially active (and busy on all full moon days throughout the year), and the *stupa* is enchantingly lit up at dusk. Climb to the highest plinth allowable and circumambulate the *stupa* in a clockwise direction for an unforgettable experience or take in the vantage from a nearby rooftop restaurant.

Mani Rimdu
May/June (Thame Monastery, Khumbu Region)
October/November (Tengboche Monastery, Khumbu Region)

A weeklong festival of the Sherpa people that takes place biannually at two monasteries in the Khumbu Region. Sherpa people travel from afar for the social and religious event. Activities include masked dance performances by resident monks, meditation, fire ceremonies and blessings.

Teechi
May/June

Celebrated in **Upper Mustang** and features **prayers for world peace**. The **three day festival** includes dances by masked monks, primarily at **Lo Manthang's Choedhe Monastery**. It is symbolic of a victory of Dorje Sonnu, believed to be an incarnation of Buddha, over a demon threatening the physical environment with storms and drought and feeding on human flesh.

Dalai Lama's Birthday
July 6th

The **14th Dalai Lama's birthday** is a time for prayer, invocation of blessings, and feasting, especially by people of Tibetans origin. Prayer flags fly overhead, and within the monasteries, butter lamps are lit for his long life and good health.

Dukpa Chesyi
July/August

Occurs toward the **end of July or early August (the sixth month and fourth day according to the Tibetan calendar).** Celebrated widely and commemorates the Buddha's first teaching. The occasion is especially lively at **Kyangjin Gomba** in Upper Langtang where the weeklong festivities include singing, drinking, dancing, and archery, among other merrymaking activities.

ANIMISM AND SHAMANIC PRACTICES

The worship of natural forces and indigenous local deities is interwoven with Hindu and Buddhist practices, each influencing the other. Animism includes the belief that certain powers and deities, often embodiments of natural phenomena, can intercede in human affairs. They can be called upon for blessings but can also turn malevolent, especially if neglected or if their space is trespassed upon and violated. When manifest in the form of a human ailment or difficulty, they must be appeased.

Jhankri **or shamans** are said to have the power to intervene and mediate between these forces and patrons. Shamans also have the duty of leading the deceased to a suitable location in the afterlife. A shaman uses ritual objects including a **double-sided drum, representative of the ability to interface between human and spirit realms**. Ceremonies, often centered around fire, can go deep into the night while a shaman enters a state that allows access to the spirit world. Sometimes the spirit speaks aloud through him describing how the affliction arose and the remedy. Certain rituals are performed to placate the disturbed forces and usually a prescription is given to the client that includes *jaDibuTi* **(medicinal herbs).**

Shamans emerge from any level of society after demonstrating connections with the spirit world early in life. They achieve status and prestige after training and elaborate initiations. Shamans are believed to renew their capacities and powers during the *Janai Purnima* festival which takes place at sacred sites including specific ridge top locations in Rukum, Dolakha and Ramechap districts as well as Gosainkunda Lake a few days north of Kathmandu Valley. Symbolic regalia includes colorful headdresses often adorned with feathers and porcupine twills, bracelets and necklaces made of *rudraaksha* (seeds of *Eleocarpus ganitrus*), stone pendants, brass bells, drums and flowing white tunics.

NATIONAL HOLIDAYS

Nayaavarsha (Nepalese New Year)
mid-April

Many people use the official New Year's holiday to get together for picnics and socializing. At **least five different New Year celebrations** are held in Nepal annually. The **New Year** according to the Bikram Samvat calendar begins in the Nepali month of **Baisakh (mid-April).** The Valley's **Bhaktapur** and **Thimi** celebrate the new year as *Bisket Jatra* with events featuring chariot processions and icons paraded on palanquins as well as tug-of-war contests, dancing and even a tongue piercing ceremony.

Tamu Losar is the **Gurung** New Year and falls at the end of December and is marked by singing, dancing, socializing and feasting. A stage and stalls are setup at Kathmandu's Tundikhel Parade Ground for celebratory activities. **Sonam Losar** is mainly **Tamang** affair with a several day affair at Tundikhel around mid-January. **Magh Sankranti** (above in Hindu Festivals) is also a time for **Tharu** people to celebrate their new year with song, dance and feasting.

The **Tibetan New Year**, called **Gyalpo Losar**, usually **falls in February**. It is heralded by feasting and celebration among the Tibetan community. The traditional **Newar New Year falls in late October or early November during the** *Tihaar* **festival** and is celebrated with sweet delicacies and colorful decorations throughout the streets of Kathmandu, Patan, and Bhaktapur.

Martyrs' Week
Late January

A time of commemoration for **martyrs**, chiefly, the people who lost their lives protesting the authoritarian Rana Dynasty of hereditary prime ministers and the erstwhile 239 year royal family hegemony. During this week, Shukraraj Shastri, Dharma Bhakta Mathema, Dashratha Chand and Gangalal Shrestha each receive a day of remembrance and have statues at Kathmandu's Shahid "Martyrs" Gate. A general day of commemoration is also observed for all other martyrs.

Ganatantra Divash (Republic Day)
(around) May 28th depending on Nepali Calendar, it falls on 15th Jestha

The day is highlighted by parades on the Tundikhel Parade ground in central Kathmandu. National ethnic groups, dancing troupes, and various organizations participate, all dressed in traditional finery. (Additionally, an annual commemoration of the ascent of Everest is usually held at the Nepal Tourism Board on May 29th.)

Rural fairs or *mela* are countrywide and occur throughout the year at various locations depending on locally chosen times. Many are in spring around planting season and in the fall after harvest. Some *mela*, such as **Khaptad Mela** in Khaptad National Park in the far west, are quite large and last several days, attracting people from surrounding districts. Others are short-lived and limited to a small region. Enterprising vendors bring raw materials and set up temporary tea and snack stalls, and some sell sundry wares on spread out blankets. The revelry is conspicuously spiced with drink.

TREK PLANNING

Trekking is more successful if the participants are prepared and have an idea of what to expect. Foremost, be prepared to be flexible and make the best of all circumstances. Trekking is essentially hiking extended routes that generally have facilities for room and board. During a trek, travelers spend nights in well-furnished hotels, simple lodges, camp or stay in the homes of local people. In Nepal, walking is the usual means of reaching most rural destinations and the road network is one of the lowest in the world relative to area and population, but a rapid increase in road building is changing things quickly.

Do not travel alone, especially on lesser-used routes, and especially as a female (unfortunately, double standards exist). Find a trustworthy travel companion. Sexual harassment is not uncommon. Foreign pornographic media is wrongly attributed to all foreigners. Dressing as conservatively as Nepalis will gain cultural acceptance. Those trekking alone would be wise to hire a guide or a porter, especially on trails with few tourists.

Please keep in mind that rare attacks on trekkers have occurred in remote areas and usually to people traveling alone. Although lawlessness is on the rise, particularly in the southern plains, due to a succession of weak administrations, travel in Nepal is relatively safer than most modernized countries. However, there are instances of assaults, theft and harassment, and foreigners have gone missing.

OUTDOOR ADVENTURE

Many special-interest activities are available these days with themes of art, flora and fauna, health, meditation, natural history, religion, yoga and more. Adventure sports include rock climbing, mountain biking, rafting, canyoning, kayaking, paragliding and parahawking, bunjee jumping, and more. These activities can be easily arranged at agencies in Thamel, Kathmandu, and Lakeside, Pokhara.

RESTRICTED AREAS

Certain areas, including the regions around Kangchenjunga, Upper Mustang, Manaslu and Tsum Valley, Humla and Mugu (northeastern Nepal), Dolpo, Naar and Phu (within ACAP), are only open to trekkers by booking with an agency. This is supposed to be an attempt by the government to lessen the environmental impact; however, financial reasons play an important role, too. Regulations are in flux, and there is pressure to make these areas more accessible to all tourists. Such a change would help to spread the wealth to the local economy rather than non-local trekking agencies. Until then, these areas are considered "restricted" by the government and require not only involvement of an agency, but a minimum of two customers and supplementary permits from the Immigration Department.

MID-HILLS

Restricted areas notwithstanding, most of Nepal is open for trekking. Outside of the publicized and regulated trekking routes, are areas not covered in guidebooks and worth exploring including much of the mid-hills or **pahaaD**, the heartland of Nepal. This broad belt of hills and fertile valleys stretching from east to west lies between the lowland plains and the Himalaya. Most visitors will discover that areas without the choicest mountain views are at least as enjoyable as the famous destinations, culturally rich and well-endowed with natural scenery. However, before venturing into some of the more remote, less popular or unpublicized areas, a guidebook trek is recommended, and hopefully the trails herein described will be your introduction. Proverbially speaking, the rest is up to you to discover.

WHEN TO GO

The most popular trekking season is autumn when the rains have washed the skies and weather and views are unrivalled, followed by spring and then winter. Generally, people avoid trekking in the monsoon season which typically begins in early June and finishes by the beginning of October, but frequently drags on for much of that month.

Notwithstanding late storms, views are usually clearest in October and November and thus, the busiest months for trekking. December and January are coldest but offer clear vistas, too, although haze often sits in valleys and reaches the upper heights, too, diminishing clarity of views. Much of the air pollution arises from the northern plains of India, one of the most densely populated regions on the planet. Haze drifts north from fires there and in Nepal for winter warmth, cooking, the burning of fields, and the incineration of rubbish, a common practice in greater Asia. The problem is exacerbated by vehicle emissions and general industrial output, especially brickmaking. February and March bring warmer weather and occasional storms but generally it is the dry season. Toward the end of March, the airborne dust and pollution can obscure distant views. At this time, it is much warmer in regions below 3000 feet (1000 m) while April and May are hottest and haziest.

MONSOON

Trekking in the monsoon (June through the end of September) can be undertaken by enthusiastic trekkers who are not troubled by getting wet. Rain and fog can be expected almost daily, making the air more oxygen-rich than it would otherwise be, and clouds part occasionally to give spectacularly evocative views of the mountains and surroundings. Generally, more rain falls in the east of Nepal as the monsoon arrives from the Bay of Bengal and moves westward. Flora is usually at its most colorful, and mid-elevation meadows are swarming with flowers and dancing with butterflies. Waterfalls are roaring at this time, too.

Although clouds cloak the mountain vistas, it is undeniably a beautiful time of year—a season when the haze of pollution is absent. Be advised that there will be occasional downpours throughout the day. When a deluge arrives, find the nearest shelter and wait it out, as cloudbursts usually do not last long—although some last for several days.

The negative side of trekking during the monsoon is that you and your gear will likely get wet. Trails can be muddy and treacherously slippery. It will be hot and humid. Roads, trails, and bridges may wash out, necessitating time-consuming and difficult detours. Travel sometimes involves wading through streams or even rivers. To make matters worse, hordes of leeches tyrannize the forests above 4000 feet (1200 m) while mosquitoes are a menace at lower elevations. Certain items of equipment are essential: a waterproof cover for your pack, sheets of plastic for covering porter loads, an umbrella, a hat with a brim, a walking stick or ski pole, and footwear with good traction.

MAPS

Maps are an integral tool for travel in Nepal and provide vital route information and terrain characteristics. Especially important are features of elevation and settlement locations. Nepal-produced, elaborate maps are available at bookstores in Nepal, especially in Thamel, Kathmandu, and Lakeside, Pokhara. Trails, villages, and some contours are shown on most of them although not always accurately; some maps have been drawn by people who have not traveled in the region.

Himalayan Map House produces excellent maps of the trekking regions in Nepal, **www.himalayanmaphouse.com**. Additionally, Pilgrims Books of Thamel and Patan has a wide supply of maps **www.pilgrimsonlineshop.com** . Some maps of Nepal are also available at online stores, such as **www.mapsworldwide.com, www.stanfords.co.uk, www.cordee.co.uk, www.omnimap.com, www.amazon.co.uk,** and **www. amazon.com.**

COSTS

Daily costs on the popular routes, depend on the amount spent on food, accommodation and extras. Rates commonly increase with elevation and remoteness. If you are traveling without porters or guides and eating food locally, $10–$15 USD per person per day might takes care of necessities, although on popular routes you may need at least $20–$25 USD per day. (With a porter, add at least another $10 a day and $15 for a guide, if you hire them independent of an agency).

In the Annapurna and Khumbu regions there are more stylish hotels, and you can spend a great deal more. Carry enough funds for contingencies. There are also national park and conservation area permit costs; for example, entry into Sagarmatha National Park is 3000 NRS, and ACAP 2000 NRS. Rrestricted areas cost much more. Additionally, since March 2010, TIMS card fees are $20 USD per person per trek ($10 for trekkers on an agency trek). Using these amounts, a two-week trek in the Solu–Khumbu (Everest) area would at least cost roughly the following:

- Daily cost of food and lodging, at least $20–$25 USD x 14 days = between $280 and $350 USD
- Sagarmatha National Park fee = roughly $35 USD
  TIMS card fee = $20 USD
- Total, not including transportation to and from the trailhead, frills like extra snacks or drinks, and porter or guide = a minimum between $335 and $405 USD.

Off the main routes, daily costs will be lower. Eat locally grown food, buy locally produced crafts, and limit purchase and use of imported products (packaged foods, bottled drinks and sauces and other items brought from Kathmandu and beyond) to save costs, support the local economy and reduce unmanageable waste.

SCHEDULE

In the hills, people generally rise at dawn, usually followed by a cup of milk tea and then work until a mid-morning meal around 10 AM. Work continues until late afternoon and is followed by a second meal in the evening. A light snack in the early afternoon is common. Until recently, activities coincided with periods of daylight, and people tended to retire indoors soon after sunset; however, with solar power lighting available in much of Nepal, activity patterns are changing.

Most trekkers stop before 5 PM regardless of season and usually depart mid-morning, after a warm drink and breakfast. Schedules are more affected by altitude and place to stay than by length of day, which has less variation from season to season than more northerly climes. Nepal is roughly at the latitude of Florida, USA and northern Egypt. In areas where there are plenty of trekker-oriented hotels, travelers can structure the day as they wish. Along the popular routes, lodges can be comfortable yet crowded during the high season. No effort has been made to evaluate the quality of lodges and services. Not only do travelers have widely ranging sensibilities, but standards, reliability, and ratings cannot be counted on in rural Nepal.

FOOD AND DRINK

Busy trailside hotels often hire staff from outside the region and offer extensive 'international' menus. Travelers can choose local food, typically **daal bhaat tarakaari** (rice, lentil soup and a vegetable dish, or sometimes *roTi* , a flatbread, is substituted for rice), which is what the hotel employees usually eat and is more energy-efficient to cook, or Westernized food. *Daal bhaat* uses local resources and although consisting of the same general ingredients, has a range of tastes depending on specific ingredients, seasonings and preparation from place to place and even day to day at the same location. It is the safest bet for a quality meal and nearly always satisfying with a delicious variety.

Unlimited quantities of *bhaat* (rice) are generally included in the meal, but the *daal* (lentils) and *tarakaari* (vegetables) are rationed. In the commercialized trekking areas, second helpings of each are usually offered but not more. The custom is to have it prepared fresh, and often quantities are misjudged prior to preparation and extra helpings might not be available. Fresh fruit is uncommon and rarely to never available in the alpine heights. Weekly markets occur in some towns and are a source of fresh food, general supplies and entertainment. The type of food available in the hills varies depending on the place and the season.

Packaged, quick-cooking noodles have become more commonplace in shops and inns throughout much of the country. They are usually insufficient as a meal replacement, contain monosodium glutamate (MSG), and vegetarians will be keen to know that the flavor packets generally contain animal by-products). Often plastic packaging is tossed away indiscriminately or burned and adds to pollution problems.

Western processed and packaged foods are available in large "supermarkets" in Kathmandu that cater mainly to tourists, expatriates and wealthy Nepalese. You may want to bring dried fruit and nuts as a supplement, and combined with a bit of chocolate you will have a nutritious energy boost. Sealable containers are convenient to carry snacks, too.

Chiyaa, or tea with milk and sugar, is the traditional beverage. Per request, lodge owners along popular routes will make it without milk or sugar. In higher territory, Tibetan salt-butter tea (*solja)* is available, although an acquired taste. You might simply ask for boiled water (*umaaleko paani*). Local alcoholic drinks include *chhyaang* (Tibetan), *jååD and raksi* (Nepali) and *tongbaa* (Tibetan and Limbu).

Chyaang and *jååD* are fermented but not distilled and the water used will not have been purified and might be unsafe to drink. *Raksi* is distilled however it is often then diluted with untreated water to increase volume. *Tongbaa* is a drink made by pouring hot water into an individual vessel (the *tongbaa* is actually the name of the container itself but has become the common name of the drink, too) of fermented millet and the liquid is traditionally imbibed through a bamboo or aluminum straw, whereas nowadays plastic is used. Hot water is refilled as needed. Commercially produced spirits are available at higher prices.

HOME STAY

Home stay can be the most memorable way of traveling and might could be the highlight of a journey. It will offer an insider's view into the culture and lifestyle of your hosts, often untouched by modern amenities.

Always be sure to remove footwear before entering a home. Visitors will likely be shown where to sit and offered a drink and perhaps a light snack to begin with and something more substantial at meal time. Otherwise, try to eat when and what the family eats. You will probably be plied with questions. A private room might be offered for sleeping or you will end up on a carpet on the floor. Relax and enjoy!

Ask whether the family has a *charpi* (toilet) or if there is a communal latrine. In much of Nepal, there are no latrines whatsoever, and you will have to use the great outdoors. Nepalese are somehow able to time this to dawn or pre-dawn in a place near the village, and they carry a *loTaa,* or small container of water for necessities. Find a corner of a field or other sheltered spot away from running water and bury the "meadow muffin" at least 6 inches (15 cm), or at least cover it with stones. If you are using toilet paper (or sanitary supplies), carry a cigarette lighter or matches and burn the used paper at once. At high altitude where there is no soil, overlaying the excreta on an out-of-sight rock is best for the environment. Whatever you do, be sure to exercise appropriate modesty and stay out of view.

If at any time you are unsure how to behave in a certain situation, follow the lead of your hosts on how to proceed. After all is said and done, when intentions are in the right place, actions will follow accordingly and mistakes, should they be made, will be easily overlooked. When departing, the amount of payment will often be up to you.

CAMPING ALONG THE WAY

Those with gear can camp along the way. Tents and stoves will certainly attract a crowd in places that have not seen much camping equipment. National parks and conservation areas will have designated fee sites. Organized treks will arrange these by the agency. On your own, look near villages for campsites on terraces that are harvested or fallow or clearings in the forest.

INDEPENDENT TREKKING

Along lesser traveled routes you will see few other tourists. Conversely, on the popular routes, your main contacts will likely be with other trekkers. If you do not have a partner, then it is relatively easy to join up with other trekkers in Kathmandu. People post for trekking partners on bulletin boards at the Kathmandu Environmental Education Project (KEEP) office and in tourist-frequented places like cafes and hotels in Thamel. The following website might also be helpful: **http://trekkingpartners.com/ads/nepal/**. Unfortunately, double standards are prevalent, and women especially should not travel alone and are advised to seek out a trekking partner or a female guide or porter (please see FEMALE CREW below). Nepalese find it difficult to understand why foreigners, especially women, would travel alone as most Nepali women do not. Although the same goes for men, it is not uncommon to see Nepali men traveling alone.

GUIDES AND PORTERS

There is a saying among independent trekkers, "No porters, no guides, no hassles!" Having a poor guide can sometimes cause needless conflict and tension and turn the journey into a struggle. That said, having an informed guide can make all the difference on a venture into the Himalaya. A guide will keep you on the correct trails and may sometimes carry a load. He or she can share a wealth of knowledge and insight on the route and culture, assist in arranging food and accommodation, and generally help to ensure your well-being. The experience can be an extraordinary introduction to Nepal.

Traveling with a porter, hired to carry a load, can also be a tremendous opportunity to get to know Nepal and its people. Porters can often be found when necessary along the trail or hired in Kathmandu before starting a trek. However, some tourists might be uncomfortable with the idea of allowing another person carry one's gear. In reality, having a porter is a mutually beneficial arrangement, providing a decent wage in a land with a dearth of employment. The tourist will have more freedom and ease to experience the sights and sounds and the journey will be enhanced in many ways. Not only will the trek be more comfortable, but often long-lasting friendships are made. In any event, trekkers are indirect recipients of porter labor carrying up food and goods purchased along routes. Hiring someone to carry gear will likely be a large pay increase over hauling other goods.

Porters use a conical basket called a *Doko* available throughout much of Nepal with a cover of plastic to keep the load dry when it rains. They carry these baskets using a wide band that goes around the forehead called a *naamlo*. Even with a modern pack to carry, most porters disregard the straps and waist belt in favor of a tumpline. Items carried by porters often receive rough treatment. It is best to carry fragile items yourself. All bags carried by porters should be locked to prevent pilfering and possible recriminations. Small locks and cheap duffel bags are available in Kathmandu.

Be aware that there are instances where a guide (and sometimes a porter) reduces the freedom of movement and choice among lodges, schedules, overnight points, and more. Often, guides receive a commission for bringing trekkers to lodges and restaurants and become insistent about patronizing certain establishments. This can result in disagreements between the guide and guest. It is important to set out guidelines before travel begins, including not only wage, but whether that includes food and lodging, and whether the guest or the guide decides on the particular lodge and restaurant and the extent and limitations of the daily schedule. Generally, there is a two-tiered pricing system and Nepalis receive a cut rate for rooms and food. However, you may want to set a limit for the daily costs.

The pay rate for guides and porters varies depending on where they are hired, the destination, the time of year, experience and language capabilities and whether the trekker provides food. It is best to have a guide who is actually from the specific area that you will be visiting. Find out current rates for guides and porters from the Kathmandu Environmental Education Project (KEEP) and from other trekkers, and inquire at trekking supply shops and agencies, too. Independently hired guides usually ask for at least $10–$15 USD per day, and porters ask for the moon but will accept $8–$10 per day. Costs will begin at least 25 percent higher if going through an agency, and the porters and guides will receive appreciably less than the above amounts.

It is also important that porters and guides have adequate clothing for the conditions. KEEP's clothing bank can help with this. All transportation costs such as bus or plane fare to the actual beginning of the trek are the responsibility of the trekker. In addition, if the trek does not leave an employee at his home or point of hiring, you are obligated to pay for his return, usually at half the daily rate. Travel is faster on the return trip, so the number of days the journey will take should be agreed upon in advance.

FEMALE CREW AND GENDER DISCRIMINATION

Nowadays, women as well as men are available as porters and guides. In order to eliminate the potential of harassment, female travelers and families with children might be especially interested in hiring female crew.

It is no secret that in Asia, women are often given a lower status, perhaps an especially striking prejudice in the motherlands of Buddhism and Yoga, considered major pathways to liberation from ignorance. Females face disadvantages in school enrollment, control over household income and work burden, employment and earnings disparities and representation in government and policy making. Some women, particularly in western Nepal, are kicked out of the household during monthly menses and forced to live in a shed to face hypothermia, hunger and insect and animal bites.

The gender bias is ominously reflected in the birth ratio statistics of Nepal's mighty neighbors, **China** and **India**. Birth rates in these nascent economic titans favor males over females by a ratio of more than 1.1. That is, out of every 110 males born, there are less than 100 females born. '**Gendercide**', in other words, excess female mortality, including **missing girls at birth** (sex-selective abortions, infanticide, and neglect), was projected in **2008** to be **3.9 million women worldwide**. **China** and **India** accounted for **more than 50%** of the estimated killings.

Tragically, in **Nepal** between 10,000 to 15,000 women and girls are betrayed and sold each year by their own families for labor and even to the flesh trade in India (with an additional 7,500 children trafficked internally). **Anuradha Koirala** co-founded **Maiti Nepal** (www.maitinepal.org), an organization that offers refuge centers in Kathmandu and along the Indo-Nepal border for women rescued from Indian brothels. She received media giant **CNN's Hero of the Year 2010** for her role in combatting sex-slavery and helping victims of human trafficking. Maiti Nepal aims not only to end abduction for the flesh trade and child prostitution but aspires to eliminate all forms of domestic abuse and exploitation (the Nepal Youth Foundation is another such organization with laudable aims, http://nepalyouthfoundation.org/).

The wide gender gap is unmistakable in **Nepal's literacy rates**, with some **differences between males and females greater than 30% in rural areas and 25% in urban areas.** Although a 2008–09 study of eight of Nepal's districts found the maternal mortality rate had been halved since 1991, there has been a disturbing rise in the suicide rate of women of reproductive age, making **suicide the leading cause of death** in the surveyed districts.

Women who are able to find employment as porters and guides can find economic and other opportunities that are unheard of for traditional Nepali women who live relatively sheltered existences determined by oppressive, patriarchal rules. Empowering Women of Nepal (http://www.3sistersadventure.com/EWN/) is a Pokhara organization run by Three Sisters Adventure Trekking that is training and promoting female guides, and The Nepali Yoga Women Trust (www.nepaliyogawomentrust.org), also based in Pokhara, aims at helping women improve their socio-economic situation.

TREKKING AGENCIES

There are nearly 1000 trekking agencies in Nepal. The industry is largely unregulated—although the Trekking Agents Association of Nepal (TAAN) and the Nepal Association of Tour and Travel Agents (NATTA) have formed powerful lobbies. A list of trekking agencies that are members of TAAN can be found at their website, www.taan.org.np, as well as other useful information on trekking, mountaineering, and tourist-related activities.

Agency travel is relatively expensive, starting at a minimum of $20–$25 USD per day to over $100 USD and varies according to the location and length of the trek, the number of people and style of travel. The larger treks are usually managed by guides called *sirdar*, some of whom are accomplished mountaineers. If you hire a porter or guide from a trekking agency, be aware that a substantial part of that pay will go to the agency. Trekkers on organized treks may be surprised to discover the low pay of the staff.

Agency treks have a predetermined route and schedule with less flexibility for diversions. Parties usually camp in tents near villages and a cook prepares meals. If you prefer to eat Nepali food rather than canned and packaged goods, suggest this beforehand. Eating locally might reduce costs as well as waste and impact on the environment.

Ask the prospective outfitter how they handle garbage. Do they carry out non-burnable items? Has the staff attended the KEEP workshop on responsible trekking as attested to by certificate? Ask whether all the cooking, including meals for the porters, is done on kerosene or gas. Ask whether porters are provided with sufficient clothing and gear. Furthermore, ask for references of people who have taken a trip that interests you, and if possible, interview the *sirdar*, too.

The following additional questions for trekking companies are suggested by the International Porter Protection Group (IPPG):

1. Does the company follow IPPG's five guidelines on porter safety?
2. What is their policy on equipment and health care for porters?
3. What do they do to ensure the trekking staff is properly trained to look after porters' welfare?
4. What is their policy on training and monitoring porter care?
5. Do they ask about treatment of porters in their post-trek feedback questionnaire to clients?

NEPALESE PORTER: TOUGH, PROUD, VULNERABLE
by Dr. Jim Duff, M.D.

Literally thousands of porters carry loads for trekkers in Nepal every season, either directly for independent trekkers or trekking companies, or indirectly by supplying trekkers' lodges. In addition they carry loads to expedition base camps. These subsistence farmers are usually not from the tiny and famous ethnic group the Sherpas, but are from the valleys of the middle hills. As a result they are not acclimatized to high altitude, and are less aware of the dangers of altitude illness and hypothermia than most trekkers. In caste-conscious Nepal, porters are at the bottom of the pile, and this has led to their neglect and exploitation by their fellow countrymen. It is estimated that several porters still die from preventable causes each year in Nepal despite improvement in their conditions of work over recent years. If you are employing porters, it is vital that you provide them with appropriate clothing and footwear for the altitude and season. Traditionally porters have fended for themselves in terms of food and shelter, but this becomes problematic when there are no villages and lodges are crowded with trekkers; make sure your porters have decent shelter and food.

Trekking agencies are in cutthroat competition for your business, and it is the porters who suffer most from price-cutting. The middleman, guide, or *sirdar* will often take a cut of their wages and any tip of cash or gear you might leave at the end of your trek. The only way to counter this is to witness or handle these transactions personally. "Overloading" is a new concept to porters who traditionally carried as much as they could possibly manage. While unavoidable in some situations, overloading is generally dangerous, exploitative, and reduces the number of jobs available. In Nepal 65 pounds (30 kg) is considered reasonable and is the legal maximum. Before signing up with a trekking agency, ask about their policy on porter clothing, food, shelter, and wages, and complain if you see any mistreatment while up in the mountains and on return. IPPG (International Porter Protection Group) recommends the following guidelines:

1. Clothing appropriate to season and altitude must be provided to porters for protection from cold, rain, and snow. This may mean: windproof jacket and trousers, fleece jacket, long johns, suitable footwear (boots in snow), socks, hat, gloves, and sunglasses. (KEEP in Kesar Mahal, Thamel, Kathmandu, has a clothing bank where the above items can be borrowed for porters' use and garment and gear donations are accepted, too)

2. Above the tree line porters should have a dedicated shelter, either a room in a lodge or a tent (the trekkers' mess tent is no good as it is not available till late evening), a sleeping mat, and a decent blanket or sleeping bag. They should be provided with food and warm drinks, or cooking equipment and fuel.

3. Porters should be provided with life insurance and the same standard of medical care as you would expect for yourself.

4. Porters should not be paid off because of illness/injury without the leader or the trekkers assessing their condition carefully. The person (*sirdar*) in charge of the porters must let their trek leader or the trekkers know if a sick porter is about to be paid off. Failure to do this has resulted in many deaths. Sick/injured porters should never be sent down alone, but with someone who speaks their language and understands their problem, along with a letter describing their complaint. Sufficient funds should be provided to cover cost of rescue and treatment.

5. No porter should be asked to carry a load that is too heavy for their physical abilities (maximum: 20 kg on Kilimanjaro, 25 kg in Peru and Pakistan, 30 kg in Nepal). Weight limits may need to be adjusted for altitude, trail, and weather conditions; experience is needed to make this decision. Child porters should not be employed. π

—Dr. Jim Duff, MD is the founder and Director of the International Porter Protection Group (IPPG), www.ippg.net ; IPPG has initiated projects for the benefit of porters' health and safety worldwide, including porter shelters, clothing banks, and rescue posts)

Things are changing for the better with groups like International Porter Protection Group (www.ippg.net), Porters Progress U.K. (www.portersprogress.org), Community Action Nepal (www.canepal.org.uk), International Mountain Explorers Club (www.mountainexplorers.org), and KEEP (www.keepnepal.org) raising awareness and setting up clothing banks, shelters, aid posts and other programs and resources for porters.

Porters are at the low end of a hierarchical society. In Nepalese terms, people in this position rarely complain, even at times when physical harm may be occurring. Thus, as the employer, either directly or through an agency, maintain a watch on the safety of your porters along the way to help ensure that the pattern of neglect and exploitation does not continue. *That said, properly engaging a porter and guide, if you are so inclined, can greatly enhance your experience while providing a valuable source of income. In fact, if you travel without a porter or guide you might be missing an extraordinary opportunity to get closer to the soul of Nepali culture.*

PORTER POETRY

Poem

Even though my soul has been torn, here I am laughing.
Even though my very being is in fragments, I have somehow survived.
As long as there is one drop of blood in my body,
Until life's last instant, I will always foster this love.
When I die I will be thinking of it – my education.
But now it is just a dream that cannot become reality.
If I was a flower, I would bloom, but I cannot for all of the thorns.
If my love was for anything else I could forget it.
I cannot forget my desire to learn, and the road is covered in thorns.
How can I laugh with my heart so filled with a love for learning?
How can I laugh?
--Santaki B.K. (translation by Ben Ayers)

Assets

Today, a Nepali's morality
Only considers possessions.

Respected porters, brothers –
Today, a Nepali's identity
Has become selfish.

Respected porters, brothers –
We're only here as long as our physical health is.
Of course, we will become wealthy and happy.

Respected porters, brothers –
If your soul is content and peaceful
Your creativity can build a Taj Mahal!

Respected porters, brothers –
Make your hardship into a possession.
Soak this earth with your sweat.
Make a storehouse for your sweat.
-- Nanda Raj Rai (translated by Ben Ayers)

TREKKING GEAR LIST

- **anti-leech oil** for monsoon treks (available at KEEP and some pharmacies in Kathmandu)
- **base layer**, long underwear of polypropylene, nylon, wool, or silk
- **camera** and photographic equipment including **extra batteries and memory cards**
- **earplugs**, more than one pair (homes and lodges can have remarkably thin walls, buses often have blaring stereos, and unruly dogs howl deep into the night)
- **elastic bands, nylon line** (parachute cord): for lashings, hanging laundry, makeshift shoestrings, or for wrapping around sole of shoes for traction on slippery trails
- **feminine hygiene materials**: women may consider bringing an ecological, reusable **menstrual cup** (*eg*, **Mooncup**) that collects menstrual fluids, as an alternative to carrying disposable tampons or other materials
- **flip-flops, sandals**, or other lightweight foam/rubber footwear: for use after the day's hike is over, around the room, lodge, and village; especially useful in toilet and shower areas
- **footwear that supports the ankles**
- **gloves**
- **handkerchief** or bandanna (more than one) , used as face mask, or to dry cups, plates, hands and more
- **hat with brim**, and **warm hat**
- **headlamp or flashlight**
- **high-energy snacks**
- **insect repellent**, including essential oils of eucalyptus or citronella
- **makeshift shelter**: emergency blanket (aluminized polyester)/plastic sheeting/bivouac shelter
- **matches** or **lighter**
- **pack**
- **pack cover** (ones made in Kathmandu are a good value)
- **pen** or pencil and **journal**
- **personal first-aid kit** (see Staying Healthy section for recommendations)
- **plastic bags**, especially useful for keeping gear dry in wet weather
- **plastic sheeting** for covering porters' loads and other uses
- **pocket knife**
- **portable music player**
- **quick drying pants**
- **rain poncho** or cape large enough to cover self and pack
- **reading materials**
- **rechargeable batteries, charger, and universal adapter**
- **skirts, mid-calf to above the ankle for women**
- **sleeping bag**
- **sleeping bag liner** or sheet for use between unwashed sheets/blankets
- **socks**, several pairs

• **spare eyeglasses or contact lenses** if you wear them
• **sunglasses** (**UV-protective**; be aware that inexpensive sunglasses might do more harm than good by dilating pupils and allowing more UV exposure)
• **sunscreen and lip balm**, ayurvedic sunblock cream is available in Kathmandu
• **sweater** (aka, jumper)
• **toiletries**, including **biodegradable soap** (ayurvedic soap is available in Nepal)
• **umbrella** if traveling in warm sunny lowlands or in the monsoon
• **universal adapter** for recharging batteries/electronic devices
• **water bottle**; at least 32-ounce (1-liter) capacity per person
• **water-purification materials**
• **windproof jacket**

Nepal's trails are steep and every addition to your load counts! Review your gear list, and pare down items beforehand.

SECOND HAND GEAR Second-hand camping and mountaineering equipment used by other trekkers and climbers on Himalayan expeditions is often available for sale or rent in Kathmandu, Pokhara, Namche Bazaar, and waypoints along popular routes. You may even find new gear that went unused on expeditions. The road forming the southern border of Thamel in Kathmandu has shops with expedition kit, and do not be surprised if the owner of the shop with whom you are bargaining is a prolific climber.

Prices vary from cheap to outrageous, and quality is not uniform. Some trekkers sell equipment by means of notice boards in restaurants, hotels, and at KEEP. Packs, jackets, and other items are locally manufactured and often carry a counterfeit label. Such gear might only last one trek if that, but some are more durable. There are now genuine outlet stores along Tridevi Marg in Thamel and Durbar Marg, the road that leads from the former royal palace, now the Narayanhiti National Museum. Some people are able to pick up everything they need in the city, but it is safer to arrive at least minimally prepared. If buying or renting in Nepal, be aware that quality is variable and a sleeping bag with an advertised rating of −20°C will not likely match expectations.

CLOTHING Hiking Nepal's steep terrain can cause a swift buildup of body heat, especially carrying a loaded pack up a sun-drenched hill. Conversely, in high altitude areas, the temperature will drop rapidly, especially in the shade of the mighty Himalaya, when the sun has set or is behind the clouds, and more so if your clothes are wet and cold from sweat. It is important to have the ability to remove or add items to adjust quickly to conditions.

Clothes made of all-cotton material, though comfortable, are not the best choice as cotton absorbs and holds moisture. A first layer of clothing should keep you dry by wicking moisture away from the skin to the next layer. There are many brand specialties in this area. Long thermal underwear is necessary at higher altitudes, especially during the winter months. Thermals made with polypropylene, a petroleum-based synthetic, might be a good inner layer, although it has a reputation of quickly becoming foul-smelling. Nylon is durable. Silk is lightweight yet needs extra care and might easily come apart at the seams. (There are now silks on the market that do not rely on mass killing of production caterpillars. These include **ahimsa** silk, also known as peace silk and vegetarian silk, and **tussah** or wild silk.)

The next layer should provide warmth. Wool clothing is traditionally chosen for the cold because it stays warm when wet. A sweater or synthetic fiber-insulated fleece (pile) jacket works well in wet weather and also dries quickly. Underarm "pit zips" allow ventilation if not removal of entire sleeves. The outer layer should add warmth and keep you dry as well. A waterproof, breathable shell that is soft and light works well. Aim for something either with a zip-out liner or large enough to cover a sweater or fleece jacket. Check to ensure that the seams have been properly sealed.

PACKS Many well-designed packs are available. Choose one that feels comfortable when loaded, allows easy access and can expand capacity when necessary. Carry a spare plastic buckle at least for the waistband (keep buckles engaged while not wearing the pack to protect them from being stepped on and possibly broken). Equipment and supplies that porters carry can be packed in sturdy, bright-colored (for recognizability) duffel bags, preferably ones that can be locked.

SHELTER Your route and preferred style dictate whether you need a tent. If you prefer to camp, or desire privacy where there aren't lodges, a tent is necessary. Generally, one large enough to sit up in and to house other people such as porters in an emergency is best. Weight, seasonality, and ease of setting up are factors to consider. A three-season tent with ventilation and rain fly over the openings is versatile enough for most trekkers. Make sure the seams are properly sealed. Check out setup instructions, and practice before you depart and do not forget a groundsheet to keep gear clean and dry and prevent dampness from being wicked up from the ground.

A lightweight "emergency blanket" (aluminized polyester), bivouac shelter, or plastic sheet can be carried for emergency shelter.

COOKING GEAR Gear is available in Kathmandu. Regulations require that trekkers and their porters, cooks, and guides be self-sufficient in national parks. Trekkers should use stoves powered by kerosene, propane, butane, or other fuel rather than wood, especially in high-altitude areas and conservation areas. Kerosene is the only fuel available in the hills, although some shops on popular routes may have mixed-fuel canisters (eg, Primus) for sale. It is better to buy canisters at trekking shops in Kathmandu that also sell stoves capable of using both portable canisters and kerosene. However, the kerosene available is often impure and clogs up most stoves necessitating frequent cleaning of the fuel jet.

Become familiar with stove operation before the trek and carry spare parts of critical components.

SLEEPING GEAR A down or synthetic-fiber sleeping bag is usually necessary for comfort at temperatures below freezing. Many lodges have quilts, comforters, and blankets, but you cannot always rely on their presence, adequacy, and cleanliness, especially during busy times. Many trekkers along the popular routes manage without a sleeping bag, but going without one is not advised on high-altitude routes. In lodges along popular trekking trails, mattresses and pillows are available, but not everywhere, especially during high season when late arrivers sometimes have to sleep in a dining hall. Although most lodges will have foam padding, those who are camping might need an air mattress, foam pad, or inflatable pad for a comfortable night's sleep.

EYEWEAR Sunglasses should absorb ultraviolet light, and sunglasses that do not can do more harm than good by opening the pupil and exposing the eye to potentially damaging UV rays. A visor to shade the eyes from the sun is an ideal addition. If you wear eyeglasses or contact lenses, bring a spare pair and copy of the prescription in the event replacements are needed. If you wear contact lenses, do not neglect regular cleaning. Infections are more prevalent in Nepal. Use water that has been boiled. If you do not want to bother with cleaning, bring disposable extended-wear contact lenses with less risk of infection, although the packaging can be burdensome to carry out.

Perhaps some people will use Nepal's trails as an opportunity to strengthen the eyes naturally by going without glasses and contacts, and training the eyes to focus alternately on things far and near and in differing light conditions. Keep in mind that of injuries and infrequent deaths of trekkers, falling off the trail is a leading cause.

WATER CONTAINERS Each person should have a water container of at least 1-quart (liter) capacity. Plastic and lightweight stainless-steel or aluminum containers can be found in trekking shops in Nepal. Stainless-steel or aluminum bottles can be ideal for storing water that has been boiled and is still hot. Encasing the bottle in a clean sock or hat or wrapping another item of clothing around it will make a source of heat that can be kept close to the body or even placed in a sleeping bag for added warmth.

OTHER ITEMS

Footwear that supports the ankles is highly recommended as well as lightweight foam or rubber sandals that can be ideal to change into at the end of the day.

A **Leatherman** or **Swiss Army Knife** gadget combination can be useful but unnecessarily heavy unless the multi-functional tools are needed. Often a simple pocket knife will do if anything at all.

Umbrellas can be used not only against rainfall but to protect against the sun on hot days and for privacy while answering nature's call.

Collapsible ski poles and **walking sticks** (*lauro* in Nepali), often made of lightweight bamboo, can help ease the load and impact on the knees.

Bring several handkerchiefs or **bandannas**. A bandanna can be useful as a makeshift face mask in windy, dusty areas and during vehicle travel, and to dry cups, plates, and hands. You can keep a separate bandana for the usual runny nose that accompanies colds and upper-respiratory infections—or learn to blow your nose Nepali style, covering each nostril in turn and blowing out the other. Petroleum jelly, Chap Stick, and lip balm are good for cold-weather to prevent or treat chafing.

For women, a reusable menstrual cup (eg, **Mooncup**) is an ecologically sound alternative to tampons and sanitary napkins, ideal for travel and lasts for years. It is recommended that you become familiar with using and cleaning before relying on it during a trek.

Pack **biodegradable soap**, a **washcloth** or towel, and a **toothbrush**.

Bring a **headlamp** or small flashlight (torch) and **spare batteries** (lithium is best), especially to power the modern camera. Outside of the main trekking routes, good batteries will rarely be available in the hills. It is better to have rechargeable batteries and to carry extra charged battery packs. Make sure to bring a **universal adapter**. Electricity averages **220 volts/50 cycle** in Nepal. As Nepal becomes increasingly electrified, there are more and more places along the popular routes to recharge. Entrepreneurs might sometimes take a fee to charge batteries. Carry spares and keep in mind that less-frequented trails might offer only solar power without the accessories to fit recharging devices. There are **no battery recycling facilities in Nepal**, and it is considered environmentally ethical to bring spent cells back to your home country for proper disposal.

Consider **earplugs** (several pairs, as they are easily lost) for noisy hotels, buses, and the occasional obstreperous dog in the depths of night.

It is wise to have at least a **Global Positioning System (GPS)** device or **compass** for high mountain travel. A GPS can be unreliable in sections of Himalayan drainages where steep gorges diminish satellite reception.

Insects are not usually a problem in the high country, and malaria is very rare in trekkers to Nepal, but visitors traveling extensively in the lowlands during the warmer months or during the monsoon might want to use insect repellent and a mosquito net while sleeping. Repellents with picardin and deet (or *N,N*-diethylmeta-toluamide) are effective against mosquitoes, or try natural repellents such as citronella or eucalyptus oil–based repellents. Insecticide sprays and powders (those containing pyrethrins or permethrin are safest) may help in the sleeping bag and can be applied to the netting. Anti-leech oil can be found in some Kathmandu pharmacy shops for monsoon treks.

A supply of **duct tape** can serve as an all-purpose, temporary fix for various situations. Several feet of tape can be wound around a flashlight handle or water bottle to store for future needs.

If you play a **portable musical instrument**, consider bringing it along. A harmonica, recorder, or flute can quickly ease communication barriers. Consider other social and entertainment skills that you might share, for example, portrait drawing or simple magic tricks.

Most trekkers carry reading matter, and writing materials, and hotels along the popular routes often have paperbacks to sell or trade. A pack of cards or miniature versions of popular board games (such as Scrabble) can be a good way to pass time and liven up a restaurant as well as get to know fellow trekkers.

It's a good idea to have a **particle mask,** to protect yourself from dust and fumes in cities and on bus journeys. They can be found in Kathmandu pharmacies.

LEAVE NO TRACE

- Dispose of Waste Properly (Pack It In, Pack It Out)
- Leave What You Find
- Respect Farm Animals and Wildlife
- Be Considerate of Others, Local Custom and Traditions

The following website has the **Minimum Impact Code** of conduct for model trekkers as suggested by ACAP and KEEP: **www.lirung.com/en/info_file/file015acap_e.html and includes the following suggestions:**

- Encourage lodges and trekking companies in their efforts to conserve environmental resources.
- Campfires and hot showers are a luxury, especially when locals use fuel only for cooking.
- Use washing and toilet facilities provided, or, if none are available, make sure you are at least 30 meters (100 ft) from any water source. Bury excreta at least 15 cm (6 in) and use biodegradable toiletries.
- Limit your use of non-biodegradable items and pack them out.
- Respect religious shrines and artifacts.
- Please don't give money, sweets or other things to begging children.
- Taking photographs is a privilege, not a right. Ask permission and respect people's desire not to be photographed.
- Dress modestly, in line with local custom and avoid outward displays of physical affection.
- You are a representative of an outside culture and your impact lingers long after you return home.

Along popular trekking trails you might see garbage bins outside lodges and shops. Usually the contents, including noxious plastics, are burned and metal discarded. Often, litter is pitched off the back side of lodges and shops or piled in a site nearby. Talk to the lodge owners and operators about your preferences for disposal. You can influence them, because they want your business.

NATIONAL PARKS, CONSERVATION AREAS, WILDLIFE RESERVES, FLORA AND FAUNA

Nepal has an extensive conservation system covering over 20 percent of the territory and safeguarding representative samples of the country's ecosystems. The task of protecting a large proportion of the country is challenging, and many of these areas are remote and accessible only by foot.

Nepal's Department of National Parks and Wildlife Conservation (DNPWC) has designated nine areas as national parks, five as conservation areas, three wildlife reserves along with Dhorpatan Hunting Reserve. The national parks and conservations areas, from west to east, include Api-Nappa, Khaptad, Bardiya, Banke, Blackbuck, Rara, Shey-Phoksundo, Annapurna, Chitwan, Manaslu, Langtang, Shivapuri, Gauri-Shankar, Sagarmatha (Everest), Makalu-Barun, and Kangchenjunga. Api-Nappa and Gauri-Shankar were proposed as conservation areas at a cabinet meeting held atop Kala Pattar, Khumbu, on December 04, 2009. The event was staged to voice climate change concerns in the Himalaya ahead of a world summit meeting in Copenhagen.

CHANGES IN HIMALAYAN GLACIAL LAKES

There are some 3000 glaciers and 1500 glacial lakes in Nepal above 11,480 ft (3500 m). Imja Glacier is considered to be one of the fastest-retreating Himalayan glaciers at approximately 243 feet (74 m) per year, and the decline is attributed to solar warming. Imja Tsho Lake has increased in size alarmingly over the last half century from mere melt ponds in the 1950s to a lake of nearly 0.38 square mile (1 km²), or 247.11 acres, with an estimated volume of 47 million cubic yards (35 million m³) of water and rising. Its moraine of rock and ice is considered unstable and a threat for a glacial lake outburst flood (GLOF).

If extensive, a GLOF could result in severe wreckage downstream. A 2002 report by the International Centre for Integrated Mountain Development (ICIMOD) and the UN Environment Program puts twenty of Nepal's glacial lakes at risk for a GLOF, and Imja Tsho is considered the worst danger. According to Nepal's Department of Hydrology and Meteorology (DHM), there have been more than fourteen GLOFs in Nepal. The most recent in the Khumbu was recorded in September 1998, which caused flooding on the Inkhu Khola. In May 2012, a massive landslide near Machhapuchhre caused flooding on the Seti River and dozens of people perished.π

Foreigners wishing to visit protected areas must pay a fee to obtain a permit in Kathmandu, Pokhara or at the entrance point (obtain permits beforehand to avoid hassles; the **Annapurna Conservation Area Project** charges double the fee for permits issued at checkposts). Buying wood from locals or taking it from the forests is illegal in the parks. All travelers doing their own cooking are required to carry stoves and fuel. Flora and fauna are protected, too.

CLASSIC TREKKING VENUES

Annapurna

The Annapurna region in the area north of Pokhara has traditionally been the most popular with trekkers, sometimes seeing over 80,000 visitors a year (nearly 75,000 tourists visited the Annapurna region in 2010, whereas about 2000 visited the adjoining Manaslu region). The Annapurna Conservation Area (ACAP) is 2946 mi² (7629 km²), with mountain scenery as spectacular as anywhere in Nepal.

The Annapurna Circuit has become threatened by encroachment of motor roads. In 2005, the government decided to build roads to the district centers on the east and west sides of the Annapurna massif. Upon completion the roads will foreshorten the world-renowned Annapurna Circuit trek by some 115 miles (185 km) from over 135 miles (215 km) to about 19 miles (30 km). In fact, a rough road to Jomsom is already in place, barring seasonal monsoon washouts, while construction work remains on the Manang side. However, ACAP officials have been hard at work and alternate paths have been developed that follow the same general circuit route, cross the Thorung La pass (17,700 feet, 5416 m) and include sensational side-excursions to Kicho (aka, Ice) Lake, Milarepa Caves and Tilicho Lake among others. **The roadway is a boon for bicyclists.**

Further north of the circuit at Kagbeni is Upper Mustang, a restricted area for limited agency treks and people willing to pay high fees ($500 USD for the first ten days). The region is in a rain shadow that is stark, arid, and strikingly beautiful.

The Annapurna Sanctuary lies southwest of the Annapurna Massif, and is a breathtaking amphitheatre set in a cirque of frosty Mountains that will not likely ever have the intrusion of a road. Settlements beyond the villages of Ghandruk and Chomrong were especially built for trekkers to whom a jeep or bus ride into the amphitheater's 4000-plus meter (over 13,000 feet) would be profane. This open-sky, inner shrine, offers nearly 360° of surrounding Himalayan goddesses. Gurung villages in the area are spectacular, too. A week to ten days is the minimum time depending on acclimatization.

Solu–Khumbu (Everest) Region

Solu–Khumbu, the district south and west of Mount Everest, in northeast Nepal, includes the highest mountain in the world, Mount Everest, 29,029 feet (8848 m), also known as *Sagarmaathaa* (Nepali) or *Chomolongma* (Tibetan). **Lhotse** (27,890 feet, 8501 m, world's 4th highest) and **Cho-Oyu** (26,906 feet, 8201 m, world's 6th highest), are part of Sagarmatha National Park, and **Makalu** (27,765 feet, 8463 m, world's 5th highest) is in the bordering Makalu-Barun National Park.

Situated in the Khumbu area of the Solu–Khumbu district, **Sagarmatha National Park** (445 square miles, 1148 sq km) is a **World Heritage Site (Natural)**. The attractions are towering peaks, villages in majestic mountain valleys with associated monasteries, and highland culture. The area has been the second most popular trekking area in Nepal, seeing 32,000 visitors in 2010, but due to the road construction north of Pokhara (despite the development of alternate routes) it is eventually likely to replace the Annapurna region as the most popular, although when the weather deteriorates, bottlenecks at entry points are a concern.

Travel choices to and from Khumbu include walking from Jiri, Shivalaya, or possibly Bhandar depending on road conditions, or flying from Kathmandu to **Lukla**, a high altitude airfield (9350 feet, 2850 m) and settlement. Lukla is one to two days south of **Namche Bazaar**, a sprawling village at the entrance to the higher Khumbu. Another route comes in from the southeast at Tumlingtar where there is an airfield or jeep service from Hille, a town also served by buses. The trek to Solu-Khumbu from Tumlingtar involves crossing three major valleys with arduous ups and downs.

Langtang, Gosainkunda and Helambu

The popular trekking region most accessible to Kathmandu includes Helambu, Gosainkunda and Langtang, north of the capital city. This area is the third most popular magnet for trekkers of the three premier venues. Langtang National Park (660 square miles, 1710 sq km), contains a wide range of habitats, from subtropical to alpine. The Gosainkunda area is the location of several sacred, alpine lakes and a pilgrimage destination for Hindus. If conditions permit, cross the Laurebina La high pass to link-up with the Helambu region. Helambu, the region closest to Kathmandu, can be approached from the northeast rim of the Kathmandu valley. It is inhabited mostly by people called Yolmo. The hill scenery and culture make up for the lack of spectacular, up-close mountain views, and the serene trails are a refreshing change of pace, especially when combined with treks in Langtang and Gosainkunda.

OTHER TREKKING AREAS

Outside of the three regions outlined above are many places undiscovered by most travelers including Manaslu, an up and coming destination to rival adjacent Annapurna. In lesser known areas, especially in the mid-hills, few lodges or facilities have been set up strictly for tourists, and some trail sections might be difficult to follow. Physical comfort along alternative trails might be at a minimum. The rewards are visiting scenic, pristine areas in the heartland of Nepal and meeting hill people, the soul of Nepali culture, in traditional settings. Areas off the beaten path will be largely unaffected by modernization and the experience will be unforgettable. Trails through these areas are not for everyone. Considerable resilience is needed, along with a spirit of adventure and an open mind. It is perhaps best to consider a first trek on a more established tourist trail. As your experience grows, take on more in-depth journeys.

WESTERN NEPAL Please see my guidebook **The Guerrilla Trek** for a description through remote Rukum and Rolpa, former strongholds of the Maoist insurgency at the epicenter of Nepal's ten year conflict (1996-2006). This region was the homeland of many revolutionaries, and during this period, even had its own autonomous government. Rukum and Rolpa are now areas of immense peace, beauty and hospitality and open, ready and willing to host tourists.

For people interested in the undiscovered areas in the west of the country, bear in mind that there are few facilities for travelers and even food is sometimes unavailable. Intrepid folk aiming for Jumla (and on to Rara Lake), can reach the destination by a hard-going seasonal road that regularly washes out or by scheduled planes from Kathmandu, but it is easier to connect through airfields in Nepalganj or Surkhet and then fly into Jumla. Travelers might share the plane with heavy bags of rice from the Nepal Food Corporation and U.N. Food Program, as the area is regularly short on food.

Rara is a three-day trek from the Jumla. An option on the way out is to trek to KolTi airport in Bajura District in three days along a route improved by locals through the U.N.'s food-for-work program (although flights out of KolTi might be precarious as air service in remote areas can be intermittent). Scant facilities along the way provide the bare minimum in food and place to sleep. Rather than fly out from KolTi, an option is to continue south to Khaptad National Park or to Sanphebagar in Accham District and meet another airstrip and the roadway. Only 135 trekkers visit the Rara area in 2010 and a mere 5 went to Khaptad.

BARDIA, CHITWAN AND WILDLIFE RESERVES

The following are lowland parks and reserves notable for wildlife. These protected areas are located in the southern plains along the border with India. Independent trekking or hiking is not possible there, but guided jungle safaris can be arranged for wildlife observation. **The website of Nepal's Department of National Parks and Wildlife Conservation provides more information on these parks and reserves, www.dnpwc.gov.np.**

Bardia National Park (and adjoining Banke National Park) is situated in western Nepal and is 374 mi² (968 km²). Together with Banke (550 km², 212 mi²) the parks cover 586 mi² (1518 km²) and encompass the largest protected area in the *tarai*. The region extends from the lowlands, which contain riverine forests and grasslands, into the Siwalik Hills, which are covered in chir pine and sal. Mammals (fifty-three different species) include tiger, swamp deer, elephant, and the recently introduced greater one-horned rhinoceros. Nearby is Blackbuck Conservation Area (6 mi², 16 km²) established in 2009 to protect the endangered Blackbuck Antelope with a recorded population in the area of 213.

Chitwan National Park and Parsa Wildlife Reserve Chitwan (360 mi², 932 km²), the first designated park in Nepal, was established in 1973 and lies in the central lowlands and is a World Heritage Site (Natural). It receives the most visitors per annum of all Nepal's protected areas (over 84,000 in 2010). **Parsa** (193 square miles, 499 sq km) is adjacent to Chitwan and established in 1984. Together they comprise riparian forests and grasslands, and extend into the **Siwalik Hills**, which are forested with chir pine and sal trees (*Shorea robusta*). Sal are said to be favored by **Vishnu**, and the **Buddha** was been born under one in Lumbini. These trees are a valuable source of hardwood in Nepal.

Chitwan is famous for large mammals including tiger, leopard, greater one-horned or Indian rhinoceros (over 400 counted in 2008), and gaur (also known as Indian bison). Bird species recorded at Chitwan total 489, a larger number than any of Nepal's other protected areas.

Sukla Phanta Wildlife Reserve Sukla Phanta (118 mi², 305 km²) lies in the lowlands of the extreme southwest and consists of sal forests and extensive grasslands (*phanta* means "grassland"). Except for a wildlife camp operating on the outskirts, there are few facilities for visitors at present. This reserve is important for grassland wildlife, notably a large herd of swamp deer, the threatened hispid hare, Bengal Florican, and swamp francolin. There are small populations of elephants and tigers here, and the greater one-horned rhinoceros has been introduced. Other animals found are wild boar, leopard, jackal, langur, and rhesus monkey. Reptiles include marsh mugger, crocodile, cobra, and python.

Koshi Tappu Wildlife Reserve Koshi Tappu (68 mi², 175 km²) lies in the Koshi River floodplains in the southeastern lowlands. The reserve consists of extensive marshes, grasslands, degraded scrub, and riverine forest. It supports some of the few remaining herds of **wild water buffalo** (*Bubalis arnee*). The 2009 buffalo population count within the reserve was 219. Koshi Tappu is also a valuable wintering area and staging point for migratory birds, especially wildfowl, waders, gulls, and terns. The number of birds visiting is in decline due to pollution and encroachment for settlement and fishing.

The Koshi Barrage area lies in the Koshi River's floodplain and was built in 1964 with India's assistance to help control floods and provide irrigation to farms. However, the Koshi drainage has an extremely high sediment load and the silt raises the height of the waters which regularly flood surrounding areas, often toward the end of the monsoon season. The river has been called the **"Sorrow of Bihar"** for its devastation in the Indian state to the immediate south. Most recently, the Koshi burst its banks in August 2008, displacing millions of people.

FLORA AND FAUNA

Nepal's species variety can be attributed to the country's extremely varied climate and topography. Nepal has some 868 species of birds, including the **Spiny Babbler (*Turdoides nipalensis*) found only in Nepal** (a worthwhile website for

Nepal bird-watchers is **www.birdlifenepal.org**), more than 650 butterflies (as well as over 3,900 moths), and about 6,500 flowering plants. Butterflies (*putali*) emerge in March and April, becoming abundant by May and June. There are at least **six butterfly species endemic to Nepal**, *ie*, believed to be found only in Nepal.

Between 1998 and 2008, **353 new species** were reported in the Eastern Himalaya (comprising Nepal, Bhutan, northeastern India, northern Burma, and southern Tibet). The discoveries include 242 plants, 16 amphibians, 16 reptiles, 14 fish, 2 birds, 2 mammals, and 61 invertebrates. Of the birds, **Sykes' nightjar** (*Caprimulgus mahrattensis*) was discovered in the Koshi Tappu Wildlife Preserve in January 2008.

In the lowlands, such as Chitwan National Park, there are subtropical forests, which support the greatest number of species. Here can be found some of the Indian subcontinent's largest mammals, including the greater one-horned or Indian rhinoceros (*Rhinoceros unicornis*), and tiger (*Panthera tigris tigris*). The World Wildlife Fund (WWF) recently estimated that there are **121 adult tigers in four protected areas of the** *tarai*.) Only small areas remain of the country's lowland grasslands, and almost all lie within protected forest areas. They are important for a number of threatened animals, including the swamp deer, the greater one-horned rhinoceros and two of the world's most endangered bustards, the Bengal and Lesser Florican.

At the other extreme towards the high peaks is the alpine zone which holds the smallest number of species. In spring and summer, alpine grasslands have a vibrant carpet of blooming flowers. A number of mammals, such as the **bharal** or blue sheep and common **ghoral** (a small ungulate that resembles both the goat and antelope) depend on high grasslands for grazing and in turn they are the vital prey of the rarely viewed and threatened **snow leopard** (*Panthera uncia*) with an estimated Nepal population of 300–400, about 10% of the world population (not including 600 in zoos). Unlike birds, wild mammals (*janaawar*) are usually difficult to see in Nepal. Many of them are active only at night.

ENTRY PERMITS, TIMS CARD
AND MOUNTAINEERING

NATIONAL PARK AND CONSERVATION AREA entry permits are processed at the National Parks and Conservation office in Bhrikutimandap, Kathmandu (please see **map** of Kathmandu for location and **KATHMANDU section** for directions), with fees up to 3000 NRS (Nepali rupees) per person, per entry. **Bring your passport, or a photocopy and two photographs (plus two more photos for the TIMS card).** Separate charges and supplementary permits are required from the Immigration Department for restricted areas, including: Kangchenjunga, Manaslu, Naar, Phu, Upper Mustang, Dolpo, Shey-Phoksundo, Mugu, and Humla.

Documents will be checked at national park and conservation area entry points and often at police check posts along the routes. It is best to obtain permits beforehand to avoid hassles and increased fees (**the ACAP fee is double at entry points**). Checkpoints are useful sources of information on trail updates and advisories. Carry a photocopy of your passport and visa as some police posts request details be written in a logbook.

TREKKER INFORMATION MANAGEMENT SYSTEM (TIMS) CARDS

There is an attempt to institute a Trekker Information Management System (TIMS) registration with a card to be presented at checkpoints along with conservation area or national park entry permits. For independent trekkers, TIMS cards are available at a separate TIMS desk at the Nepal Tourism Board (NTB) office in Bhrikutimandap near the counters where national park and conservation area permits are obtained, as well as through trekking agencies and at the offices of the Trekking Agencies' Association of Nepal (TAAN) in Kathmandu (Maligaon) or Pokhara. **A copy of your passport and two passport-size photographs are needed.**

Is it necessary to obtain and carry a TIMS card for each trek? NTB, which exists to promote and develop tourism in Nepal, and TAAN collect information on trekkers via these cards, purportedly for the safety of the trekker. Previously, TIMS cards were distributed free of cost (despite some agencies charging a fee). Some people have suggested that the cards were first introduced in early 2008 for collecting marketing data which required a visit to a trekking agency, providing them a chance to pitch services. Apparently, NTB and TAAN realized that the cards could be a source of funds (NTB is also involved in the "departure tax" implemented in 2005 for all travelers departing Nepal via Tribhuvan International Airport, 1356 NRS for travel to SAARC countries and 1695 NRS for all other countries. This fee is now incorporated into airfare ticket prices and a collection counter no longer exists at the airport. Note, there is no such departure tax for overland exits). As of spring 2010, TIMS cards cost $20 USD per card/trek for each independent trekker on top of conservation area, national park, and restricted area fees ($10 USD for each person trekking through an agency).

When the cards were free, there was little to no enforcement at checkpoints and some trekkers did not bother obtaining them. With assignment of fees, NTB and TAAN have a financial incentive, and monitoring has been stepped up and enforced at park and conservation area entry points. Nevertheless, changes to trekking policy occur frequently, and it is difficult to predict how this will settle out and what adjustments will be made. In any case, **TIMS cards will not likely be required outside of popular routes.** Otherwise, it is a good idea to obtain one to avoid bureaucratic difficulties. For more information, see **www.timsnepal.com**, a website put up by TAAN.

MOUNTAINEERING

According to the Nepal Tourism Board, there are 326 peaks in Nepal open for mountaineering. Climbing permits for expedition peaks are issued by the Mountaineering Section of the Ministry of Culture, Tourism and Civil Aviation.

Besides expeditionary peaks, thirty-three minor peaks, or so-called "**trekking summits,**" can be attempted. Permits are issued by the Nepal Mountaineering Association (NMA). Eighteen of these are the original trekking peaks, opened in 1981, and are categorized as **Group B**. An additional fifteen peaks were added in September 2002 and referred to as **Group A** peaks.

That they are called trekking summits in no way implies that they are for casual travelers. Some are difficult and dangerous, and some have only had a few ascents. These high altitude peaks are not suitable for trekkers who do not have substantial experience in climbing. Further information on the eighteen Group B climbs can be obtained from Bill O'Connor's book *The Trekking Peaks of Nepal*.

To attempt one of these peaks, apply to the Nepal Mountaineering Association (NMA), located in Naxal, Nag Pokhari, Kathmandu (www.nepalmountaineering.org). Fees, payable at the time of application, are nonrefundable. Climbers can apply after arrival in Nepal. There are specific regulations, and although it is not necessary to use a trekking agency, most climbers do, and having an NMA guide along is a requisite.

The following trekking peaks are grouped according to region and the term *Himal*, means "range" (if there is a number to the right of peak name, it indicates the number of climbers in 2010):

Annapurna Himal

Group B
Hiunchuli-8 (21,132 feet, 6441 m)
Mardi Himal-7 (18,218 feet, 5553 m)
Singu Chuli, aka, Fluted Peak-22 (21,329 feet, 6501 m)
Tharpu Chuli, aka, Tent Peak-80 (18,579 feet, 5663 m)

Ganesh Himal

Group B
Paldor Peak-23 (19,449 feet, 5928 m)

Kangchenjunga

Group A
Bokta-9 (20,154 feet, 6143 m)

Khumbu Himal

Group A
Abi-1 (20,003 feet, 6097 m)
Chhukung Ri (18,238 feet, 5559 m)
Cholatse-12 (21,129 feet, 6440 m)
Kyajo Ri-49 (20,295 feet, 6186 m)
Lobuje West-6 (20,161 feet, 6145 m)
Macchermo (20,463 feet, 6237 m)
Nirekha-5 (19,898 feet, 6065 m)
Ombigaichen (20801 feet, 6340 m)
Phari Lapcha-9 (19,741 feet, 6017 m)

Group B
Imja Tse-2,843 (Island Peak) (20,210 feet, 6160 m)
Khongma Tse (19,094 feet, 5820 m)
Kusum Kanguru-10 (20,889 feet, 6367 m)
Kwangde-22 (19,721 feet, 6011 m)
Lobuje (Lobuche) East-463 (20,075 feet, 6119 m)
Mera Peak-1,400 (21,247 feet, 6476 m)
Pokalde-112 (19,048 feet, 5806 m)

Langtang Himal

Group A
Langshisa Ri-9 (21,086 feet, 6427 m)
Yala Peak-112 (18806 feet, 5732 m)
Yubra Peak-1 (19,800 feet, 6035 m)

Group B
Naya Kanga (19,173 feet, 5844 m)

Manang Himal

Group B
Chulu East-153 (21,601 feet, 6584 m)
Pisang-96 (19,984 feet, 6091 m)
Chulu West-101 (21,060 feet, 6419 m)

Manaslu Himal

Group A
Larkya Peak-71 (20,502 feet, 6249 m)

Rolwaling Himal

Group A
Chekijo (20,528 feet, 6257 m)

Group B
Pharchamo-295 (20,299 feet, 6187 m)
Ramdung-45 (19,439 feet, 5925 m)

SUBCONTINENTAL GAS CHAMBER

Atmospheric Brown Cloud (formerly referred to as Asian Brown Cloud) is a layer of airborne pollutants up to 3 km thick that covers much of the northern subcontinent and is especially heavy in the dry seasons. It is estimated that 75-80 percent of the smog is **anthropogenic** and contaminants can move halfway around the world within a week.

A similar bloc of particulate air, referred to as **Asian "Dust"**, occurs over East Asia, carrying among the soot and aerosols from industry and human activity, fine sand particles from the Gobi Desert and steppes of the Mongolian Plateau. The combined effect of these masses of airborne pollutants on health in Asia, which has over half of the world's population, is a major concern (according to a 2002 United Nations Environment Programme report, an estimated 2 million deaths a year in India are attributed to atmospheric pollution).

The southern *tarai* of Nepal is part of the Indo-Gangetic plain, which has one of the highest population densities in the world. People in Nepal, India, Bangladesh, and Pakistan regularly use unclean fuels such as wood, coal, and kerosene for domestic cooking fires, and often burn waste produced from everyday commerce, including plastics. Other practices that produce smog include the setting ablaze of harvested fields and industrial processes such as combustion in kilns for brick making along with vehicle emissions.

The problem becomes compounded from November to April when precipitation that would otherwise scrub the air is scant and cool winter temperatures lead to more wood and garbage burned for warming fires. The subcontinent's haze is not limited to urban areas but extends beyond 10 million square kilometers. It adversely affects health, and absorbs sunlight which in turn impacts agriculture and can mask global warming with effects on the regional climate and beyond.

The smog haunts the air up to the ramparts of the Himalaya and spoils views of the well-endowed scenery. Along with a threat to the tourism industry and consequently Nepal's economy, the fragile alpine ecology is at risk. The high elevation black carbon deposits on snow and ice can result in greater solar absorption and a concomitant rise in temperature with accelerated glacial melting. According to Nepal's Department of Hydrology and Meteorology, the temperature in the Himalaya may well be increasing more rapidly than other areas of the world.

Although Nepal is said to be one of the lowest-per-capita emitters of greenhouse gases, the haze has far reaching effects as does the common practice of using waterways for waste disposal and toilet activities which infect them with excreta and other contaminants. Water is critical for survival of life on earth and the lower its quality the harsher existence becomes. It is doubtful that defiling of rivers, burning of rubbish and fields, and widespread use of cooking fires and kilns are fully included in popular carbon footprint calculations; however, there is no doubt of the impact on the environment.

Clearly, industrialized nations have amends to make for ecological neglect. It is not likely that phlegmatic machinations of governments will legislate improvements to ameliorate problems. Tackling pollution requires **individual participation** *en masse*. Rather than looking at what others are contributing and waiting for worldwide consensus to mandate a plan, each person can adjust personal behavior to lessen the amount of pollution individually contributed, and trekkers can start with the trails of Nepal. (At the same time, reducing the consumption of meat and the immense resources for its supply might play a significant role. As suggested by **Albert Einstein**: "Nothing will benefit human health and increase chances for survival of life on Earth as much as the evolution to a vegetarian diet.") π

KATHMANDU

It would be difficult to visit Nepal without, at some point, passing through Kathmandu (4383 feet, 1336 m), the seat of parliament and a teeming metropolis in the throes of transformation. The legendary city is the site of a present day battle between the 21st Century and medieval times. Modernization is inexorably overtaking and vanquishing ancient architecture and infrastructure but not without disorganized resistance from the fading era. A high population density and dearth of general services and basic facilities intensify growing pains, including extensive power cuts, fuel shortages and rationed water, especially during winter and spring when rainfall is scarce.

Recently, the city has been receiving a makeover in the paving of roadways, lane dividers put into place, and police directing traffic at major intersections and checking vehicle licensure. It is a far cry from the chaotic, anything goes flow of traffic of a few years ago with frequent bottlenecks, backups and horn-blowing ensnarlments. Additionally, morning crews regularly sweep the streets and garbage collection bins have been placed at some points around the city, a significant improvement to the litter strewn streets of the recent past. Solid waste disposal is still sorely problematic, as collected rubbish has to go somewhere and often winds up at waterways. Nevertheless, **the city is beautifying and construction of new homes, apartment complexes, businesses, private schools, large malls and shopping centers are signs of increased wealth and a burgeoning middle class.**

As a necessary stop for most travelers, there are many activities to bide your time in this remarkable city. The contrast between hectic urban life and trekking trails can make the time on the Himalayan trails all the more cherished. What follows is a brief description of the valley and a few options for leisure, either preparing or waiting for a journey or general recreation.

KASTAMANDAP The city takes its name from a centuries-old structure, Kastamandap, which humbly translates to "wooden pavilion" It sits majestically in the busy World Heritage Site of Durbar Square among other regal temples. Legend has it that this large, three-story structure was built from the timber of a single sal tree in the eleventh or twelfth century CE at a trade crossroads. A shrine with an icon of the **Hindu yogi Gorakhnath** (his emblem is usually a pair of footprints and statues are rare) is housed within the central sanctum, with four nearby statues of Vinayak, aka Ganesh, protector of the Valley, and a busy Ganeshstan shrine abutting Kastamandap to the northeast.

AIRPORT Kathmandu is served by Nepal's only international airport, although Pokhara is under consideration for an upgrade and an international airport is planned for Bara District in the south with a major highway corridor linking that proposed airport with Kathmandu.

ECCENTRICITY AND CHAOS Many people revel in the havoc and eccentricity of Kathmandu's myriad bazaars and bustling streets with shrines and restaurants in every nook and cranny, while others take the first available chance to be rid of the crowds, noise, grit and grime for higher ground. Indeed, the city can be extremely polluted, from the roads to the skyline, and many people wear particle masks to filter the air and extra caution is needed with food and water. Tourist areas are relatively well-maintained and garbage collection takes place, although sometimes erratically. Piles of garbage are often set alight before they can be removed, especially in the cold season when both garbage and wood are used in the city as fuel for warming fires.

POPULATION AND AIR QUALITY The population of Kathmandu Valley in 1980 was around 350,000. The 2011 census estimates that now there are over **2.5 million residents in Nepal's largest city and greater valley** in which it sits with over 4% percent annual population growth. With a high density of people and a lack of adequate measures to control pollution, the joint aggregate of human and industrial activity often blankets the valley in a cloud of smog that travels to the bulwark of the Himalaya and spoils views. However, on windy days, or just after a rainstorm clears out, the urban sprawl reveals the valley's heavenly setting with a broad panorama of the distant Himalaya standing guardian to the north and east. At these times, a visit to a rooftop restaurant will reward onlookers with a dazzling mountain vista.

Air quality is much better than it used to be in the days when garbage was more widely burned and swarms of diesel *tuk-tuks*, small three-wheeled taxis, roamed the lanes and billowing kilns dotted the valley. Even nowadays, kilns are the second largest source of air pollution in the valley, after vehicles. The valley's uninhibited growth requires upwards of 1.2 billion bricks a year. Since 2002, regulations have been implemented that reduce pollution from inefficient kilns, and with the addition of electric, public transport vehicles, air quality has improved dramatically but still has a long way to go. Cooking on wood and coal by some people in the valley adds to the haze. At the ground level, a constant cacophony of horns arise from motorbikes plying the streets and narrow passageways, many of which are crowded with vendors.

HYDROPOWER OPPORTUNITIES Despite Nepal's bulging, Himalayan fed rivers with a vast potential for hydroelectric power, Kathmandu endures daily outages of electricity **(rolling blackouts referred to as 'load shedding')**, especially in the winter season when demand is much higher than capacity with reduced water flow at generating stations. Simply put, the power supply is insufficient and Nepal has neither the facilities nor infrastructure despite many foreign aid projects aimed at improving the situation. Not a few of these immoderately funded projects have been mired in corruption and failed to materialize. With two power hungry neighbors in India and China, Nepal's hydropower potential has been likened to the Middle East's reserve of oil, but the treasure remains untapped and the country remains impoverished.

WATER Kathmandu also suffers from a shortage of potable water. According to Kathmandu Upatyaka Khanepani Limited, the corporation that manages the valley's water supply, daily demand is about 85 million gallons (320 million liters) while supply is merely 24 million gallons (90 million liters) during dry months and 42 million (160 million liters) during the rainy season. Groundwater depletion and quality is a growing concern. One solution to the water woes might be the **harvesting of rainwater**. It has been calculated that over ten times the current water demand falls on the valley's 250 square miles (640 sq km) every year.

EARTHQUAKE DANGER A 2001 study listed Kathmandu as the world's most earthquake-vulnerable city, and the country is in a seismically active zone. Over 1000 minor earthquakes occur annually in Nepal, with a magnitude range of 2 to 5 on the Richter Scale. It is the collision of the Indo-Australian Plate and the Eurasian Plate that led to the uprising of the world's highest range and Nepal's greatest natural attraction, the Himalaya. The 2001 study focused on the following three criteria: building frailty, potential for landslides and floods, and the capability of local authorities for rescue, firefighting, and life-saving operations.

The tragic earthquakes that struck Haiti in January 2010 and Japan in March 2011 raised the call for better readiness in the valley. Worries intensified after a September 2011 earthquake in Sikkim, India, just beyond Nepal's eastern border, registered a magnitude of 6.9. Over 100 people were killed, with six deaths in Nepal. Three people met their demise when a wall at the British Embassy, of all places, collapsed in Kathmandu.

Preparedness has improved little since 2001, while population density has only increased and most buildings are made of poured cement and masonry and erected without regard to building code. Should a heavy trembler hit, it would be catastrophic given Kathmandu's overpopulation and pathetic infrastructure. A major earthquake struck the valley in 1934, killing over 4,500 people in the sparsely populated valley and destroying one-fifth of its structures. Another earthquake in 1988 in eastern Nepal claimed the lives of 721 people and 22,000 houses collapsed.

TOURIST ACCOMMODATION AND FACILITIES The majority of tourists stay in or near an area named **Thamel**. To some, this **globetrotter ghetto** may seem like paradise, whereas to others it is sensory overload. The area has an abundance of facilities and profusion of signs promoting hotels, restaurants, bars, bakeries, and more, including a broad range of shops with everything from Tibetan *thangka* paintings to cheap Chinese snack goods. It also has a fleet of street hawkers, drug pushers, and young, glue-sniffing street beggars. It can seem oddly incongruent with the rest of Kathmandu, not to mention Nepal, and may be overwhelming, especially after a return from the mountains. However, tourism is a mainstay of Nepal's economy and, despite the seeming mayhem, Thamel is a suitable place for arranging travel logistics and picking up gear.

A wide range of equipment and clothing is available, and many shops sell varying quality replicas of brand names (referred to as "North Farce" and "North Fake"). Authentic outlets are along Tridevi Marg and Durbar Marg including Nepal's own **Sherpa Adventure Gear** (with a main showroom near Jai Nepal Cinema Hall).

More difficult to find are genuine mountaineering gear and supplies, found in shops run by mountaineers themselves when they retire or are not away climbing. Some of this gear is left over from prior expeditions and some is new. The road at the southern border of Thamel, perpendicular to Kantipath Road, has several of these shops. Do not be surprised if the owner with whom you are striking a bargain has been to the summit of Everest several times, as well as the tops of other titans. The operator of a shop frequented by the author has scaled Everest thirteen times at last count.

KEEP AND HRA The **Kathmandu Environmental Education Project (KEEP)**, with an associated Porter's Clothing Bank, and the **Himalayan Rescue Association (HRA)** have locations in Thamel. A visit to either will provide a chance to register for free with your respective embassy. Both organizations have notice boards with valuable information for travelers, including people looking for trekking partners. KEEP is a particularly worthwhile visit for unbiased resources and materials, including trekker logbooks with the latest trail information and supplies such as water purifiers, anti-leech oil, biodegradable soap, and more. Contact KEEP at telephone (01) 4410952, info@keep.org or find more information at www.keepnepal.org. As of July 2011, the KEEP office has moved to the Kesar Mahal section of Thamel, a few hundred meters off of Tri-Devi Marg.

HRA (tel. 4440292, 4440293 is currently located on a second floor office of the Sagarmatha Bazaar complex in the nucleus of Thamel, along Mandala Street, one of the few "walking streets" (vehicles not allowed) in Kathmandu, however, this branch is closed during slow times. HRA's main office is in Dhobichaur, Lazimpat, along the road to the north of the former royal palace compound, now Narayanhiti National Museum.

HRA has saved innumerable lives in 40 years of operation and the organization runs two aid-posts: Manang on the Annapurna circuit and Pheriche in the Everest region. Foreigner visitors pay a service charge or can leave a donation. Nepalis are treated free of cost with only a 50 NRS consultation charge for those who can afford it. HRA estimates that annually 5,000 people visit the high altitude posts, and the organization helps coordinate helicopter rescue.

ACCOMODATION BEYOND THAMEL Additional areas to stay in that are popular with tourists include **Paknajol** to the northwest of Thamel, the Chetrapati area to the southwest of Thamel and an area referred to as **"Freak Street" in Basantapu**r near Durbar Square (Kathmandu). Additionally, the area around Baudhnath Stupa has many lodges. These locations have a wide range of accommodation, restaurants, travel agencies, and other shops that cater to tourists. Several upper-end hotels are found along Durbar Marg, the road leading to the front gate of the former palace as well as in the Lazimpat area of town and in the nearby city of Patan (also known as Lalitpur).

GETTING AROUND The city has a public transport network of buses, minivans, and smaller box-shaped vehicles known as *tempos* (the white-and-green *safaa tempos*, aka clean tempos, run on electric power) that travel throughout the valley on specific routes. This is an inexpensive way to get around and allows insight into the lifestyle of city dwellers. Public vehicles are usually brimming with commuters. Placards with numbers and destinations (usually written in Nepali) are posted on windshields.

People seeking transport hail the driver from the roadside along a specified route. To use this system requires more effort than a casual visitor is likely to expend, and some language ability would be useful. That said, the conductors, mostly adolescent boys who announce routes and collect money, are usually, but not always, helpful if not amused by foreigners willing to attempt this public transit network. Otherwise, taxis are ubiquitous and drivers are required to use meters (meters are occasionally tampered with and unreliable). Nonetheless, most taxi drivers will try to negotiate an inflated set fee. Other than walking, traveling via bicycle rickshaw, when they can be found, is the most environmentally sound method of getting around and provides a source of income to some of the poorest inhabitants of the valley while offering a relatively restful, open vantage of the busy streets. Rickshaw *wallah* (drivers) usually lease a rickshaw on a short term basis and can often be seen sleeping in them along the roadside at night as many are homeless.

OBTAINING PERMITS FOR TREKKING Entry permits for national parks and conservation areas as well as **Trekkers Information Management System (TIMS) cards** are available at **Bhrikutimandap** along Pradarshaan Marg (Exhibition Road); passport-size photos are needed, two for each conservation or national park permit as well as two for each TIMS card. (TIMS cards are also available at trekking agencies and at the TAAN Headquarters in the Maligaon section of the city; however, this office is difficult to locate). Bhrikutimandap is also the location of the main offices of the **Nepal Tourism Board (NTB)** and **Tourist Police** headquarters. The NTB has a small visitor center with brochures and leaflets and runs daily programs at its lecture hall open to the public. There are less than forty tourist police for over 500,000 tourists who visit Nepal each year. They report that an average of 600 cases are lodged every year, 80 percent for theft.

RESTRICTED AREAS AND VISA Permits to restricted areas and visa renewals are obtained at the Central Office of the Home Ministry's Immigration Department (www.immi.gov.np) in the Kalikastan section of the city (north of the compound housing parliament, Singha Durbar). To get to the **Immigration Department**, see directions in the VISA EXTENSIONS section of the PRACTICALITIES Chapter. In **Pokhara**, the Immigration Department office is near Ratna Chowk in the southern area of town, west of the airport.

WORLD HERITAGE STRUCTURES The whole Kathmandu valley has been declared a World Heritage Site because of seven structures cited by the United Nations Educational, Scientific, and Cultural Organization (UNESCO) as demonstrating historic and artistic achievements. The World Heritage Sites of Hanuman Dhoka (Kathmandu) Durbar Square, Patan Durbar Square, and Bhaktapur Durbar Square were the respective courts of kings ruling the Kathmandu valley at a time before the country was unified in the late 1760s. An entry fee is required to enter these magnificent areas **(the Valley's tourist attractions have toll gates for foreigners with tiered pricing and steadily rising fees).**

Three other World Heritage Sites are the sacred temple of **Pashupatinath** honoring Shiva, near the airport, and the fabled *stupa* (Buddhist shrines) of **Swayambhunath** and **Baudhnath**, which are centuries-old landmarks and also require entrance fees.

Pashupatinath is Nepal's foremost Shiva temple and receives pilgrims from all over the world and is home to a number of ascetics who have renounced secular life. Pashupati is one of 1,008 names of Shiva and invoked as Nepal's divine benefactor as well as a guardian of all animals. The compound is built along the banks of the Bagmati River where there are cremation platforms. Only Hindus are allowed within the main temple, considered to have been the site of an ancient, pre-Hindu shrine. Pashupatinath receives large crowds during festival times as well as certain days of the month according to the lunar cycle.

Swayambhunath is especially revered by Newar Buddhists and the site dates back to the 5th century. Nicknamed The Monkey Temple (with no shortage of furry but ferocious creatures abiding there), it is perched atop a hillock that rises above Kathmandu's bustling streets and provides a sensational panorama of the valley. Swayambhunath is within 2 km (1.2 mi) walking distance west of Thamel.

Baudhnath is on the NE edge of the city in a section largely populated by people of Tibetan descent. The *stupa* is especially revered by Vajrayana Buddhists and receives visitors from around the world. The monument dates to the early 7th century is roughly 121 ft (37 m) high. Every day, thousands of devotees circumambulate (*kora* in Tibetan) the *stupa* in clockwise fashion, a deed that is said to earn merit. The area is especially active on evenings when the moon is full. More than a dozen extravagant Tibetan monasteries thrive in the surrounding area representing four main Tibetan Buddhist lineages of Gelug, Nyingma, Sakya, Kagyu.

The final, seventh World Heritage Site farther out in the northeast of the valley is **Changu Narayan Temple**, one of the valley's oldest existing temples believed to have been constructed in the third or fourth century. The pagoda is dedicated to Vishnu, whose ten incarnations are molded in its struts and the temple has other elaborate woodcarvings, stone sculptures and metalwork. (Additionally,

UNESCO has tentatively listed the Durbar Square of **Panauti** as a World Heritage Site. Panauti is a Newar town 30 km southeast of Kathmandu).

STREET KIDS Tourists in Kathmandu will inevitably encounter children living on the street. For guidelines on how to respond to begging, please see **"Victims of Kindness"** in the **COUNTRY BACKGROUND** section.

STRAY ANIMALS The Kathmandu Animal Treatment Centre, in Chapali Gaon, Budhanilkantha, is dedicated to the welfare of Nepal's animals, especially Kathmandu's stray dogs. Reach them at www.katcentre.org.np, KATinfo@KATCentre.org.np, and tel. (01) 4373169.

THINGS TO DO IN KATHMANDU

SPORTS AND RECREATION

JOGGING People wishing to keep their legs in shape for the strenuous ups and downs of Nepal's steep trails can visit the **National Stadium**, about a thirty-minute walk down Kantipath Road from Thamel. The stadium is also known as *Dashratha Rangsaalaa* after the martyr Dashratha Chand, executed by firing squad in 1941 CE for inciting a protest against the then ruling Rana regime. The stadium is usually open to all comers from sunup to sundown unless a sporting event is taking place. The track is especially alive in the early morning with joggers and martial arts enthusiasts. You might also connect with the Hash House group in Kathmandu as well as trail runners at **www.trailrunningnepal.org** and join an annual race, the Shivapuri Vertical Kilometer.

SWIMMING AND TENNIS High end **hotels** usually sell day passes for swimming and some have tennis courts as well.

Behind the stadium is the **National Swimming Pool** which guests can visit for a fee of 100 NRS for gents and 90 NRS for ladies. It is closed Sundays and for about 3½ months during the winter cold season. Otherwise, the following three time slots are available: 10 AM–noon, 1 PM to 3 PM, and 4 PM to 6 PM (the cost is increased 50 NRS during this time slot), and 6 PM to 8 PM, members only.

Adjacent to the pool is the complex of the **Nepal Lawn Tennis Association** with three, rough *clay* courts that can be used for a fee. Racquets, partners, and even coaches are available for temporary hire. Costs are 150 NRS/hr/person (75 NRS for Nepalis). Racquets and balls may be rented at 550 NRS/hr and a hitting partner is 40 NRS/hour while a coaching session costs 500 NRS/hr. Monthly memberships are available at 2,200 NRS/month (1,100 for Nepalis) and 6,000 NRS for 3 months, or 20,000 NRS yearly. Hours are 6 AM to 5 PM, and the courts are often busy with members before noon.

On the opposite side of Exhibition Road from NTB at Bhrikutimandap (where conservation area and national park permits are issued), is the **Nepal Police Health Club**. It is open for day visits for a fee; long-term memberships are available, too. Facilities include a large swimming pool, badminton courts and a restaurant. Aerobics and yoga classes are sometimes available in the morning. Costs are activity-based and for swimming, the fee is 200 NRS for non-members (150 NRS for students with identification cards).

YOGA Pranamaya (www.pranamaya-yoga.com) offers daily classes, workshops and retreats and has a studio in Patan and another at '1905' off of Kantipath Road just down from Tridevi Marg (1905 also hosts a Saturday Farmer's Market). Additionally, just down from the former location of the Kathmandu Environmental Education Project (KEEP) office in the Jyatha area of Thamel is the **Brahma Kumari Rajyoga Center**, which offers free week-long introductory courses in **Raja Yoga** and has a meditation hall.

BICYCLING The Valley offers numerous opportunities. Arrange a day out with one of the many agencies specializing in bike tours, or, if feeling adventurous, rent a bike and set off on your own. Once you break away from the congestion of main thoroughfares, discoveries are endless. Bring a mask for dusty roadways! The hamlets along the southern fringe of the valley are especially enchanting.

A recommended long route is a ride to ancient Panauti, 30 kms (19 mi) southeast of Kathmandu by a backroad from Lubhu to Lamatar and up to Lakuri Bhanjyang pass (6870 feet, 2094 m). From the pass it is less than 16 kms (10 mi) downhill to the Newar town of Panauti and a visit to its majestic temple complex is suggested. A short ride to Banepa connects with the Arniko Highway for a return by way of Sanga Pass, where you can pay homage to a **colossal statue of Shiva overlooking Kathmandu Valley.**

VISIT FOREIGNERS IN JAIL Along the way to the stadium from Thamel, in an area named Sundhara, to the right hand side of a gas (petrol) station and near a large shopping complex, is Kathmandu's Central Jail. At any given time, many foreigners are retained there from around the world, most incarcerated for visa or drug violations. Visitations are encouraged, and a smaller women's jail sits behind the men's compound.

MEDITATION RETREATS AND BUDDHIST STUDIES

Those wishing to join a Buddhist meditation course in the land of Buddha's birth (he was born in Lumbini, in the southern Nepal district of Rupandehi) can visit the **Vipassana Foundation**. Regular courses are available on a donation basis. Their main office and nearby meditation hall is just off Kantipath Road. The retreat center, Dharma Singha, is on the outskirts of the valley to the north. The center is above a Hindu shrine known as **Budhanilkantha** and also near a shrine honoring the late **Khaptad Baba**; a large golden *stupa* inside the compound resembles Burma's famous **Schwedagon Pagoda**.

To find the main office in Kathmandu, follow Kantipath to the right (south) from Tridevi Marg. Within five minutes, there is a complex with a Nepal Bank office and Hero Honda motorbike sales shop and combined Honda/Hero-Honda service shop. The office is inside this complex at the basement level and the meditation hall is behind the motorcycle workshop. Courses are run by donation. Visit www.dhamma.org/en/schedules/schshringa.shtml for further information.

The **Himalayan Buddhist Meditation Center (HBMC)** has moved frequently in the last few years and is currently on the top floor of the Himalayan Yoga Hotel in Thamel and offers **meditation, yoga and tai-chi,** and **reiki classes** (please keep up to date at **www.fpmt-hbmc.org**). HBMC holds regular talks on meditation and Tibetan Buddhism, and is under the auspices of Kopan Monastery in Baudhnath and the Foundation for the Preservation of the Mahayana Tradition.

There are many Tibetan monasteries near Baudhnath, some of which regularly hold teachings. The following institutions have courses that cater to interested foreigners: the **International Buddhist Academy** (www.sakyaiba.edu.np), **Rangjung Yeshe Institute** (www.shedra.org), and **Kopan Monastery** (www.kopan-monastery.com).

Most monasteries in the Baudhnath area and elsewhere open their doors to visitors. Please respect the setting (even while some of residents may seem not to). If you visit during daily prayer and chanting ceremonies, you are in for an otherworldly experience, as the sing-song rhythm of the chanting accompanied by bells, conch shell blasts, horns, drums, and cymbals leave quite an impression. These ceremonies usually take place in the early morning or early evening. If you enter a monastery, do not sit against pillars or on cushions unless invited to do so, and obtain permission before taking photographs of the monks.

ADDITIONAL SIGHTSEEING AND MORE

The religious sites of Namo Buddha and Budhanilkantha are worth a visit. **Namo Buddha** is a site where the Buddha, in a prior lifetime, is told to have sacrificed his own flesh out of compassion to save the lives of a famished tigress and her cubs too weak to hunt for themselves.

Budhanilkantha is a 7th century Hindu shrine that features a 23 ft (7 m) long, stone-carved image with a recumbent Vishnu (in the form of Jalasyan Narayan) lying on a serpent representing the cosmic ocean. The former kings of Nepal were considered a manifestation of Vishnu; a soothsayer warned them not to view this particular statue for fear of death upon seeing their own visage (they were, however, allowed to visit a similar, smaller statue in Balaju). The name *Budhanilkantha* (BuDhaanilkaNTha) may seem a bit of a mystery. '*Budha*' refers to 'old' rather than the homonym (at least to foreign ears) of 'Buddha'. '*Nilkantha*' is a reference to Shiva and his blue neck, a result of ingesting a poison that was threatening the destruction of the universe. He was cured by drinking the cool waters of Gosainkunda Lake which he created near a meditation area in the Himalaya for the purpose of soothing his burning throat. The waters at Budhanilkantha are mythically linked to Gosainkunda Lake, and hence, the reference to Shiva, despite Vishnu as the featured deity. **Clamorous evening**

prayers make for a mesmerizing din of devotion and fire. An active Laxmi Shrine lies just above with surrounding totems to Saraswati, Ganesh and more.

Ancient **Pharping** is a 9 mile (15 km) trip outside of the valley to the southwest and is alleged to have existed while Kathmandu Valley was still a lake. Pharping is the site of Nepal's first hydroelectricity station (and Asia's second), built in 1912 when the autocratic Rana dynasty was ruling. Nearby are caves of **Asura** and **Yangleshö**, said to have been used by **Padmasambhava**, also known as **Guru Rinpoche** and yogi **Gorakhnath**. Supposedly, head and handprints of Padmasambhava are impressed on Asura's rock face. There are many majestic Tibetan monasteries in this area where retreats are undertaken.

DAKSHINKALI AND BLOOD SACRIFICE

The slaying of animals is believed to propitiate certain bloodthirsty deities and merit boons. Even human sacrifice, a ghastly practice that began in the Licchavi era is alleged to have continued until last century at a few locations around the Valley. The Dakshinkali Hindu temple complex is not for the squeamish and lies in a gorge about a half mile (1 km) below Pharping. The site was established some five centuries ago and animal sacrifices are made year-round. On busy days, the hectic bazaar surrounding the temple is buzzing with thousands of devotees. Offerings on sale include marigold flowers and garlands, coconuts, and even **raw eggs** and **pumpkins, subsititutes for butchering sentient animals**. The area also has many souvenir and snack stalls for the horde of visitors.

According to a contested interpretation of Hinduism, sacrifice is appeasing (many Hindus are appalled by the practice) and goddesses rather than gods are the usual recipients. At this temple, it is **Kali**, a fierce demon-goddess thought to be easily flattered by supplicants and quick to grant blessings. Kali wears a garland of human heads and is said to have mastered time and is a partner of **Kala (one of Shiva's 1,008 names)**. Legend has it that Shiva was summoned to quell her killing rampage and did so by lying on the ground in front of her. She stopped the massacre only when she realized that she was standing atop her consort, a grave insult. Kali has four hands: one holds a severed head symbolizing the sacrifice mortal beings make to reach ultimate reality (dissolution of the personal ego), another holds a drawn sword to cut away ignorance and reveal divine knowledge, the other two are making gestures of protection and wish fulfillment.

Pujare, or priests who do the slaughtering, perform the sacrifice as supplicants bring animals, mainly roosters, goats and the occasional water buffalo, to the temple and pay the *pujare* as they deem fit (sometimes nothing is given but the severed heads are kept by priests and a candle might be lit atop it to denote that the slain beast's mind has been enlightened). Wealthier Hindus often bring a coterie of animals and their own family priest to perform the rites. According to some views, sacrificial animals represent particular human faults that a donor wishes to relinquish. **Buffaloes are believed to embody the defilement of anger, whereas goats signify lust and desire, sheep represent foolishness, ducks are for laziness and roosters, fear.**

The animals' heads are first sprinkled with water and reflexive head shaking is taken as consent to be ritually decapitated. Icons of the goddess are ceremonially splattered with blood and the carcass is hauled away by the family that brought it and often roasted and consumed nearby at a picnic spot in the forest. Most people arrive before noon, and the busiest bloodletting days are Tuesdays and Saturdays.

Getting there and away: Travel agencies offer trips to Dakshinkali as part of packaged tours. Another option is to hire a taxi for the day and explore nearby Pharping and the Newar villages of Kirtipur, Bungamati and Khokana, too. Arriving by bicycle is relatively pleasant once you gain distance from Ring Road and pass the gateway of Tribhuvan University (Nepal's oldest with one of the largest enrollments worldwide and 7,000-plus professional faculty). Otherwise, find public buses from Old Bus Park (aka, City Bus Park and Ratna Bus Park), and Shahid (Martyr's) Gate.

KIRTIPUR, CHOBHAR, BUNGAMATI, KHOKHANA, GODAWARI Rustic hamlets around the southern fringe of Kathmandu Valley well worth a visit for an inkling of a way of life unchanged for centuries.

Within the valley are the cities of **Bhaktapur** "the city of devotees," and **Patan**, an upscale haven for NGOs. The national zoo is in the Jawalakhel area of Patan (should you desire to witness suffering animals in meager facilities).

NEWAR are the original inhabitants of the valley and their cuisine, language, and culture are unique. Visit a Newar restaurant and try ***chataamari***, a type of Newari pizza among other traditional dishes.

MOMO A plate of *momo* is one of the most satisfying and popular dishes in Kathmandu and often the best value on the menu. These round or crescent-shaped dumplings are common in Nepal, Tibet northeast India, and Bhutan The outer portion is made of dough and usually contains a filling of minced meat, chicken or 'buff' (water buffalo), mixed with onions, garlic and coriander. For "veg *momo*," shredded cabbage is the mainstay in lieu of meat. In local food stalls, the *momo* are splashed with sauce whereas the dipping sauce is provided separately in tourist restaurants.

Usual preparation is steaming in a large gas-fired container. *Kothey momo* are pan-seared after steaming. Another greasy variation is to deep fry the whole *momo*. For those who like it spicy, *C-momo* are smothered in a sauce of chili (the 'C' is for 'chili'), onion, green pepper, and tomato. In tourist places, scrumptious cheese-filled *momo* are sometimes available as well as more decadent varieties with sweet apple filling or even candy bar chunks.

DOHORI Kathmandu has many *dohori* restaurants that provide live Nepal folk music with call and answer repartee between traditionally costumed male and female singers. This is a staged version of a courtship ritual that still exists in villages, and you might be able to witness the genuine version in the hills away from tourist trodden paths.

CINEMA There are several large cinema halls in Kathmandu, mostly showing Bollywood productions with occasional Nepal-made films and other foreign films as well. Kathmandu Guest House, a Thamel landmark, regularly screens movies in their small hall, and in high season, informational lectures and videos documenting popular trekking routes are offered for a fee.

DHARAHARA is located in Sundhara, near the central post office and is also known as Bhimsen Tower. The tower was built in 1932 for Prime Minister Bhimsen Thapa. It stands 165 ft (50 M) high and has a viewing platform near the top with an entry fee of 299 NRS for tourists (160 NRS for SAARC Nationals, and 50 NRS for Nepalis). Incidentally, another tower stood beside the current one, however, it was destroyed in the 1934 earthquake.

SHOPPING AND GAWKING

For a fascinating look at one of city's busiest and most vibrant bazaars, visit the narrow street linking **Asan Chowk** and **Indra Chowk**, and beyond to New Road and Durbar Square. This is a pulsating market area with a seeming endless variety of items on sale and display, from colorful spices to hand-woven carpets and more. However, it is not for the claustrophobic, as the alleyway is packed with merchants, shoppers, onlookers, general pedestrian commuters, and honking motorcyclists.

Many vendors also set up daily in **Ratna Park** and the open grounds just south of it peddling a variety of low-cost items, mostly clothing and bric-a-brac. **Hong Kong Bazaar** (aka, Bhrikutimandap Market) although 1.5 mi (2 km) and full of merchandise, this tarp covered cavernous marketplace is well-hidden and as temporary as the rise and fall of the sun. Goods are hauled in daily in the morning and lugged away each evening. **Situated behind NTB** (where trekking permits and TIMS cards are obtained) the horseshoe-shaped bazaar passes by Singha Durbar before returning to Pradarshan Road. The exit is 125 meters west of Ram Shah Road near Ichhamati Temple which lies along the banks of the putrefying Tukucha, a sluggish stream overburdened with refuse and excreta from a livestock pen.

Basantapur Square, nearby Freak Street fills up daily with unique curios that make fine souvenirs. A former Rana resort, '**1905**', located off Kantipath Road just down from Tridevi Marg, hosts a Saturday morning Farmer's Market featuring savory delicacies.

MUSEUMS

Narayanhiti, the former royal palace and site of the royal family massacre of 2001, is located at the northern end of Durbar Marg in central Kathmandu. After the monarchy was abolished in May 2008 and Nepal declared a republic, the palace was turned into **Narayanhiti National Museum** and opened its doors to the public in February 2009. The museum entry fee is 250 NRS for SAARC and Chinese nationals and 500 NRS for other foreigners. It is closed Tuesday and Wednesday and otherwise open from 11 AM to 4 PM.

The **National Museum (Rastriya Sangrahalaya)** in **Chhauni** is also worth a visit (a Military Museum lies on the opposite side of the road). The entry fee is 100 NRS, and an additional 50 NRS for cameras. The summer hours are 10:30 AM to 4:30 PM (closed Tuesdays; Monday hours are 10:30 AM to 2:30 PM). In winter it closes an hour earlier. The official website is www.nationalmuseum.gov.np

The **Natural History Museum** is located to the southern side of Swayambhunath. The entry fee is 50 NRS and hours are 10 AM to 5 PM (10 AM to 4 PM in the winter), closed Saturdays and public holidays. The official website is http://nhmnepal.org/index.php

BOOKS, MEDIA AND NEWS

There are plenty of book dealers, both new and used, small to behemoth, in Kathmandu, often operated by genuine aficionados of literature. Nepal also has several daily and weekly newspapers that provide goings-on within the valley, mostly of a political nature. Keep in mind that independence of the press is under threat in Nepal with between 288 to 342 incidents of press freedom violations in 2008 (including physical attacks, imprisonment, and more), 155 incidents in 2009, and 107 in 2010 (including 3 murders and 2 abductions).

Some of Nepal's news sources can be accessed online. The following portals provide up to-date news and more about Nepal: **www.thereporter.com.np, www.ecs.com.np, www.nepalnews.com, www.myrepublica.com, www.ekantipur.com/the-kathmandu-post, www.thehimalayantimes.com, www.himalmag.com, www.nepalmonitor.com, www.nepalitimes.com,** and **http://travel.nytimes.com/travel/guides/asia/nepal/overview.html**

HIKES IN THE VALLEY FOOTHILLS

There is much to explore. Please see the guidebook **The Kathmandu Valley Rim and Beyond** for an excursion beyond the ridge to the northeast of the valley. The route offers a three to four day trek that can still be undertaken when a transport halting *banda* (strike or closure of businesses and roads) occurs, or if you have time on your hands and need a break from the turbulent city.

Below are route descriptions to the valley's two highest peaks, **Shivapuri**, to the north, considered a hangout of Hindu deity Shiva, and **Phulchowki**, **"Flower Fortress"**, to the south with staggering views of the valley and Himalaya beyond.

APPROACHING SHIVAPURI PEAK FROM BUDANILKANTA:

To reach the gate of the Shivapuri National Park at Buddhanilkantha, find minivan transport along the road that fronts the **Nepal Airlines Corporation** building (formerly the **R**oyal **N**epal **A**irlines **C**orporation and still referred to as **"RNAC"**) near the gate to New Road where there are many street vendors. This minivan staging area lies to the west of **Tundikhel Parade Ground**. You will need to find the minivan to **Budhanilkantha** or **Mohan Pokhari**. The one that goes to Mohan Pokhari delivers passengers at the gate of the park itself. An onward van to Mohan Pokhari can also be transferred to from vans ending at Budhanilkantha.

Vehicles to Budhanilkantha reach a parking lot 100 meters below the temple complex (¾-1 hour ride from Tundikhel in central Kathmandu). From that drop off point, head through an archway to the right of the taxi stand and up a one-way road. The temple complex is 100 yards/meters up the road on the left side (see the beginning of this section above for more information on this shrine).

About 25 minutes up the road from the temple complex, reach the Shivapuri National Park payment counter (entry fee is 250 NRS for foreigners, 500 NRS for mountain bikers) and army check post (the Nepal Army is tasked with guarding Nepal's National Parks). Across the road from the payment counter is **Dharmasingha**, a Buddhist meditation retreat center. Please see the section above, **MEDITATION RETREATS AND BUDDHIST STUDIES,** for more information on making a retreat here. A large golden *stupa* inside the compound was built to resemble Burma's famous Schwedagon Pagoda.

Inside the park gate the ticket will be registered in a log book and is good for one-entry up to seven days. Just beyond is a large signboard detailing paths to Shivapuri Peak. One way is to travel via **Vishnudwara**, considered the origin of the Vishnumati River that follows a stone staircase much of the way. Another option is by way of Nagi Gomba nunnery and **Baghdwara**, considered to be the source of the Bagmati River. A third option is to travel more directly bypassing **Nagi Gomba**. These three options are outlined below as well as a recommended optional start from Baudhnath and Kopan Monastery.

Option 1: SHIVAPURI PEAK BY WAY OF VISHNUDWARA

Head left from the signboard area (the sign indicates that it is 6 km, or 3.7 mi, to Vishnudwara), cross a bridge and follow a wide set of stone steps. After about 1¼ to 1½ hours reach a built up tap marking the origin of the Vishnumati River. Unfortunately, the surrounding area is often littered with refuse from picnickers. 5 minutes beyond is a trail junction. To the left is a trail that descends steeply towards a road that can be followed west to Kakani (5 to 6 hours away through a jungle without facilities). Follow the path to the right to ascend for 30-45 more minutes before the steps finally end and the single path track continues steeply. Eventually pass below the remains of an old army post and hermitage of the late Shivapuri Baba and the summit beyond in 15 minutes from the end of the stone steps.

Option 2: SHIVAPURI PEAK BYPASSING NAGI GOMBA

From the signboard at the gate to the park, head right up the dirt road. Follow this road, in 20-25 minutes a view of the valley opens up and just over five minutes beyond a set of stone stairs leads off to the left (north) before immediately ascending to the right (east) for a steep climb to the summit (5.5 km away according to a sign, about 3.4 mi). There is a roofed shelter a minute from leaving the road. In 30-35 minutes the stairs end and a single dirt trail begins. The trail ties in with the wider trail from Nagi Gomba in 15 to 20 more minutes. Head left and in less than 30 minutes reach Baghdwara (to continue from **Baghdwara**, then see the section immediately below)

Option 3: SHIVAPURI PEAK BY WAY OF NAGI GOMBA

To travel by way of **Nagi Gomba**, rather than ascend the stone steps to the left of the road described immediately above, keep along the road and in 15 more minutes, ascend another set of stone steps that lead up to the left (the vehicle road continues to Sundarijal, about 9.5 km or 6 miles away). A lower shrine hall is reached in 10 minutes.

Nagi Gomba is a nunnery of the Kagyupa and Nyingmapa lineages of Tibetan Buddhism with some 100-110 residents, mostly Tamang, Tibetan and Newari. The convent has a small shop as well as six guest rooms should you need a stopover. The rooms are often booked by spiritual pilgrims, and more rooms are under construction. To the right of the upper shrine room and small clinic, pass through the compound's gate and follow the prayer flag-lined trail as it climbs through the jungle on a single track. Stay with the widest path and reach Baghdwara in 1¼ hours. Nearby are two cave shelters sometimes occupied by hermits.

Baghdwara is considered to be the source of the sacred Bagmati River. There are three built up spouts and a small pond with a seated Shiva holding a trident. Two *chorten* and several *lingam* have been put up in the area.

A couple of minutes more along the trail is the **ashram** of two yogis and a small, usually unmanned *gombaa*. One of the yogis, ToDke Baba, is from India and has been here 19 years. The name ToDke refers to a hallowed out area at the base of a tree. This baba used to stay in such a place just above on the way to the summit and hence the name. Another yogi goes by the name Pashupati Baba. He has been here 8 years and hails from the Godawari area of Kathmandu Valley.

The path onward splits at the ashram. To the right bypasses Shivapuri Peak and heads to Chisapani, a village on the way to Helambu. The path to the left ascends to Shivapuri Peak and a nearby sign indicates that it is 1 km (.6 miles). To continue to the summit, then follow the path up and in a minute it branches into three trails. Stay with the middle path that ascends steeply and in less than 10 minutes reach 2 hermitages built into a space at the base of trees where ToDke Baba once stayed. Continue on to the summit in about 10 minutes from the tree hermitages. To the west of the summit are the remains of an old army post and hermitage of the late **Shivapuri Baba**. The army post was abandoned during the 10 year civil war (1996-2006) because of threat of Maoist attack and lack of nearby water source. Shivapuri Baba stayed here many years and passed away in 1963, reputedly at the age of 137.

ALTERNATE APPROACH (RECOMMENDED) BAUDHNATH STUPA/KOPAN GOMBA TO NAGI GOMBA

To begin from **Baudhnath Stupa**, then start from Ram Hiti Chowk (intersection) along the road 10 minutes north of the *stupa*. From this intersection, follow the road north about 25 minutes to reach Kopan Chowk (also known as Krishna Chowk) near a small Krishna shrine. This intersection is just above Kopan Bus Park and below Kopan Gomba monastery. From this intersection, follow the road to the right (northeast) passing a secondary school and below Kopan Gomba and Rigpe Dorje Gomba.

In 10 minutes, come to a junction of several roads near the gate of a police training center. Follow the road that leads to the northeast and after 100 yards/meters from the police gate and just beyond a building, head left along a single track that passes to the left (northwest) side below Pulahari Gomba. In 10 minutes reach a road near a secondary school of **Jagadol Bhanjyang** (to the right up this road leads to a gate to Pulahari Gomba).

Stay left and immediately turn left again away from the paved road along a dirt road and reach a *pipal* tree with a small shrine dedicated to Krishna at a junction. Do not follow the roads but ascend the pine tree covered hill to the north (northeast). The first section is steep and crisscrossed with pasturing trails, the route then contours while gradually ascending along the ridgeline toward the north through a peaceful pine forest. Keep to the widest trail and enjoy sensational views along the way.

Reach a large open ground (5577 feet, 1700 m) within an hour with outstanding, open views of Kathmandu Valley to the south and southwest. Nagi Gomba can be seen above to the north and Tare Bhir Village to the northeast. Stay to the right of the ridge and continue on its east side and in 5 minutes, pass a large gate on the left and keep gradually ascending on the wide path and in less than 2 more minutes, branch sharply back to the left and ascend to a pair of houses (to the right continues to Tare Bhir Village) and continue to the right (north), climb steeply along the ridgeline. Pass a small monastery affiliated with Nagi Gomba and just above reach a road in 15 minutes from the pair of houses. Head left, north, (to the right heads to an army guard post and Tare Bhir in 10 minutes). Contour along the road and in a few minutes it branches. Follow the road branching to the right up to Nagi Gomba (6528 feet, 1990 m) in 10 minutes. Please see the section above on **SHIVAPURI PEAK BY WAY OF NAGI GOMBA** to continue from Nagi Gomba.

PHULCHOWKI PEAK, KATHMANDU VALLEY'S HIGHEST SUMMIT

This route leads to the highest summit in the valley, Phulchowki meaning "Flower Fortress". The peak is so named for the abundance of flowers that fill the ridge top near the army post in the summertime. The first section visits villages with sensational views of the mid hills as well as Kathmandu Valley. Further along the trail becomes isolated and passes through dense forest with few facilities, and although rare, attacks have been reported. Use caution and do not travel this area alone.

GETTING TO THE TRAILHEAD The starting point of this hike is **SURYA BINAYAK** (a reference to the sun, Surya, and the Hindu god Ganesha, aka, Binayak) near Bhaktapur on the Arniko Highway. Buses to Bhaktapur leave from City Bus Park (also known as Old Bus Park and Ratna Bus Park) as well as nearby Bhaktapur Bus Park in central Kathmandu. You will need to reach Surya Binayak, the twon adjacent to Bhaktapur along the Arinko Highway, the highway to the border with Tibet. Specifically, begin from **Surya Binayak Chowk** (intersection). At this intersection, follow the side road south away from the highway towards **Surya Binayak Temple** (also known as Ganeshtan), dedicated to the Hindu deity Ganesha. Reach the steps up to the temple within fifteen minutes. The main temple is a short climb from the gate and Aamaasthan (Mother's Temple) is a few minutes higher.

From the main Ganesha Temple area, continue from the south gate to descend to a road in 2 minutes. Head right for a minute and then keep right again. In just over 5 more minutes, reach a small shrine at a branch of the road. Ascend to the right and the road branches again after about 35 more minutes. This time stay left (south) and within 10 more minutes, a road to the right branches to the first houses of **Ghyampedada**. It takes a little less than 10 minutes to pass through the hamlet with a splendid view of Kathmandu Valley to the west.

Continue heading south and within two minutes the wide trail branches. Stay left and within 2 to 3 more minutes avoid a trail that branches to head down to the east but stay on the main trail. Just beyond, take the trail up to the right (west) away from the main trail. Ascend steeply for several minutes to tie in with a road above and follow it left.

Reach **Rankikot** (6345 feet, 1934 m) in about 10 more minutes. Be advised that the route onward passes through an unpopulated area and theft has been reported. Do not travel alone. Stay to the right (west) for Lakuri Bhanjyang and the most direct route to Phulchowki. In a few minutes, the road ends at **Bhag Bhairab**, a rock shrine said to resemble a tiger. Take the upper of two trails to the left that pass below Bhag Bhairab and then follow along the ridgeline with magnificent views of the Kathmandu Valley on the right side.

Reach a few houses in a little over 20 minutes and follow the wide trail to the right (north) that descends and stay left at a branch to a school and collection of shops and restaurants at **Lakuri Bhanjyang** in less than 10 minutes.

Lakuri Bhanjyang is at a crossroads. To the right (west) the road descends to buses at Lamatar about 1¼ hour (3.4 miles, 5.5 km) below with bus service to Kathmandu. To the left (east), the road continues to Panauti, 9.6 miles (15.5 km) away.

LAKURI BHANJYANG TO PHULCHOWKI SUMMIT

To continue to the peak, head east for a about 100 meters/yards before ascending to the right (southwest) away from the main road along a wide track. Stick to the main trail and within 10 minutes pass a set of stairs branching to the right (the stairs ascend to a viewpoint 2 minutes above). In less than 5 more minutes, the trail branches. Stay right to ascend gradually and contour and descend to a school at a saddle (6890 feet, 2100 m) in 20-25 minutes. Find the fainter path on the southeast side of the saddle rather than the wider trail that ascends to the east, although both tie in beyond. Reach **Champakharka** (6844 feet, 2086 m) in just over 10 minutes. From here, cross to the southwest (the road to the right (west) descends to Godawari and the road to the left (southeast) heads into Nuwakot District).

From Chapakharkha to the peak the trail passes through dense forest without facilities. Ascend to the southwest and in 15 minutes avoid a trail heading downward to the left (east). Within 10 more minutes the trail branches. Stay to the right and generally head south and stick to the main trail. In 20-25 more minutes, the trail branches again. Both branches head to the road above, whereas the left branch is the more direct, albeit steeper option. Reach the main roadway to the peak in less than 10 minutes. Head left and follow it to the summit, about 1¼ hours or 2.8 miles (4.5 kms) away.

The summit (9039 feet, 2755 m) has an army post guarding signal towers as well as a small Hindu shrine, **Phulchowki Mai**. Views are somewhat obstructed by the towers, barracks and boulders at the top.

Godawari lies below and to the northwest of the summit, and transport to Kathmandu can be found there. Follow the road from the top all the way down to the micro-bus stand just below Saint Xavier's school. The journey of 8.7 miles (14 kms) and takes nearly 3 hours with no facilities and few to no water sources along the way until the valley floor.

Just above St. Xavier's and a bus staging area is the Hindu **Nau Dhara Temple**. To the east of the bus stand is a paved road to the **National Botanical Gardens**, a 10 minute walk away. The entry fee is 10 NRS for Nepalis, 25 for SAARC country members and 100 NRS for non-SAARC foreigners. Nearby the gardens is the Hindu shrine dedicated to **Godawari Kunda**. To the west of the bus stand is a quarry and marble factory. To reach Kathmandu, you will likely have to transfer to two other minivans before reaching City Bus Park (aka, Old Bus Park or Ratna Bus Park in central Kathmandu).

KEEP (KATHMANDU ENVIRONMENTAL EDUCATION PROJECT)

A visit to KEEP in the Kesar Mahal section of Thamel is highly recommended. KEEP strives to provide unbiased information on tourism and trekking. Their goal is to maximize the benefits of tourism while minimizing the negative impact. Register with your embassy for free there, and maps are on hand, along with logbooks in which trekkers record up-to-date experiences along the trails. These logbooks are invaluable sources of current information on trail conditions and facilities. There are also notice boards announcing the latest news and regulations, with postings by travelers looking for trekking partners. KEEP has an in-house Green Café and store that sells eco-friendly trekking products such as biodegradable soap, anti-leech oil, and water purifiers. There is a convenient library as well with free videos, such as the BBC's documentary on porters, *Carrying the Burden*, and a viewing room, too.

KEEP runs a Porter Clothing Bank—established by D. B. Gurung of KEEP and Ian Wall of Community Action Nepal (CAN), and financed and stocked by the IPPG, Porters Progress UK, the Mountain Fund, and International Mountain Explorers Club—where you may get clothing for porters (a deposit is required) and donate garments and gear as well. KEEP will also arrange collection of donations from your hotel (contact information below). The clothing bank is managed by a former porter who lost part of his feet to frostbite.

KEEP welcomes volunteers to conduct English language courses (and sometimes German and other languages), mostly for porters and guides. They also provide training for tourism professionals in trekking responsibly, first aid, mountain safety, flora and fauna, and cultural heritage, and conducts environmental awareness programs for all-comers. Financial donations are accepted directly at their office where you can also become a member of this exemplary organization. Funds go towards the aforementioned activities as well as ongoing outreach projects. KEEP might also help place travelers who wish to volunteer in some capacity in Nepal. Contact KEEP at tel. (01) 4410952, info@keep.org or find more information at www.keepnepal.org π

KATHMANDU TO POKHARA

There are regular **flights** between these two cities, best arranged through a local travel agency. Air time is 30 minutes. For Himalayan views, request a seat on the right side on the way to Pokhara and left for the leg to Kathmandu.

Tourist Bus tickets can be purchased from travel and trekking agencies, and many depart from Kantipath Road, a few minutes south) from Thamel's Tridevi Marg road and other convenient sites. The 200 km journey takes roughly 7 hours. Public buses to Pokhara can be found at Balaju Bus Park (aka, *Nayaa Bas Park* or New Bus Park) and mini-vans across Ring Road from it. Additionally, same day buses and mini-vans can also be found at the intersection to the west of Kathmandu's Ring Road named **Kalanki Chowk**.

Kalanki Chowk is at a crossroads for vehicles leaving the valley via the Thangkot escarpment. The journey follows the Prithvi Rajmarg highway, the major artery for vehicles traveling to eastern and western Nepal as well as south to India. The road out of the Valley climbs gently to a pass and then descends laboriously on a winding road. It is slow going to Mugling, halfway to Pokhara and point of confluence of the Marsyangdi and Trishuli rivers, which become the Narayani River. Most vehicles turn south at Mugling to follow the Narayani 22 miles (36 km) to the highway that runs the east-west length of Nepal, the Mahendra Rajmarg. Roads are planned for a direct southern link between Kathmandu and the Tarai to a potential new international airport in Bara District as well as a link to eastern Nepal. However, until completed, the current route is likely to remain clogged with traffic.

POKHARA

Pokhara (2,690 ft, 820 m) is an attractive lakeside city 125 miles (200 km) west of Kathmandu and a restful hub for deeper ventures into the Himalaya as well as post-trek rejuvenation. Its busiest tourist months are October, November and March followed by September and April. Visitors relish the city's many offerings including adventure sports (paragliders can be seen throughout the day as they make their way down from a nearby ridge top), shopping, and a busy restaurant, bar and music scene. The tourist area has a laid back atmosphere with many facilities for travelers.

On clear days, Pokhara's setting is breathtaking with white-capped mountains looming large as they peek over the hills into the city. The mountains are best seen from the southern fringe of the valley where high end hotels are located. The highlight is magnificent **Macchapuchhre "Fishtail"** (6,997 m, 22,956 ft), considered sacred and therefore off limits to climbing.

PHEWA LAKE AND PEACE PAGODA (AKA, SHANTI STUPA)

Most tourist accommodation lies along the north shore of Phewa Tal, a 1.7 mi² (4.5 km²) lake that has been dammed for hydropower. The lakeshore offers a pleasant place for a stroll. Phewa is also a source of some commercial fishing, mostly to the northwest.

Boats can be hired to reach **Barahi Temple** set on a small island and for general leisure. One method to reach the Peace Pagoda (the white *stupa* on the hilltop to the south) is to travel across the lake by boat and hike up from the far shoreline.

The **Peace Pagoda** is otherwise accessed by a rough road that leaves from Siddhartha Highway (the road link to Butwal and the *tarai*) at the southeast end of the lake. The shrine was built in 1996 with Japanese support and on good days, the views from it are jaw-dropping with the lake and valley below and the snowy mountains as a backdrop including three of the world's ten highest: Annapurna (8091 m, 26,545 ft, world's 10th highest), Dhaulagiri (8167 m, 26,794 ft, world's 7th highest) and Manaslu (8156 m, 26,758 ft, world's 8th highest).

Accommodation has been recently constructed for those wishing to spend the night and catch sunset and sunrise vistas.

Circuit Loop Day Hike around Phewa Lake From **Peace Pagoda**, follow along the ridgeline east to Lukunswara Village and stay right to continue to Pumdi where you will descend to the marshlands of the lake. There are makeshift wooden bridges to head directly to the other side or contour around the valley to meet the road and local bus service at Pame Village. Otherwise, follow the road for a pleasant stroll along the north shore of the lake back to Pokhara.

PANCHASSE TREK (4 to 5 Days) The route follows a high ridge above and south of the Polkhara Valley. Highlights are stunning views from Panchasse Peak (8257 ft, 2517 m) and vistas from the ridgeline along the way as well as the luxuriant village scenery in an area that sees few tourists. The trail begins near the Damside area of Pokhara and climbs northwest before continuing north to Naudanda and the Baglung/Beni Highway where transport back to Pokhara is available. Otherwise you follow the ridgeline to Sarangkot and descend to Pokhara from there.

SETI RIVER GORGE AND SURROUNDING LAKES

Not many visitors are aware of the gorge that runs through Pokhara, at times very narrow. The Seti Khola ("White River"), so named for its chalky waters, has created deep canyons best experienced at the north and south ends of the city.

Begnas Lake lies about 18 km out of town and has a few tourist facilities, too. Other smaller and more remote lakes in the area include **Rupa** and **Lipang**.

DEVI'S FALLS, CAVES AND TIBETAN SETTLEMENTS

Devi's Falls (also known as *Patale Chhango*) is located a few kilometers south of the airport along the Siddhartha Highway and is a hustling tourist attraction that requires an entrance fee. The cascading waters of the Pardi Khola, a tributary of the Seti Gandaki, emerge from Phewa Tal. The falls disappear into an underground gorge and reappear a half a kilometer away. Across the road is **Gopteswar Mahadev Cave**, which also requires an entry fee, **Mahendra Gufaa, also known as Bat Cave,** lies to the north of the Pokhara-Baglung/Beni Highway.

TIBETAN REFUGEES When China invaded and captured Tibet in 1959, thousands of Tibetans fled south to Nepal. Pokhara lies on an old trade route between India and Tibet and was a likely place for asylum. Three Tibetan encampments have been set up in the region. **Tashi Ling** is a settlement just up the road from Devi's Falls and has a *gomba* as well as Tibetan medical clinic. **Tashi Pakhel**, near Hyangja village, lies on a shelf of land overlooking the Seti Gandaki, five kilometers from Pokhara along the Baglung/Beni Highway and has guest house accomdation and a monastery. Paljor Ling is associated with the Tibetan Handicraft Center near the center of town.

ADVENTURE SPORTS

White water **rafting trips, mountain biking, rock climbing, canyoning, ultra-light aircraft flights, a zipline** and **paragliding** can easily be arranged at agencies in Pokhara as well as Kathmandu with programs for beginners to experts. Recently, a company has been offering **"parahawking"**, paragliding accompanied by a magnificent bird of prey. The birds assist in finding thermal uplifts and occasionally land and take off from the paraglider's gloved arm. Magnificent birds are provided by **Himalayan Raptor Rescue**, a rehabilitation center for injured raptors. Unfortunately, many wild birds in Nepal are succumbing to illness and death after feeding on carcasses of animals fed on pharmaceuticals poisonous to birds.

Daily hatha yoga classes are available at the Nepali Yoga Centre (www.nepaliyoga.com), a few hundred meters/yards along the main road (east) from Hallan Chowk. Additionally, there are two nine-hole golf courses with driving ranges within 4.5 miles (7 km) from Pokhara. The Yeti Golf Course is associated with the Fulbari Resort.

SARANGKOT

This village lies an hour hike's up to the north of Pokhara and is a popular take off point for paragliders and has a newly built 1.8 km (1.1 mile) **zipline** that drops over 600 m (2000 ft) in 2 minutes. Reach it by motor road from nearby Baglung Bus Park. Otherwise hike up for about an hour from the northern shore of the lake. Tourist accommodation and facilities are available but prices are higher than Pokhara, and the panoramic views make it worthwhile!

MOUNTAINEERING AND GURKHA MEMORIAL MUSEUMS

The large **Mountaineering Museum** is dedicated to the Himalaya, its people and climbers. Fascinating displays feature historical information about the ascent history of the world's highest mountains and include mountaineering gear and personal accounts. Other exhibitions cover culture, plant and wildlife as well as climate-change in the Himalaya.

Pokhara and the surrounding area is a primary recruiting ground for the world-renowned Gurkha soldiers. The **Gurkha Memorial Museum** is on the grounds of the British Camp north of the Mahendra Pul area of town and contains memorabilia from Gurkha history and warfare exploits including uniforms, medals and photographs.

SHOPPING BAZAARS

Many tourist oriented shops and street peddlers line the main strip in the Lakeside area. Locals flock to a bustling commercial sector near an intersection known as **Prithvi Chowk** and up to **Mahendra Pul** (recently re-named Bhimsen Chowk). The area has many shops, restaurants and street-side vendors dealing mostly in clothing and knickknacks.

GETTING AROUND

City buses and minivans ply the major thoroughfares of the city. Hail them from the roadside as they approach. It will help to know the pronunciation of the destination and the attendant, often a teenage boy, can alert you at the appropriate place. Fares are nominal, however, vehicles are often packed and might offer standing room only. Taxis are comparatively expensive but quicker and more comfortable.

Consider **hiring a bicycle** near **Hallan Chowk** or from a guesthouse for the day or even a **motorbike** to get outside of the metropolitan area into the beautiful countryside. Roads link Pokhara to the south to the *tarai* via the Siddhartha Highway, Kathmandu via the Prithvi Highway, and up to Beni and now even on to Jomsom and soon a linkage to the Tibetan frontier will be unlocked.

For a highly recommend side-trip to **Bandipur**, 70 km southeast of Pokhara, please see **Dumre** in the section below, **TO MANANG AND OVER THORUNG LA,** *Eastern Valley of the Circuit.* Dumre lies along the Pokhara-Kathmandu (Prithvi) Highway and is an access town for a counterclockwise trip around the Annapurna Circuit. Bandipur is an enchanting hamlet perched on a ridge a 2 hour hike west of Dumre and sensational place to explore and unwind.

GETTING THERE AND AWAY

Please see the end of the Kathmandu section for arranging **flights** and **buses** between Kathmandu and Pokhara.

There are **three main bus parks** in Pokhara. One is convenient for tourists, located in southeast end of the **Lakeside** area on the way to the airport near the intersection known as Mustang Chowk. This Tourist Bus Park, aka Mustang Bus Park, has tourist buses to Kathmandu, Chitwan and beyond.

Baglung Bus Park is for travelers to the ACAP trailheads of Phedi, Kande and Naya Pul as well as Baglung, Beni and further into the remote hills north of Pokhara including Jomsom (about 150 km to the northwest). It lies 2 km up (north) from the intersection known as **Zero Kilometer**, aka Baglung Chowk. The main **public bus park** to the east of **Prithvi Chowk** has buses heading east to Kathmandu as well as to the south including **Bhairawa** near the **Indian border** town of **Sunauli**, and many more destinations.

POLLUTION WHERE IT'S PRETTY

An increasing downside to scenic Pokhara Valley is the issue of solid waste management. In the evening, shops away from tourist zones burn garbage from daily commerce, including noxious plastics and the smoke fills the valley. Additionally, towns and villages along roadways often dispose of refuse into nearby rivers.

STAYING HEALTHY

Gastro-intestinal issues and respiratory infections are the primary causes of illness in travelers to Nepal, and slips from the trail are the leading cause of death to trekkers. Trail safety should not be overlooked among other concerns. Bear in mind difficult conditions might be encountered at high elevations far from help. Unexpected weather can arrive swiftly and without warning. Consider obtaining travel and evacuation insurance in addition to standard medical coverage. Insurance will not prevent you from having to arrange payment for helicopter rescue should it be necessary, but will help to recover substantial costs.

The Himalayan Rescue Association (tel. 01- 4440292, 4440293, hra@mail.com.np, www.himalayanrescue.org, might help arrange insurance in Kathmandu. Inquire at The Himalayan Rescue Association's main office in Dhobichaur, Lazimpat (along the road to the north of the former palace), or the Nepal Mountaineering Association, tel. 01-4434525, www.nepalmountaineering.org, in the Naxal area of Kathmandu.

VACCINATIONS

Visit your physician to obtain vaccinations at least **4-6 weeks before the date of travel** to ensure that you are current before arrival. If your status is incomplete in Nepal, vaccinations are available in Kathmandu with several options for health care service (check with embassies for advice).

Many travelers and expatriates select the **CIWEC Travel Medicine and Dental Center**, tel. 01-4424111, fax 4412590, www.ciwec-clinic.com, across the road from the British Embassy (just down from the Indian Embassy) on Kapurdhara Marg road in the Lainchaur area of Kathmandu. CIWEC stands for Canadian International Water and Energy Consultants - the clinic was originally started to provide medical care for employees of this organization and expanded to the general public. The **Nepal International Clinic** (NIC), tel. 01-4434642, fax 4434713, www.nepalinternationalclinic.com has Western trained Nepali doctors. It is located between Durbar Marg and Naxal, near the front gate of the former palace, now Narayanhiti National Museum. The **Patan Hospital** in Lagankhel offers decent care. Other less modern facilities include the crowded Tribhuvan University Teaching Hospital near the U.S. Embassy in Maharajganj affiliated with Nepal's first medical school.

The following immunizations are recommended for Nepal: **DPT (diphtheria, pertussis, tetanus), MMR (measles, mumps, rubella), Hepatitis A (or immune globulin), Hepatitis B, poliovirus, typhoid fever**, and **seasonal influenza**. You might also consider vaccines for **Japanese encephalitis** and **rabies**.

Rabies is spread by infected animal saliva as it penetrates the skin. In case of an **animal bite**, treat by washing the wound immediately with soap and water as well as a dilute solution of salt water. If rabies is suspected, seek medical treatment as soon as possible. Prevent bites by not moving suddenly toward any animals, especially on first encounter. When dogs threaten, approach with a stick or stones. Most dogs and beasts of burden in Asia shy away from the merest hint of being struck. An alternate approach is offering a scrap of food. Kindness to dogs is a rarity in Asia and might fast earn a friend and four-legged trekking partner. Keep in mind the manifold risks to a dog of displacing it from an area to which it has become accustomed and has found means to survive.

Japanese encephalitis is a potentially fatal viral infection spread by a certain species of mosquitoes. Cases have recently been reported in Nepal, mostly in the *tarai* (lowland plains), during August and September, and Kathmandu Valley post-monsoon. Japanese encephalitis is rare among casual visitors.

Malaria was once endemic in the *tarai*, but today has been controlled and risk is low. The current protection for malaria is one of the following suppressants: atovaquone/proguanil, doxycycline, or mefloquine. The chance of contracting it while trekking in the hills and mountains is slight, especially above 4000 feet (1200 m).

A useful **health information resource** is the (US) Center for Disease Control's country-specific website for Nepal, www.cdc.gov/travel/destinations/nepal.aspx

Additionally, an informative website run by diabetics regarding mountain activities is www.diabetic.friendsinhighplaces.org

THE TREKKER'S PERSONAL FIRST-AID KIT

- **Altitude Medicine** Acetazolamide (Diamox), 250-mg tablets
- **Antibiotics**, eg, azithromycin, ciprofloxacin or norfloxacin (broad spectrum, especially useful for bacterial diarrhea and other infections)
- **Anti-fungal cream**
- **Antihistamine/decongestant** for colds and allergies
- **Anti-motility medicine** loperamide (2 mg) for unavoidable travel while suffering with diarrhea
- **Antiseptic** for cleaning wounds, eg, Betadine
- **Band-aids**
- **Elastic Bandages/Gauze Pads**
- **Moleskin, Secondskin, Blister Pads** Felt or foam for the prevention of blisters
- **Motion Sickness tablets** for vehicle travel
- **Oral rehydration powder** aka, *Jeevan Jal*, can be purchased in pharmacy shops, health posts, and general shops
- **Painkiller, anti-inflammatory, anti-fever tablets**
- **Sunscreen** ayurvedic sun block creams are available in Kathmandu
- **Throat lozenges**
- **Temporary filling material** for dental emergencies and/or eugenol, oil of cloves, used as a topical analgesic and antiseptic

- **Tinidazole** for *giardiasis* and *amoebiasis* (protozoan infections)
- **Water purification materials** (see below)

DIARRHEA

The CIWEC website has an informative web page , "Understanding Diarrhea in Travelers" at www.ciwec-clinic.com/articles/understanding_diarrhea.php

Bacterial infection is the most common cause of travelers' diarrhea in Nepal. Symptoms generally include quick onset often accompanied or preceded by chills or fever and cramps. **Ciprofloxacin**, 500-mg, is the antibiotic of choice for infectious bacterial illnesses. The dose is one capsule every twelve hours until symptoms subside. Alternatively, **norfloxacin** may be tried, one 400-mg capsule taken every twelve hours until symptoms subside. **Azithromycin** would be a good choice for children. The dose can range (depending on body weight) from 5 to 20 mg per kg body weight per day. The adult dosage for azithromycin is 500 mg, one capsule per day.

Giardia is the cause of about one in ten cases of travelers presenting with diarrhea at CIWEC. It generally takes a longer time to acquire than bacterial infections, usually two weeks and sometimes longer, after ingesting cysts. Stools often contain mucus and, as with some bacterial cases, might smell like rotten eggs or sulfur, as will expelled gas. A churning stomach, cramping, and bloating are common, vomiting and fever are rare. The treatment is 2 grams of tinidazole as a single dose, repeated in 24 hours.

Cyclospora is a protozoan parasite acquired through contaminated food or drink. Risk of infection is mainly during the monsoon season, June through September. Common symptoms include watery diarrhea, bloating, gas, loss of appetite, and prolonged fatigue. Vomiting, fever, and other flu-like symptoms may present, although some infected people may be asymptomatic. Without medical intervention, the illness might self-limit within a few days to a month or longer, and relapses can occur. Treatment is co-trimoxazole (TMP/SMX) every twelve hours for seven days. *Cyclospora* cysts are resistant to disinfectants and can survive chlorine and iodine, which then leaves boiling as the surest means of purifying water.

WATER PURIFICATION

Although boiling is the safest means to obtain drinking water, it is not usually feasible and requires scarce fuel resources, especially in rural areas. Bottled water is available on popular treks but will be difficult to find on trails that see few tourists. It is claimed to be treated, although studies repeatedly find contaminated supplies. Disposal of empty bottles is burdensome, too. Using a filter, even a piece of clean cloth, is a good idea as **most microorganisms are not free floating but attached to particles in water**.

Chlorine Dioxide **droplets or tablets**, though not easily found in Nepal, are better than other chorine-based options available in Kathmandu, which do not offer full protection.

Troclosene sodium (sodium dicholoroisocyanurate), chlorine disinfectant now widely available in Kathmandu under different names including **Aquatabs** and **Micropure**.

Iodine Tablets, use one tablet per quart (liter) of water. Available in Kathmandu at KEEP and elsewhere.

Tincture of Iodine (**USP – United States Pharmacopeia**), 2% solution. Add five drops per quart (liter), wait 30 minutes before drinking

Strong Iodine Solution (**BP - British Pharmacopeia**), 10% solution, one-two drops and wait 30 minutes

Lugol's Solution (iodine), available in some pharmacies in Kathmandu as well as the larger stores that cater to wealthier clientele. Solution strength may vary; if 2% solution, then 4-5 drops per quart (liter).

Filtering, water filters are effective but bulky to carry.

UV Light (SteriPEN), small handheld device with reputed ability to purify a liter of clear water in less than 2 minutes. It requires expensive batteries. Devices are available in Kathmandu at KEEP and some trekking supply shops. Don't depend on it without a backup system.

Drink mixes can be added to improve flavor to chemically treated water after the disinfection period has elapsed.

FOOD HYGIENE

Food contamination may occur from the preparation and handling of the food by unclean hands (hand soap is not widely used in Nepal), unclean plates, cups and utensils, flies and airborne contaminants. Be vigilant but realize that lack of complete sanitation is a fact of life in Nepal and comes with the territory. Food can otherwise be assumed to be safe if it has just been cooked and not left out for a long period of time.

RESPIRATORY INFECTIONS

Upper-respiratory infections, including the common cold occur frequently in Nepal. Physicians in the high-altitude Khumbu region have noted that the three most common ailments are **bronchitis**, aka, "Khumbu cough," brought on by cold, arid conditions, **gastroenteritis**, and **viral upper-respiratory infections**.

THE TYRANNY OF LEECHES DURING THE MONSOON

Sanguivorous leeches thrive during wet conditions, vying for a trekker's 10 some pints of blood. During the monsoon, they are abundant in forests above 4000 feet (1200 m)...and the author once became attached to one at over 12,000 ft (3700 m). These jawed, terrestrial parasites (*Gnatbobdellida* of the suborder *Hirudiniformes*) are sensitive to light and attracted to movement, warmth, and by-products of respiration. They can drop from vegetation or "crawl" in inch-worm fashion (by using suckers at each end of the body) up from the ground as well as attach from leaves or rocks. Leeches find hosts by detecting shadows, mechanical stimuli of vibrations and heat as well as chemicals (carbon dioxide and skin oils).

As ecto-parasites, they attach themselves by means of tiny teeth or sharp cutting edges. Although leeches feed off the blood of a host, bites usually go unnoticed because a concomitant anesthetic is released. They also disperse an anticoagulant (the peptide *hirudin* is in their saliva) to keep the prey's blood flowing and eventually, will drop off once sated. This may take twenty to forty minutes or longer, in which time the leech can swell many times in size.

A single feeding is enough to sustain a leech for several months and they burrow into the ground to survive long dry periods. Leeches are hermaphroditic and deposit eggs in a cocoon after copulation and exhibit advanced care of young not usually seen in the phylum *Annelida*. They are sometimes used medically during recovery in plastic and reconstructive surgery cases and are helpful in the drainage of pooled blood, especially to relieve venous congestion and maintain circulation.

To remove a leech, use the leading edge of a fingernail (or other flat object) scraped along the skin to dislodge the thinner, anterior end at the attachment site. Keep the wound clean. **Other means of removal—such as pulling or using heat, salt, alcohol, or insect repellent—can cause the leech to release the contents of its stomach which contain bacteria and may infect the bite area.** Jawed leeches are not known to be transmitters of disease, however, because of anticoagulants there might be considerable blood flow. Control the minute lesion with pressure, and watch for signs of infection later. Rarely, some people have an anaphylactic or other allergic reaction to leech bites, requiring serious medical attention.

If embarking on a monsoon trek, certain items of equipment are essential: a waterproof pack cover, sheets of plastic for porter loads, an umbrella, a hat with a brim, a walking stick, footwear with good traction and **especially leech protection**. The best preventive to bites is to cover the skin. However, leeches often find a way through clothing. Some insect repellents work when applied to boots, lower legs and exposed skin. "**Anti-Leech Oil**," a potent elixir of five oils, is available in some pharmacies and shops in Kathmandu and at the Kathmandu Environmental Education Office (KEEP) in Kesar Mahal, Thamel. Other options include eucalyptus oil, lemon juice, or smearing bath soap over dry skin and leech-proof socks could be worn over regular socks. With preparation, a foray into the leech infested heights can be relatively trouble free, and the rewards memorable.

ALTITUDE ILLNESS AND ENVIRONMENT-INDUCED HEALTH PROBLEMS

While trekking in the lap of the highest mountains on Earth, certain precautions are necessary. Visitors must pay attention to the environment and to messages that their own bodies are giving as well as signs that fellow travelers are in need of assistance. Information sessions about altitude illness are given by the Himalayan Rescue Association in Kathmandu and at aid posts in the Khumbu (Everest Region) at **Pheriche** and **Maccherma** and in **Manang** (Annapurna Region). (Additional information on altitude illness is available from CIWEC at www.ciwec-clinic.com/articles/altitude_illness_advice_for_trekker.php)

Physically fit, active people might be at increased risk given that strength and energy allows them to ascend more quickly and they might also be accustomed to pushing through discomfort, especially dangerous at elevation. Altitude illness can strike anyone regardless of fitness level and is prevented by acclimatization, ascending gradually while allowing rest days and being watchful of symptoms. **Acetazolamide** (Diamox) is beneficial in helping the acclimatization process, too. The preventative dose is 125 mg by mouth two or three times a day, begun a day before ascending to higher elevations, and can be increased to 250 mg when symptoms present.

If any of the following **mild Acute Mountain Sickness (AMS)** symptoms are present, then do not ascend higher but remain at the current elevation or descend until better. If symptoms worsen, descend to below where symptoms began and **DO NOT ASCEND HIGHER:**

- **headache**
- **nausea**
- **loss of appetite**
- **difficulty sleeping**
- **fatigue**
- **dizziness or light-headedness**

Serious symptoms of altitude illness require immediate descent without delay, regardless of hour and by porter, pack animal or other means if necessary. These symptoms include:

- **lack of balance, loss of coordination, staggering, inability to walk a straight line (this is the most serious indicator of altitude sickness and requires immediate descent)**
- **breathlessness at rest, difficulty breathing**
- **mental confusion**
- **severe headache**
- **rapid resting heart rate—120 or more beats per minute**
- **persistent cough, coughing up fluid**
- **blueness of face and lips**
- **persistent vomiting**

FROSTBITE (frozen body tissues) is rare in trekkers. Prevent cold injuries with adequate clothing and equipment, by eating enough food, and by avoiding dehydration and exhaustion. (Conversely, to counter hot weather, soaking bandannas, hats, and shirts in water can be helpful, too.)

EMERGENCY CARE AND RESCUE FACILITIES

Nepal aims to provide secondary health care in each of the 75 districts with hospitals staffed by physicians. Primary health care is provided by health posts scattered throughout each district. If an emergency occurs, local schoolteachers may be a helpful resource and usually can speak English.

Additionally, keep in mind that a main reason behind a TIMS card charge is to provide rescue funds for trekkers and staff. It may be a challenge convincing TAAN and NTB to reimburse you, however, rescue is a service they consented to when implementing TIMS card fees, and there ought to be a large reserve of funds.

HELICOPTER RESCUE

The Himalayan Rescue Association (HRA) reports that Nepal has over 150 helicopter evacuations annually. The cost of helicopter rescue is high—nearly $2,500 per hour and companies charge a minimum of three hours for roundtrip rescue flights from Kathmandu to the Annapurna and Everest regions. This has to be underwritten by the party involved, unless rescue insurance has been taken out previously; alpine clubs in your home country sometimes provide insurance as will some organizations in Nepal. HRA www.himalayanrescue.org, and NMA www.nepalmountaineering.org might have more information on registered agencies in Kathmandu.

Pheriche (Everest) rescues are corrdinated by HRA's Mr. Basyal +977 9841320378, and 038-540214 and Manang (Annapurna) by HRA's Mr. Acharya +977 9841355667 and +977 993664515. Register at your embassy in Kathmandu to facilitate the process in the event they receive a rescue message.

EMERGENCY NUMBERS

If air rescue is necessary, send a message to Kathmandu for a helicopter. City area codes are 01 for Kathmandu and 061 for Pokhara (you may have to omit the zero depending on from where the call is made). The phone numbers of the agencies and rescue facilities should be checked once you reach Kathmandu. Phone numbers change frequently. There is no emergency network in Nepal. You can try the police emergency numbers 100, 110, and 122. Rescue messages should be sent to one or more of the following (redundancy helps ensure that at least one message will arrive) in order of preference:

• **Himalayan Rescue Association** (tel. 01-4440292, and 4440293, mobile +977 9851033046, hra@mail.com.np, www.himalayanrescue.org)
• **The embassy or consulate of the victim** (for U.S., tel. 01-4007200, 01-4007266, 01-

4007269, fax 01-400-7281, http://nepal.usembassy.gov; for Canada, tel. 01-4415193; for U.K., tel. 01-4410583; for Australia, tel. 01-4371678)

• **The trekking agency that organized the trek**, if applicable; (get the home phone number of the managing director before you leave Kathmandu)

Helicopter Operators
• Fishtail Air (tel. 01-4112217, 4112230; mobile, +977 9751000120, 9851026185)
• Mountain Helicopters (tel. 01-4111031; fax : 01-4111049; mobile, +977 9751020015)
• Air Dynasty Heli-Services (tel. 01-4497418, 4477562; fax,01- 4468802; mobile, +977 9851030013)
• Simrik Air (tel. 01-4155340)
• Nepalese Army (tel. 01-4246140, 01-4246932, 01-4241731, fax 977-1-4269624)
• Manang Air (tel. 01-4496253)
• Shree Airlines (tel. 01-4220172)

MAOBAADI (MAOISTS)

Nepal's communists first emerged from behind the scenes as part of the opposition to the Rana dynasty of hereditary prime ministers who overmastered the monarchy for more than 100 years, condoned by the British in India. The oligarchy was successfully overthrown in 1951 through combined efforts of several groups including communist factions and the newly independent government of India. The re-instated monarchy flirted with democracy from 1957 until 1960, and the communists claimed a meager four seats in Nepal's first general election.

The system was not to then King Mahendra's favor and he dissolved the nascent parliament and outlawed political parties. At the time, Sino-Soviet communists supported the king and his anti-democratic rule and did so until the mid-1960s while other communists sided with the Nepali Congress Party and pro-democracy forces and operated underground from India.

Political parties re-emerged in 1990 as part of the successful *Jana Andolan* "People's Movement". Among the parties that surfaced at that time were several variations on communism. One of these groups, The Maoists, was barred by a court ruling from the electoral process on trivial issues. In reaction, they boycotted elections and rebelled against police and ruling class harassment in Rolpa and Rukum districts. **The democractic developments in the early 1990's had failed to address discrimination and segregation, apartheid really, along ethnic lines, that became deep-rooted during the** *panchayat* **years.** Autocratic rulers used political protection to establish and maintain domination with systematic oppression of the disenfranchised who suffered chronic poverty. Maoists formally declared their "People's War" in February 1996. The uprising quickly gained local support in western Nepal, and spread like wildfire throughout the country.

The circumstances of the insurgency took a dramatic change following the poly-regicide at the Royal Palace in June of 2001. The successive king authorized the Royal Nepal Army to pursue the Maoists, a move that his brother had avoided as the royalists and the Maoists shared an implicit opposition to the presiding government. The king's decision changed the political landscape and the Maoists in turn began targeting the army.

During the war, Maoists gained notoriety for human rights abuses, only to be outdone by the police and army. At one point during the ten-year insurgency, Nepal had the shame of leading the world in disappeared persons (people who went missing while in custody, assumed to be executed by captors). The Maoists gave women positions in battle and were accused of recruiting minors and the paramilitary youth wing of the party, the Young Communist League, gained a reputation for intimidation.

Known as *Maobaadi* in Nepali, the party's official name is the Unified Communist Party of Nepal-Maoist (the official party website is www.ucpnm.org). They embraced the name of an authoritarian figure whose policies led to the demise of an untold amount of people by famine and persecution. Many of Chairman Mao's tenets have been discredited, and in his homeland China, he is euphemistically considered as less than perfect. During Nepal's civil war, the provocative party name did nothing to elicit foreign support but caused reflexive negative reactions, and they were not even endorsed by Mao's motherland. Nepal's Maoists overlook his shortcomings and unrealistic implementation of agrarian reform and cultural upheaval.

They called for armed revolution, foremost to ameliorate miserable inequalities that amounted to apartheid with social stratification that has plagued Nepal for centuries. Their aim garnered support among the long-harassed multitudes. However, overturning traditional, supremacist structures and prejudice inherent in a caste and class based society does not happen without forceful resistance from those in privileged positions with the most to lose.

In late 2005, the Maoists came to the table and joined a coalition of seven leading parties to oppose the monarch's attempt to re-assert royal rule by dissolving parliament. Widespread protests began in 2006. During this second people's movement, **Jana Andolan II**, hundreds of thousands of people marched in the capital defying martial law. The king capitulated, which eventually led to a formal dismantling of the crown and the end of the ten-year insurrection.

The Maoists had the strongest role in ousting the 239 year-old monarchy. However, during the decade-long "People's Revolution", 1996-2006, upwards of 15,000 Nepalis died including many civilians. State forces were behind a majority of the deaths, and Amnesty International accused both sides for "unlawful criminal deaths" among other abuses.

Nationwide elections were held at the beginning of 2008 and ten million people voted in the polls. The Maoists unexpectedly won the highest number of parliamentary seats (202 out of 601, or 33.6%), giving them a mandate to lead Nepal and immediate legitimacy with China, India and beyond. The new government formally declared Nepal a secular, federal, democratic republic on May 28, 2008 with none other than the chairman of the Maoist party, Pushpa Kamal Dahal, a former schoolteacher, nicknamed *Prachanda* ("the fierce one"), as the first Prime Minister and leader of the republic. Since coming to the political forefront, they have entered a lion's den of traditional politics and a few Maoist politicians have proven to be as megalomaniacal as leaders anywhere.

Despite increasingly bad habits, they are trying to reform the system beyond casteism or elitism. Otherwise, it remains tainted by patronage, nepotism, prejudice and preferential treatment. Beyond that, Maoist philosophy is inscrutable; interchange it with any of the opiates of the masses for a similar mindset. Nevertheless, having entered the mainstream, they have become less inclined to ideological dialectics. They have gained insight into a more comprehensive reality of world affairs beyond India and China and beyond choosing between communism or the wretched hierarchies that Nepal knows too well. Despite supplementary rhetoric, Maoism was primarily used to chip away at the walls of state-sponsored discrimination and administrative malfeasance that has impoverished Nepal for centuries.

The royal family was stripped of privileges including legal immunity. Henceforth, the king must pay his own bills and his image is no longer embossed on bank notes. The royal palace subsequently became a national museum.

The Sari Soldiers (2008), by Julie Bridgham is a documentary of the lives of six Nepali women of contrasting affiliations filmed over three years during the insurgency.

The People's Nepal (2010) is a documentary film by Jim Wills about the decade-long war, the demise of royal rule, and the emergence of democracy. π

Yarsagumba, aka Himalayan Viagra

The epic search for **Yarsagumba** has been an economic blessing for high hills residents as well as people who arrive from surrounding areas. They travel to the highlands in large groups in the spring to forage for its outgrowths. *Yarsagumba* is the **larva of the Himalayan bat moth (*Hepialis armoricanus*) that has been transformed by the fungus *Cordyseps Sinensis*.** Moth caterpillars form a cocoon to nest underground but the hibernating larvae play host to the fungus which consumes them. The fungus eventually sprouts from the earth in the spring similar to a grass bud. *Yarsagumba* is relished in China and commands a high price, and revenue from its harvest helped fund Nepal's Maoist insurgency. It is believed to enhance energy, male virility and general health but these putative properties await conclusive research.

Yarsagumba was mentioned in Tibetan medical literature around the 15th century, but first achieved world headlines in 1993 when unheralded Chinese distance runners achieved astonishing success at the World Championships in Germany. Their coach partially attributed record-setting victories to the fungus. Later, when testing became standard, some of his athletes would fail checks for performance enhancing drugs.

The price is increasing exponentially, largely driven by China's *nouveau riche*, and a desire to be fashionable. Prices over 11,500 per pound (more than 25,000 USD per kg) have been reported. The desiccated caterpillar husk is generally pulverized and added to food or boiled in tea, and sometimes plopped whole in soup.

Lokta paper, another local product, is made from the inner fibers of the Daphne bush. The Himalayan variety of this shrub, *Daphne bhoula* or *Daphne papyracea,* is evergreen at lower altitudes but deciduous in higher realms. Traditionally, the luxurious, pliable paper was used for religious texts and government documents but is now made into tourist products such as stationery, greeting cards and even lamp shades.

THE ROUTES

Nepal's popular trails can, at times, seem to be nothing but a series of hotels, albeit majestically draped with extraordinary natural appeal, yet lesser cross-cultural interaction. Rural Nepal is rich in heritage; traveling away from the main tourist track and visiting nearly anywhere in the mid-hills and higher can be an immensely rewarding endeavor. The hospitality of the hill people is unmatched, as is their spirit, and many areas remain relatively untarnished by modernization. People will be enthusiastic to meet you and honored to have a visitor. Away from the tourist highways, foreigners in rural areas are few and far between. Without electronic devices impinging, there are more interactions between people. If you have a chance, diversions from the main route and home stay are highly recommended.

While trekking, the author encourages the use of local products. Do your best to eat the same fare as your hosts and support the region's farmers. As much as possible, try to avoid packaged foods which contribute to rubbish that locals do not know how to deal with adequately, especially away from the main trekking venues. (Garbage is usually disposed of openly in villages, or otherwise stockpiled in a few locations to rot or be burned.) Be aware that monosodium glutamate (MSG), known as *TesTi pauDar* (*ie*, tasty powder) or *ajinomoTo* in Nepal, may be in use, even in far-flung villages; if you prefer food without this "flavor enhancer," request that it not be added to your meal in lodges (please see language section below).

GETTING STARTED

In the route description that follows, times do not include stops. That is, only actual hiking time is recorded in calculations given. Overall times, including stops, are longer than indicated times.

Additionally, trail conditions and routes change for a variety of reasons over time and there may be inaccuracies in the following description. When trails do change, it is usually due to a landslide, erosion and damage and finding more suitable routes as well as the result of rapid road construction taking place throughout Nepal (tongue-in-cheek referred to as "tractor terrorism".)

During the winter season, there is less daylight than at other times, but regardless of season, most people finish before 5 PM and depart mid- to late morning, after breakfast.

Altitudes listed in the descriptions are taken from several sources, including maps and GPS.

A *chautaaraa* is a rest area with a platform and often an accompanying tree for shade. The trees are usually *pipal* or banyan, both of the fig family. The **Bodhi** or **Bo Tree** that sheltered Buddha at his enlightenment, was a *pipal (Ficus religiosa,* ie, sacred fig). These trees are considered sacred to Hindus and Buddhists alike and have characteristically **heart-shaped leaves**.

A *chorten* is a Buddhist religious monument, often cubical or conical. A *stupa* is a large *chorten*. *MaaNe* walls are rectangular with stone tablets inscribed with *mantras*.

During the day, especially along less trekker-frequented trails, you may pass many Nepalese who will greet you and ask where you are coming from and where you are going, a time-honored way of expressing concern for a traveler's well-being. The accepted form of greeting (and leave taking) is '**Namaste!**'

THE TAMANG HERITAGE TRAIL

route outline

The Tamang Heritage Trail lies west of the third most popular trekking venue in Nepal, the Langtang valley. The route was developed and "launched" by the United Nations along with the Tourism for Rural Poverty Alleviation Program (UN/TRPAP) in 2005, and passes through mainly Tamang villages in the mid-hills that receive considerably fewer tourists than the traditional, adjoining Langtang trek.

Although the mountain views are farther away, the village vistas are sensational and home stay enables a deeper cultural experience than can be had on the more established routes. Additionally, a trek along the Tamang Heritage Trail can be combined with the Langtang valley trek. The trails coincide at Syabrubesi or along the high route from Syabrubesi to Rimche where they tie in at the village of Khangjim (to be distinguished from the similarly sounding village of Kyangin Gomba, often referred to as Kyangin).

The Tamang ethnic group comprises about 6 percent of the total population of Nepal, and Tamang are the predominant inhabitants of Rasuwaa District where this trek and the Langtang valley lie. Rasuwaa District is named after a fort located at the border with Tibet several days ahead on this trek. Tamang also comprise a large percentage of the populations of Sindhupalchowk, Kathmandu Valley, Bhaktapur, Lalitpur, Dhading, Makwanpur, Nuwakot, Ramechhap, Dolakha, Chitwan and Kavreplanchowk. In fact, their ancient capital named Yambu was in Kathmandu Valley long before Nepal's state formation and artifacts from that period date back to the Stone Age.

Tamang are believed to have originally arrived from Mongolia north of the Himalaya. The origin of the name Tamang is under scholarly dispute. Some claim that it simply means horse (*Ta*) rider (*mang*), while others propose that *Ta* indicates 'entrance' in Tibetan and *mang* refers to people, the idea that for Tibetans, the area south was a gateway to the

Tamang people. The Tamang ethnic group has also been referred to as *Rongpo* in Tibet and *Murmi* in Nepal.

Most Tamang follow Buddhism and Shamanism and practice ancestor worship. Ram Bahadur Bomjang, the so-called *Boy Buddha*, from Bara District in the inner *tarai* is Tamang and has gained a large following and has spent much time in the jungle meditating and is now teaching.

Tamang have a distinct language of the Tibeto-Burman family which is closely related to the languages of the Gurung and Thakhali. Tamang also have a distinct manner of dress, ornamentation and craftsmanship, and many homes along this route have ornately carved wooden windows and porch fronts. Important festivals for the Tamang include Saga Dawa (Buddha Jayanti), Dasai, Tihaar, and Sonam Losar (see RELIGION AND FESTIVALS for more information).

The hospitable people of this area have unique customs and traditional dances, including the welcome dance, *jhankri* dance, and the Mendomaya Dance between men and women. *Mendo* means 'flower' in Tamang language and *maya* means 'love'. *Dohori* is also popular in these parts with call and answer repartee between male and female participants. Many dances are a type of courtship ritual, complemented by folk music. Some of the dances depend on the time of year and usually take place during festivals.

QUICK FACTS AND HIGHLIGHTS:

best time to visit: all season (views are clearest from fall to spring)
environment: mid to high-hills
maximum elevation: Naagthaali (10,640 feet, 3243 m)
minimum elevation: Syabrubesi (4813 feet, 1467 m)
facilities: lodges and hotels, teahouses, home stay
duration: up to a week and longer
difficulty level: easy to moderate
formalities: Nepal Visa on arrival ($25 USD for 15 days, $40 USD for 30 days, or $100 USD for 3 months); Langtang National Park Entry Fee, 3000 NRS ; Trekking Information Management System (TIMS) card, $20 USD, will be checked if passing through Dhunche (rather than walking in from Betrawaati)
food and lodging costs: minimal
typical Nepali dish: *daal-bhat tarakaari* (rice, lentil soup and vegetables)
typical drink: *chiyaa* (sweet milk tea)
highlights: Tamang ethnic group, cultural interaction, village scenery and lifestyle, Nepali hospitality, Himalayan panoramas, hot springs, Buddhist monasteries, cheese factory, Naagthaali, Taaruche and Gottegang Kharka viewpoints

THE TAMANG HERITAGE TRAIL AT A GLANCE

WALKING TIME BETWEEN WAYPOINTS (RESTING TIME NOT INCLUDED)	DURATION
Syabrubesi (4813 feet, 1467 m) to **Thaambuchet** at (5774 feet, 1760 m)	2¼-2½ hours
Thaambuchet at (5774 feet, 1760 m) to **Gatlaang** (7343 feet, 2238 m)	1½ hours
Gatlaang (7343 feet, 2238 m) to **Taatopaani** (8530 feet, 2600 m),	3¼-3½ hours
Taatopaani (8530 feet, 2600 m) to **Naagthaali** (10,640 feet, 3243 m)	1¾-2 hours
Naagthaali (10,640 feet, 3243 m) to **Timure** (5781 feet, 1762 m)	3½-3¾ hours
Low route: Timure (5781 feet, 1762 m) to **Briddam** (7218 feet, 2200 m)	2¾ hours
High route: Timure (5781 feet, 1762 m) to **Briddam** (7218 feet, 2200 m)	4-4¼ hours
Briddam (7218 feet, 2200 m) to **Syabrubesi** (4813 feet, 1467 m)	2-2½ hours

WALKING IN: BETRAAWATI TO GATLAANG

Betraawati (2050 feet, 625 m) to **Mailung** (3035 feet, 925 m)	3 hours
Mailung (3035 feet, 925 m) to **Gogaane** (4888 feet, 1490 m)	1½-1¾ hours
Gogaane (4888 feet, 1490 m), to **Thulo Haaku** (6890 feet, 2100 m)	2½ hours
Thulo Haaku (6890 feet, 2100 m) to **Gatlaang** (7343 feet, 2238 m)	3-3½ hours

getting to the trailhead

The usual starting point is either Syabrubesi (a starting point for the Langtang trek as well) or Thaambuchet. There is a daily direct bus from Kathmandu to Thaambuchet; otherwise, three buses depart daily for Syabrubesi from the Baleju Bus Park (also known as Gongabu and New Bus Park). The road rises out of the Kathmandu valley to the northeast. Enjoy refreshing sights of fertile hills along the way and the occasional symphony of cicadas (if they can be heard over the din of the bus!). Along the way they might be glimpses of Ganesh Himal and west to Himal Chuli and the Annapurna Range.

Trishuli is a large town and the administrative center of Nuwakot District, and is less than 45 miles (70 km) (up to 3–4 hours) by road from Kathmandu. The vehicle journey continues to Betraawati, 5 miles (8 km) away. To avoid the bus ride over a rough road to Syabrubesi (39 miles or 63 km from Trishuli) via Dhunche, an option is to start the trek from Betraawati, and then meet the Tamang Heritage Trail at Gatlaang village in 3 days. Villages along this alternate route rarely see tourists facilities are minimal along this portion. It is better to start from Syabrubesi unless you are an experienced trekker with some language facility and a few treks under your pack's waist belt. The description will begin from Syabrubesi, a typical starting point. The ambitious alternate route from Betraawati will be described later.

Langtang National Park area. Park entry permits are inspected along the road just before reaching Dhunche (6594 feet, 2010 m), the headquarters of Rasuwaa District, 30 miles (48 kms) from Trishuli. The check post and national park office and information center are just over ½ mile (1 km) before Dhunche or a 10-minute walk. The road continues 9 miles (14½ kms) on to Syabrubesi and farther west to Thaambuchet (and continues farther west into the Ganesh Himal area to lead and zinc mines neay SomdAng by private vehicle) or north to the border with Tibet. Occasionally, vehicles from Syabrubesi can be arranged to Gatlaang, a cornerstone village on the Tamang Heritage Trail, otherwise the route via Thaambueht is outlined below.

KATHMANDU TO SYABRUBESI AND THAAMBUCHET – DAY 1

Syabrubesi lies at the confluence of the Bhote Kosi and Langtang rivers and is a staging center for the Langtang Valley trek as well as the Tamang Heritage Trail. It is the final destination for buses from Kathmandu with the exception of a single bus that continues on to Thaambuchet after a brief stop in Syabrubesi. Thaambuchet lies along the Tamang Heritage Trail. The bus from Syabrubesi to Thaambuchet departs Syabrubesi between 4:30 and 5 PM after first arriving from Kathmandu. The curvy dirt track travels from Syabrubesi at 4813 feet (1467 m) and zigzags up over Bahundanda Pass at 7175 feet (2187 m) and then drops down to Thaambuchet at 5775 feet (1760 m) in about an hour. Rather than travel by bus, a recommended option is to hike from Syabrubesi to Thaambuchet, outlined below.

To hike rather than ride, follow the motor road that heads toward Tibet from the north end of Syabrubesi and along the west side of the Bhote Kosi river. Just before the road drops to cross the Chilime Khola (river) and then over the Bhote Kosi, a footpath heads left /west from the road up through a canyon of the Chilime Khola valley. First pass through a few fields near a dwelling before dropping down to cross the **Chilime Khola** on a suspension bridge, **45 minutes** from Syabrubesi. From the bridge, follow the trail upstream/left (rather than to the right, which heads to Thuman village). The trail ascends to cross a ridge and then contours to cross another nearby ridge where it diverges. The lower path is more direct to Thaambuchet but through an section prone to landslides, and the route might be difficult to follow. The upper path heads to Paajungbensi (*Lower* Paajung) with few facilities, and from here it drops back down to the river to meet the lower trail to Thaambuchet (or continues higher along the way to upper Paajung, Bremdaang, and Taatopaani villages).

Reach a long suspension bridge to cross back over to the south bank of the Chilime Khola in **1 hour 10 minutes** from the previous bridge over the same river. On the other side of this bridge is the small Newar village of **Goljung Besi** (*Lower* Goljung) with an atypical preponderance of Christians. The village of (Upper) Goljung is high above on the hillside. Looking back from the south side of the bridge, on the other side of the river, you will notice a large Christian cross mounted atop a hillock, a peculiar sight in Hindu-predominant Nepal (Christians make up less than 1% of the population). On a plateau just above Goljung Besi is a church as well as the nearby ruins of a former palace. To reach and explore the ruins, take the trail out of Goljung Besi that ascends toward Goljung. Then head right/west away from the trail and through fields past the church to the ruins beyond.

Villagers say the ruins were an estate of a Newar king predating Prithvi Narayan Shah, the king from Gorkha District who conquered and united Nepal in the 1760s. The large, dilapidated stone structure is surrounded by fields along with more ruins built up around a nearby *pipal* tree (a sacred fig, *Ficus religiosa*). These trees are holy to Hindus and Buddhists alike with characteristic heart-shaped leaves.

To head directly to Thaambuchet from Goljung Besi, the trail follows from the long suspension bridge to the right along the Chilime Khola. Eventually pass a hydropower project just before the village of **Thaambuchet** (5774 feet, 1760 m) in **30 minutes**, less than **2½ hours** from Syabrubesi. There are lodges here, and electronic items can be charged. There is also a health post in the village. Tibetan refugees inhabit the upper part of the hamlet. A motor road with bus service reaches as far as Thaambuchet. Daily service includes a bus **from Thaambuchet** to Syabrubesi and onward to Kathmandu, leaving around 7 AM (time subject to change); and a bus **to Thaambuchet** departing Kathmandu at 6:30 AM from Baleju Bus Park (again, time subject to change). Thaambuchet lies at the confluence of the Bremdaang Khola river and the larger Saangjen Khola river, and is also the location of the Chilime Hydro Power Project.

THAAMBUCHET TO GATLAANG – DAY 2

From Thaambuchet, cross over the Bremdaang Khola on a suspension bridge at the upper (west) end and pass through fields to a long *maaNe* wall. Head left (southwest) at the *maaNe* wall and reach a wooden bridge to again cross the Bremdaang Khola and follow the trail upriver before ascending steeply through a forested area. (Another, non-recommended route continues to follow the river, crossing it a few times before then steeply ascending to Gatlaang.) Reach a large boulder with painted arrows pointing the way. Gatlaang can be seen up the valley. The scenic trail eventually emerges from the woods into fields and gradually ascends to Gatlaang, passing many *chorten* and *maaNe* walls along the way. Reach **Gatlaang** (7343 feet, 2238 m) in **1 hour 35 minutes** from Thaambuchet.

Gatlaang is an impressive Tamang village with picturesque, closely linked houses with slate roofs. Gatlaang also has a Christian church (missionaries have been afoot in this area) as well as a school and a post office. According to legend, Padmasamhava, aka Guru Rinpoche, was in the area and fell ill, he recovered in the location of Gatlaang and the name means subsequently means happiness or relief.

There are three lodges here, two privately run at the top of town and a community lodge toward the lower end. Guides for this area and beyond can be arranged at one of the upper lodges. Home stay is also encouraged in this village.

The church is above the settlement by the school. Much higher above is a Buddhist *gombaa* and farther above the valley and high above Gatlaang is an army post. A side trip from Gatlaang up to the *gombaa* and Parvati Kund, a nearby sacred pond, and cheese factory is described below. If weather permits, the Langtang peaks are vibrant from Gatlaang. Landline phone is available, and power sockets for charging batteries, mobile phones, and more available in the lodges.

Side Excursion to Parvati Kund pond and Cheese Factory

The trail ascends from the upper part of **Gatlaang** village, passing *maaNe* walls and crossing a road. From there you ascend along a stream for a while before reaching a so-called "abandoned village" in 15 minutes (the main village was moved to its present location to be closer to fields). Many of the stone houses here are in ruins while some of the houses are still occupied. Keep ascending and reach **Parvati Kund** (8415 feet, 2565 m), in approximately **40 minutes** of steep uphill climbing from Gatlaang. Parvati Kund is a pond with a stone wall built around it. Inside the walled area is a ceremonial platform, along with a bathing *ghaaT* (platform) and *chorten*. Outside the rock enclosure is a rest area as well as a small Hindu temple containing a stone image of the goddess Parvati with Shiva. Two Buddhist *chorten* are located beside the temple. The area receives many pilgrims for 4 to 5 days during the Janai Purnimaa festival

From Parvati Kund are views of the Langtang and Gosainkund range. Across the road (which continues to Dhading District's SomdAng) from Parvati Kund is a fenced-in apple orchard, above which sit the remains of a destroyed compound. Previously,the villa of a Nepal Army general, the compound was demolished by Maoists (the general was away at the time) during the civil war (1996-2006). A 5-minute walk farther along the road will bring you to a few shops known as Gyang Danda. From here, a path heads right/north to a *gombaa* just above the hill and a nearby, newer, isolated building with a curious signboard that reads "The Community Creativity Centre."

From the left /south side of the road, a trail leads above to a **cheese factory** in **10 minutes**. Cheese and *ghiu* (or *ghee*, clarified butter) are produced here to be sold in Kathmandu. This factory is run by the governmental Dairy Development Corporation (DDC), and its initials are emblazoned on the cheese discs.

Return to Gatlaang via the same route. (Another return option from here, if doing the Tamang Heritage Trail in reverse, is to use the route described at the end of this section to walk out to the road at Betraawati, 5 miles (8 km) from the large market town of Trishuli and bus service.)

GATLAANG TO TATOPANI – DAY 3

Depart for Taatopaani at the bottom (eastern) end of **Gatlaang**. A minute from leaving the village, avoid the branch that heads down steeply toward the river. Instead, continue on the gradually descending trail as it passes through fields and by rows and rows of *chorten* and *maaNe* walls. Pass a final *chorten* and leave the fields behind to descend through trees to the level of the river. Continue along the riverside, crossing the **Bremdaang Khola** on a wooden bridge in 1¼ hours. The trail then follows a long *maaNe* wall towards Chilime. (Thambuchet can be reached from a branch that leads right from the *maaNe* wall.)

From the *maaNe* wall, contour up the Saangjen Khola valley. (Chilime Khola is the name given to the river after the confluence point of the Bremdaang and Saangjen rivers.) The Chilime Hydro Power Project is visible alongside the river. (Incidentally, electricity for both Thaambuchet and Chilime arrives from Trishuli rather than this large, privately owned project.) Pass by a few houses and lodging in the lower part of Chilime, and then pass the upper settlement of **Chilime** (6000 feet, 1829 m), an enthralling village to explore, about **1½ hours** from Gatlaang.

The trail passes below Chilime to reach a suspension bridge over the **Saangjen Khola** within **20 minutes** from the wooden bridge over the Bremdaang Khola. From the east/far side of the bridge, do not ascend, but take an immediate left to follow the trail upriver for a couple of minutes before heading away from the river up through fields. After crossing through the fields, the trail branches. Take the wider trail to the right to ascend steeply. As you ascend, the houses of Chilime can be seen below as well as a bird's-eye view of the Chilime Hydro Power Project and nearby Thaambuchet, and farther beyond Thaambuchet, the village of Goljung on the far side of the valley.

Reach **Gonggaang** (7300 feet, 2225 m) in **1 hour** from the Saangjen Khola crossing where simple lodging is available. (From Gonggaang, a high trail contours down and out of the valley to the village of Paajung, and on to Syabrubesi.) Follow along the trail from the upper end of the village and ascend to round a ridge from where Taatopaani is visible high up the valley. Continue ascending through fields and trees for **45 minutes to 1 hour** to reach the collection of inns at **Taatopaani** (8530 feet, 2600 m), a well-developed hot springs bathing area. (*Taato* means "hot" in Nepali and *paani* is "water," or, in other words "hot springs.")

Above the lodges is the eponymous bathing area with six spouts (two each for three bathing pools) and dingy changing rooms nearby. Drains have to be closed before the bathing pools fill up. Keep an eye to belongings, as thieves have been known to strike while unsuspecting bathers are rejuvenating in the water. Solar power is available in the lodges along with landline phones. A 5-minute walk to the northwest provides an inspiring view up the Saangjen Khola valley with a beautiful glimpse of snow-capped peaks of the Kerung Range in Tibet.

TATOPANI TO TO NAAGTHAALI – DAY 4

Meet the trail onward to Bremdaang by the bathing area above the lodges. Bremdaang is at a higher elevation than Taatopaani and back down the valley. Gray langur, also known as Hanuman langur, are an old-world monkey and the furry creatures frequent the forested area between Taatopaani and Bremdaang. From Taatopaani, ascend gradually through the woods, crossing a few small streams, and after 5 minutes the trail forks. Both branches lead to Bremdaang. The newer trail heads right to contour more gradually, while the older trail ascends steeply for 5 minutes before contouring and dropping down slightly to a meeting point with the new trail after approximately 10 minutes.

Continue to climb through the woodland, pass through a small open meadow, and shortly thereafter cross a small stream and reach a fork in the trail just beyond, 30 minutes from Taatopaani. A painted sign on a rock with an arrow pointing the way to Naagthaali might be visible. Follow the sign to take the trail to the left and ascend steeply through a forested patch to reach a rock wall surrounding the fields that abut the village of Bremdaang. The trail passes between this wall and a large boulder topped with prayer flags. Follow along the wall to the village of **Bremdaang** (9350 feet, 2850 m) **1 hour** from Taatopaani. (Along the wall, just before reaching Bremdaang, a trail from below joins the trail from Taatopaani. If doing this route in reverse, avoid taking the trail down to the left, but continue to follow the wall to where the trail passes between it and a large boulder.)

Simple lodging and solar power are available in Bremdaang as well as phone service. There are elaborate carvings around the windows and doors of the houses here. A small *gombaa* sits above the hamlet, along with a built-up viewpoint area where Paldor Peak can be seen. A large prayer wheel stands beside the entrance of the *gombaa*. If the doors are locked, a villager may help locate the key. The trail to Naagthaali emerges from the upper part of the hamlet and winds through the trees to round a ridge with views available of the adjoining valley. The trail follows this ridge from which the Trishuli River valley can be seen as well as settlements along that valley including Dhunche. Reach a large open meadow named **Naagthaali** (10,640 feet, 3243 m) with a scattered collection of well-furnished lodges in **50 minutes** from Bremdaang.

Look for *chAUmri* here, a cross between cows and yaks. Two small *gombaa*, the older stone structures surrounded by prayer flags, are located in Naagthaali; one lies at the high end of the meadow and the other is more centrally located. If the *lama* of either is present, he might let you into a throne room with Buddhist iconography. A monetary request will likely be made (it is customary to leave a nominal donation when visiting religious sites.) There are caves nearby that locals say have long been used for meditation. You might need a local guide to find them somewhere in the area above and behind the uppermost lodge and higher *gombaa* at the high end of the meadow.

Side Excursion to Taaruche Viewpoint

As advertised on a sign at a **Naagthaali** lodge, "Visit Taruche with kaleidoscope views of Ganesh Himal Range, Kerung Range (Tibet), Langtang Himal Range and Gosainkund Range." the panorama is truly outstanding. To reach this viewpoint, the trail leads away from the upper end of the meadow and passes below the higher *gombaa*. Follow the trail to ascend through pine forest, and keep to this wide trail along the ridge overlooking the Saangjen Khola valley with occasional vistas through the trees. At one point the lodges of Taatopaani can be seen below. On the way to Taaruche, there is a small, seasonal cheese-making operation in a hut among the trees below the trail. Milk is gathered and hauled up from *chAUmri* herders around Naagthaali, and their products are sold locally and in Kathmandu.

Emerge from the trees and contour away from the valley rim and up through open hillside, then ascend to round another ridge and pass through a lush grove of moss laden trees including rhododendron. Water is likely to be available here. Pass out of the trees and round another ridge to reach the top of an open ridge. This area is known as **Taaruche** (12,224 feet, 3726 m), **1½ hours** from Naagthaali, marked with prayer flags. Here you will find nearly 360° of immense views (if Mother Nature, ie, the weather, cooperates) and a herder's seasonal shelter. No facilities are available, but keep a lookout for grazing *chAUmri*. Mountain views north to Tibet, as well as west to the Ganesh Himal Range and Paldor Peak, and east to the Langtang range, are sensational. No sounds impinge but that of insects, the rustling of the wind, birdsong and perhaps the occasional jingle of a bell on a grazing animal. π

NAAGTHAALI TO THUMAN AND BRIDDAM – DAY 5

Note that from **Naagthaali** to **Thuman**, the trail can be unclear with several diversions. Catch the trail to Thuman at the lower end of the Naagthaali meadow. The trail here might be difficult to follow given the amount of heavy-footed ungulates plodding around the soft earth in a slow, never-ending search for fodder. Descend while heading northeast, and after approximately 5 minutes the trail to Thuman branches off to the right (east). This might be easy to miss as the widest trail continues straight (northeast), but it only descends to a pasture in a few minutes where it then becomes a maze.

The right branch heads down through a grove of trees with abundant rhododendron for a few minutes, then straight across an open area. Continue heading straight to descend through forest. In 30 minutes from Naagthaali, the trail emerges to cross a large, splendid meadow and continues its descent. In another 15 minutes the trail forks. Continue straight (rather than left) down through fields above Thuman. Pass by a school on the right and arrive at **Thuman** (7546 feet, 2300 m) in **1 to 1¼ hours** from Naagthaali.

Thuman is a large Tamang village with closely placed houses and elaborate wood carvings around doors and windows. Lodging and a health post are available here. A *gombaa* lies at the lower, southern end of town. The *konyer*, or keyholder, lives nearby. Trails to Thaambuchet and Chilime up the Saangjen Khola valley and to Syabrubesi leave this end of the village. A trail to Taatopaani that bypasses Naagthaali also branches off the same trail to Chilime. The settlement is powered by hydroelectricity from a nearby stream, and sockets are available for charging batteries, phones, and other devices. However, electricity is usually only available from evening to morning (6 PM–6 AM).

THUMAN TO BRIDDAM

The Tamang Heritage Trail offers two options from Thuman. One route is to travel north to the border post of Rasuwaa Gaadi along the trade route with Tibet with a return to the village of Briddam, seen opposite Thuman on the other side of the valley. Another option is to head directly to Briddam from Thuman. The direct trail will be covered first as an alternate route, then the longer option via Rasuwaa Gaadi at the border.

Direct Route from Thuman to Briddam

The trail descends steeply from **Thuman** to a bridge over the Bhote Kosi (5151 feet,1570 m) and up the other side to Briddam (7218 feet, 2200 m). From the *gomba* at the southern end of Thuman, descend along a ridge past a series of *mani* walls in **20 minutes**. The trail drops down from the left side of the lowermost *mani*, away from the ridge line through the trees in the lush gully below the fields of Thuman. Reach a bridge over the Bhote Kosi in **1½** hours. Climb to cross the road to the lower end of the village of Ling Ling in 15 minutes. Find the trailhead after passing a *maaNe* wall and lodge and before reaching a small stream. The route passes ascends between houses, through a field, and steeply up to a group of prayer flags and in ¾-1 **hours** meets a trail from Timure that bypasses Ling Ling. Keep ascending and round another ridge with *chorten*. Briddam can be seen on the other side of the hill. Drop down steeply to cross a stream over a cement bridge. Pass through trees and ascend to **Briddam** in 3¼-3¾ **hours** from Thuman. See below for a description of **BRIDDAM** village. π

THUMAN TO RASUWAA GAADI AND THE TIBETAN FRONTIER

NOTE: The area north of Timure is occasionally closed to trekkers. The trail from Thuman to Daahaal Phedi leaves the north end of **Thuman**. Contour through fields and pass old *mani* walls to a junction with a sign painted on a rock indicating the path to "Dalphedi/Timure," the upper trail, or "Timure," the lower trail circumventing Daahaal Phedi.

To continue to Daahaal Phedi, climb steeply to cross a ridge marked by a *chorten*. From here, the town of Timure is seen up the other side of the Bhote Kosi river valley. The trail descends to **Daahaal Phedi**, in 1¼ **hours** from Thuman. Daahaal Phedi is a small Tamang village with scattered houses. Continue down through houses and fields directly toward the river below. Reach a resting point marked by a tall wooden pole in **15 minutes**. (To bypass Daahaal Phedi for a more direct route to Timure, take the lower route at the rock signed junction mentioned above and avoid branches to the right that descend to the river. In 45 minutes the two routes tie in near the resting point below Daahaal Phedi, marked by the tall wooden pole.)

The trail descends steeply to the Bhote Kosi river to a **suspension bridge** in **30 minutes**. On the other side of the river you enter Langtang National Park, specified by a park sign. Head upriver and ascend to the motor road through rubble created in its making. In 15 minutes, pass a built-up hot springs area with three concrete pools built in the summer of 2009.

Follow the road and reach **Timure** (5781 feet, 1762 m) in 45 minutes from the suspension bridge or 2½-3 **hours** from Thuman. is a prosperous, trade-route village with many facilities. The area north is sometimes restricted, otherwise, to continue to Ghattekhola and Rasuwaa Gaadi at the border with Tibet, the trail leaves the upper end of Timure and follows along the motor road. Reach an army post with checkpoint just beyond. Bags will be inspected and due to sensitivities at the border, cameras and mobile phones might be held until you return. The road follows the Bhote Kosi to **Ghattekholaa** in **20 minutes** from Timure. Ghattekholaa is a beguiling hamlet that does not see many tourists and is worth a visit. Most houses have traditional wooden carvings and paintings around doors and windows. The mantra *"Om Mani Padme Hum"* is carved in Tibetan script in big, colorful letters on a large boulder in the center of the village. Glimpses of snowy peaks can be seen from the village up the GhaTTe Khola valley. **Rasuwaa Gaadi** (5955 feet, 1815 m) is another **20-30 minutes** from Ghattekholaa. Simple lodging is available along with a few shops stocked with Chinese snacks. Rasuwaa is the name of a fort built in this area in 1912. Only the foundation remains. The Rasuwaa District of Nepal, which includes the Tamang Heritage Trail and Langtang National Park, is named after this fort. It lies at the confluence of the Lendi Khola and Kerong Khola, which join to form the Bhote Kosi. The road to Tibet passes up through the Kerong river valley. An area for camping is available below the shops and the remains of the fort.

There is a suspension footbridge and a bridge for vehicles over the Lendi Khola. Both bridges have gates blocking free passage across. The first gate of the suspension bridge is located midway across the bridge. At this point a Chinese soldier will come to meet you to see if you have proper documents to pass into Chinese territory. The Chinese side is much more built up than the Nepali side and has heavy security in the presence of soldiers.

The return route to Timure is the same way, along the road. From Timure, there are two routes to reach Briddam. The lower route begins by following the road back down past the hot springs. Alternatively, there is a high route leaving from Timure village, and if you do not mind a few steep inclines and descents, then this high trail avoids the motor road and is more pleasant and scenic although 1¼–1½ hours longer.

TIMURE TO BRIDDAM ALONG THE HIGH ROUTE VIA KHAIDI

From the lower end of a mid-village *maaNe* wall head east and pass by the police post below the monastery. The route follows power lines most of the climb to **Khaidi** (7480 feet, 2280 m), **1½ hours** from Timure. There is a tea shop here and small veterinary clinic, but no other facilities. Fresh apples, peaches, and plums might be available depending upon the season. (From Khaidi, a path leads a few hours higher to Gumling, where there is a *gombaa*, and beyond that to a seasonal pasture area known as Braanga Kharka at about 10,500 feet, 3200 m, with spectacular views. However, no facilities are available, and trekkers must be self-sufficient in food and shelter to ascend higher from Khaidi.)

Contour and enter a tributary valley. The trail passes above rock bluffs and descends steeply to a bridge over the **Phenglung Khola** in **1 hour**. The route onward is a lesser-traveled path with relatively few other users. The next section may be challenging to follow, and foliage sometimes closes in on the trail making it particularly damp and leech-infested during the monsoon. Ascend and contour through a wooded area. Be conscientious to follow the widest path as there are several off-shoots to the main trail. The path eventually rounds a ridge with a *chorten* and ties in with a lower trail to descend to the Briddam Khola. Two bridges span the stream, side by side, one steel and the other cement. **Briddam** is a 5–10-minute ascent or **1¾-2 hours** from the Phenglung Khola crossing.

TIMURE TO BRIDDAM ALONG THE LOW ROUTE

As you follow the motor road from **Timure**, it is possible to catch a trail that contours along the hillside above the road for some time rather than walking along the road itself. This trail can be found approximately 5 minutes downriver from the hot springs and branches to the left (east) side of the road. However, this trail or parts of it will likely come into discontinuance as the road gains prominence. Follow this trail above the road and river to reach a bridge in 1 hour from Timure. After 30 more minutes the trail branches in two. The upper path ascends to Briddam while the lower passes through the village of Ling Ling in another 5 minutes.

The upper path ascends through the small village of Pelku with a tea shop and simple lodge. Keep ascending and avoid any forks along this trail that head lower. Cross a stream straddled by a prayer wheel and then round a ridge marked with prayer flags. Keep ascending and round another ridge with *chorten*. Briddam can be seen on the other side of the hill. Drop down steeply to cross a stream over a cement bridge. Pass through trees and ascend to **Briddam** in approximately **2¾ hours** from Timure.

BRIDDAM

Briddam (7218 feet, 2200 m) is a large village with lodges and many options for home stay. A number is assigned to each participating home-stay house. Signs are posted on the houses with the number as well as the names of the owners. Electricity is available 24 hours per day (power cuts notwithstanding) along with sockets for charging electronic devices.

A health post and primary school are also located here, and a *gombaa* lies at the top of town. Another older and smaller *gombaa* is built around an overhanging rock a few minutes farther up/east from the village. Inside, the main figure is Guru Rinpoche, also known as Padmasambhava. To get to this *gombaa*, follow the trail from the central village area up toward the main *gombaa*. The trail branches to the right just before reaching the houses and community center next to the main *gombaa*, and passes behind these houses and through fields to the older *gombaa* a few minutes beyond. π

Side Excursion to Gottegang Kharka

There are no facilities on this long, arduous day trip from **Briddam** involving a 3500-foot-plus (1100 m-plus) ascent and the same return descent. You'll enjoy breathtaking views from the pasture at the top. Water sources along the way will be scarce, and few to no other people will be on this path.

Find the trail at the top of the village to the right of the houses that lie before the main *gombaa*. Pass behind the houses and to the left of the smaller, older *gombaa* which is just above and marked by prayer flags. The trail ascends to reach a ridge in less than 10 minutes where it forks. Take the lower, left trail down to Briddam Khola and cross branches of the stream twice on wooden bridges before ascending steeply up the opposite hill to cross a ridge marked by prayer flags. Briefly contour to the next ridge and then ascend steeply, following this ridge to pass through a luxuriant forest abundant with rhododendron.

Eventually, contour northeast through pine, enjoying views west and north along the way. Reach an open meadow in **2½–3 hours** from Briddam. Seasonal *goTh* huts used by summer herders dot the meadow. **Gottegang** is considered to be the area at the top of the meadow. However, the trail up becomes overrun by grazing tracks. **Take care to notice where you leave the main trail behind so as to be able to find it on return, especially if the weather deteriorates.** Make your way up to a large rock at the top of the meadow marked with a cairn and prayer flags for the best views (11,066 feet, 3373 m, GPS coordinates, N 28° 12.537', E 085° 23.156'). Dhunche can be seen down the valley and Naagthaali and Paldor Peak to the west, as well as the Kerong range to the north in Tibet. From Gottegang, the trail ascends farther to more *goTh* of Pangsang, but you must be self-sufficient to continue as there are no facilities.

BRIDDAM TO KHANGJIM AND THE LANGTANG VALLEY OR SYABRUBESI – DAY 6

The trail from Briddam to Khangjim departs from the upper, southeast corner of **Briddam** and ascends gradually to cross a ridge and pass through an archway near a rest area in 15 minutes. From here, the wide trail gradually descends through forest. In another 10-15 minutes (30 minutes from Briddam), reach a junction. The high trail continues to **Khangjim,** an **hour** from Briddam and connects to the route to the upper Langtang Valley; the lower trail descends to Wangal and out to Syabrubesi. Khangjim has satellite dishes, a renovated *gombaa*, as well as abundant lodging, and batteries can be recharged as well. Above the village is a Tibetan refugee camp..

DIRECT ROUTE TO WANGAL AND SYABRUBESI

To head directly from Briddam to Syabrubesi, where buses can be found to Kathmandu, take the right fork to Wangal and descend through a lush forested area in 1 hour from the junction south of Briddam, the trail narrows and descends steeply for 20 more minutes to **Wangal** (5358 feet, 1633 m) **1½–1¾ hours** from Briddam, with a tea shop and simple lodge. The trail to Syabrubesi heads south out of the village. Descend gradually following along the river below and reach the older part of **Syabrubesi** in **40 more minutes**.

A hot springs lies below along the banks of the Trishuli River. It has five concrete bathing pools which may or may not have water but are likely to be in disrepair and a bit polluted. **Buses to Kathmandu depart three times daily at 7 AM, 7:30 AM, and the last bus departs around 9 AM after first arriving from Thaambuchet (times subject to change).**

WALKING IN: BETRAAWATI TO GATLAANG

Be advised that this is a challenging route with few facilities for trekkers for up to 3 days. If you are not camping, then home stay and arranging meals will be necessary along the way. It is better to start from Syabrubesi unless you are an experienced trekker with some language facility.

To take this adventuresome option of walking in to the Tamang Heritage Trail, rather than staying on the bus to Syabrubesi, then disembark at **Betraawati** (2050 feet, 625m), 5 miles (8 km) from the large bazaar of Trishuli. (Alternatively, a single, daily bus plies the track to Pairebesi, a village 1 hour's walk ahead, from Kathmandu's Maccha Pokhari/Baleju Bus Park area, departing at 11 AM. The return trip to Kathmandu leaves Pairebesi daily at 9 AM. Bus times are subject to change.)

From Betrawaati, take the bridge crossing the Phalaakhu Khola river to the north side where a sign announces entry to Rasuwaa District, the location of Langtang National Park and the Tamang Heritage Trail. Rasuwaa District is named after a fort located at the border with Tibet, nearly a week ahead on this trek. Over 60 percent of the inhabitants of Rasuwaa are of the Tamang ethnicity.

Follow the road as it inclines to the left (west). A short distance (500 feet, 150 m) from the bridge, a trail to the left breaks away from the road to Dhunche (the road keeps climbing slightly). Follow this trail to the left, a wide double-tracked trail which drops down from the road and contours above the nearby Trishuli River. In 10–15 minutes, you will come to a suspension bridge across the Trishuli River. (You can cross here to walk up the west side, then cross the Salaakhu Khola on another suspension bridge to tie in with the east-side route near Pairebesi.) Keep hiking up the east side of the river, passing through the fields and houses of KaidaleTaar village, following the wide double track along the east side of the Trishuli River. The trail gradually rises to the village of Pairebesi (2230 feet, 680 m) **1 hour** from Betraawati. Simple lodges are available in Pairebesi.

From Pairebesi, take a suspension bridge to the west bank of the Trishuli River to more houses and simple lodges. You can take an immediate right to pass a row of shops, then find your way through fields along the Trishuli Khola while gradually rising to Shanti Bazaar (2460 feet, 750 m) with several restaurants and shops. Otherwise, continue straight from the bridge and head right on the dirt road that leads up to **Shanti Bazaar** in **20–25 minutes**. (Two daily buses ply the road on the west side of the river from Maccha Pokhari/Baleju Bus Park area in Kathmandu to Shanti Bazaar. The road from Shanti Bazaar continues to Mailung, but there may be no regular vehicle service. Road construction along this valley bottom all the way to Syabrubesi is underway. The plan is for a road that avoids the climb to Dhunche by following the river basin all the way to the border with the Tibet Autonomous Region to the north.)

Reach **Simle** (2493 feet, 760 m) in **20 minutes** from Shanti Bazaar while traveling alongside the Trishuli River. There is good camping about halfway between Shanti Bazaar and Simle in a low-lying area near the river. From Simle, the wide track continues to contour along the Trishuli Khola for 15 minutes before climbing and then descending gradually back to the river level. As the path gradually ascends along the river, with cliffs occasionally overhanging the path, you'll pass splendid rock walls and waterfalls on both sides of the valley. On the opposite side of the river are magnificent multilevel waterfalls that have cut deeply into the rock over the years; changes in the course of the waterfalls can be traced from the scars left behind by previous watercourses.

One hour from Simle is ChipleTi, with landline phone service and simple lodging. A little farther along, **1¼ hours** from Simle, is **Mailung** (3035 feet, 925 m), a larger village than ChipleTi with a few lodges and landline phone. From here up the Trishuli Khola valley, snowy peaks in the Langtang range can be seen. Keep to the double-track road and approximately 650 feet (200 m) from Mailung, take a trail that branches to the right, dropping from the road to cross the Nyam Khola on a wooden bridge. The service road not taken is part of the Mailung Khola hydropower project and continues ¾ mile (1.2 km) farther up the Nyam Khola.

After crossing the Nyam River, the route passes over a former rockslide and follows the Trishuli River. In 20 minutes find a trail to the left that abruptly ascends away from the river. (Just near this fork there is a basket-and-pulley system for crossing the river to a trail on the other side that leads to Dhunche.) The trail to Gogaane heads directly and steeply up the side of the hill before contouring and ascending more gradually up the Trishuli Khola valley. It is an isolated area with no water sources from the point of departure near the river until reaching Gogaane. In 1 hour 20 minutes the trail forks (10 minutes before reaching the village); the upper branch climbs steeply and enters **Gogaane** past a school. From here it is necessary to pass through people's front landings to continue; the lower trail passes below the village and ties in on the north side. Gogaane (4888 feet, 1490 m), a

Tamang village, is reached in a little over **1½ hours** from Mailung. This picturesque and rustic hamlet, with houses decorated by simple paintings around the front doors, sees very few foreign visitors. There are no facilities in Gogaane.

Water is scarce and there are no facilities between Gogaane and the next settlement, Thulo Haaku, and few people will be encountered other than herders and those out collecting wood. From Gogaane, avoid the trail that drops down steeply to a suspension bridge over the Trishuli River and on to Dhunche; instead, follow the trail that contours and climbs above the valley. About **1 hour** from Gogaane the trail levels off and then drops down slightly to cross a **stream**. Near the stream there are several large overhanging rocks favored by herders that provide shelter suitable for camping or getting out of the rain if necessary.

From the stream, the trail ascends out of the canyon and climbs steeply to a ridge, then steadily ascends while contouring north up the Trishuli River valley. About 30 minutes beyond the stream, you round a ridge to a view of several snow-capped peaks from the Langtang range, including the peaks of Langtang I, II, and Kimshung. Pass the open, communal latrine along the side of the trail as you reach **Thulo Haaku** (6890 feet, 2100 m), in **1½ hours** from the stream (**2½ hours** from Gogaane). (If doing this trail in reverse, from Thulo Haaku to Gogaane, then avoid an upper trail branch 10 minutes out of Thulo Haaku on the way to Gogaane.) Thulo Haaku is a large Tamang village with simple facilities, including a post office, monastery, secondary school, and view of the Langtang range. Landlines that will reach overseas are available here, and some mobile networks are covered. Houses here have elaborate carvings around the doors and windows, mostly of Tibetan Buddhist motifs. The small monastery is above the hamlet nestled in a copse of trees including several tall Juniper. Across the valley, the road to Dhunche can be seen about the same level as Thulo Haaku, and farther up the valley along a ridge, houses of Dhunche can be seen.

From Thulo Haaku, take the upper trail from the high end of the village. Sano Haaku is just up the valley. The first section of trail out of Thulo Haaku is a communal latrine, as on the other end of the settlement. Contour over a boulder-strewn stream and cross several more streams, some with water-powered mills and one with a cascade that is ideal for a waterfall shower. Reach **Sano Haaku** (6562 feet, 2000 m), also a Tamang village, in approximately **25 minutes** with an elementary school and a police post. Many houses have elaborate carvings around windows and doors. Follow the trail to the north from the upper part of the village, to reach a rock imprinted with a *mantra* in Tibetan script in large colorful letters. The trail forks here with the lower fork leading to a village named Gre (described below as an alternate route). Take the upper trail to go on to Naising and the Balbuto Pass before descending to Gatlaang, a prominent village on the Tamang Heritage Trail.

Sano Haaku to Balbuto Pass via Gre (ALTERNATE ROUTE)

This path is less direct and takes longer than Sano Haaku to Naising to the Balbuto Pass. At the trail juncture outside of **Sano Haaku** near a large rock with *"Om maaNe padme hum"* written in large and colorful Tibetan script, take the lower trail to Gre. The trail travels up the valley high above the Trishuli River, passing down through a canyon below Naising and crossing a stream on a concrete bridge before ascending out the other side of the canyon, continuing with occasional steep drop-offs at the trail's edge. Cross a final ridge and pass *chorten* before descending slightly to **Gre** (6562 feet, 2000 m) in **1½ hours** from Sano Haaku. Gre is a Tamang village with few facilities other than a tea shop, school, and a *gombaa* as well as a Christian church. From Gre, a trail to Dhunche/Bharku heads east out of the village and drops to the river. The steep trail to Syabrubesi can be seen across the way on the opposing hillside to the north. Perhaps unbelievably, this trail ascends up and over the ridge to the north before descending to Syabrubesi. To head to Gatlaang, follow the trail west out of the village. It ascends steeply to **Balbuto Pass**, reached in **1½ hours** from Gre.

SANO HAAKU TO BALBUTO PASS (DIRECT ROUTE)

To continue to Naising, after approximately **30 minutes** from Sano Haaku, reach a ridgeline with a *maaNe* wall. Just beyond more *maaNe* walls is the village of **Naising**, a predominantly Tamang village with a Christian church established in 2003 which sits above the trail. According to locals, many people in the village fell sick and some were dying in 2000 when a Nepalese missionary visited the village. He was able to convince the villagers to convert from Buddhism to Christianity to avert further health problems.

From Naising, do not take the trail from the high end of the hamlet which leads up to grazing areas. Instead, the trail emerges from the lower edge of the village and immediately branches. The trail to the right drops down to the hamlet of Gre. Take the upper fork that snakes through fields on the way to Balbuto Pass and the Tamang Heritage Trail. After approximately 15 minutes of gradual descent from Naising, the trail passes a few huts used for milling as it crosses a stream on a wooden bridge. The trail then begins climbing out of the canyon. After approximately 10 minutes from the bridge, avoid a faint fork that again heads to Gre. Stay on the main upper trail, which climbs steadily and steeply to the ridge top above. Cross the ridge (8218 feet, 2505 m) and then climb gradually through a broad-leaf forest to a *maaNe* wall at **Balbuto Pass** (8628 feet, 2630 m).

From the pass, Gatlaang can be seen below as well as the road to SomdAng. Leave the Trishuli valley as the trail drops down steeply to wind along the hillside. Avoid any diversions to the right that head directly to the village of Godam. The trail passes through a few fields to emerge along the road from Syabrubesi to lead and zinc mines at SomdAng. At the point the trail meets the road, the village of Godam is approximately 450 yards (400 m) down the road itself. To continue to Gatlaang, cross the road; approximately 25 yards/25 m up on the other side of the road, the trail drops away from the road, down to the cluster of houses of **Gatlaang** (7343 feet, 2238 m) approximately 10–15 minutes away from the road crossing and **2¼ hours** from Naising. See above for more information on Gatlaang village including a side trip to nearby Parvati Kund pond and a cheese factory as well as continuing along the Tamang Heritage Trail. π

Langtang, Gosainkunda and Helambu

The popular trekking region most accessible to Kathmandu includes Helambu, Gosainkunda and Langtang, north of the capital city. This area is the third most popular magnet for trekkers of the three premier venues. Langtang National Park (660 square miles, 1710 sq km), contains a wide range of habitats, from subtropical to alpine. The Gosainkunda area is the location of several sacred, alpine lakes and a pilgrimage destination for Hindus. If conditions permit, cross the Laurebina La high pass to link-up with the Helambu region. Helambu, the region closest to Kathmandu, can be approached from the northeast rim of the Kathmandu valley. It is inhabited mostly by people called Yolmo. The hill scenery and culture make up for the lack of spectacular, up-close mountain views, and the serene trails are a refreshing change of pace, especially when combined with treks in Langtang and Gosainkunda.

LANGTANG

QUICK FACTS AND HIGHLIGHTS:

best time to visit: all season (views are clearest from fall to spring)
environment: mid to high-hills
maximum elevation: Laurebina La (15,121 feet, 4609 m)
minimum elevation: Syabrubensi (4813 feet, 1467 m)
facilities: lodges and hotels, teahouses, home stay
duration: 7 days and more
difficulty level: easy to moderate
formalities: Nepal Visa on arrival ($25 USD for 15 days, $40 USD for 30 days, or $100 USD for 3 months); Langtang National Park Entry Fee, 1000 NRS ; Trekking Information Management System (TIMS) card, $20 USD
food and lodging costs: medium
typical Nepali dish: *daal-bhat tarakaari* (rice, lentil soup and vegetables)
typical drink: *chiyaa* (sweet milk tea)
highlights: Himalayan vistas, Tamang and Yolmo ethnic groups, cultural interaction, village scenery and lifestyle, Nepali hospitality, Buddhist monasteries, yak cheese, Viewpoints of Kyangjin Ri, Menchamsu, Tsergo Ri

getting to the trailhead

Start from Syabrubesi or Dhunche. There are three daily buses from Balaju Bus Park (also known as Gongabu Bus Park and New Bus Park). The sluggish 84 mile (133 km) road excursion to Syaburbesi via Dhunche takes up to 9–12 hours due to poor road conditions and frequent stops.

Langtang National Park entry permits are inspected along the road before **Dhunche** (6594 feet, 2010 m), headquarters of Rasuwaa District, 30 miles (48 kms) from Trishuli. The check post and national park office with information center are ½ mile (1 km) from town. The road continues 9 miles (14½ kms) to Syabrubesi and even farther west to Thaambuchet (on the Tamang Heritage Trail) to a remote mine. Another road continues north along the Bhote Kosi to the Tibetan Frontier.

SYABRUBESI TO LANDSLIDE AND KYANGJIN GOMBA

Syabrubesi (4650 feet, 1417 m) lies at the confluence of the Langtang Khola with the Bhote Kosi, which flow together and become the Trishuli River. The new part of town is to the south. Below it on the true right bank of the Trishuli River, are hot springs with five small pools that have become polluted and are in disrepair. Inquire locally if they are operational.

Cross the Bhote Kosi and then Langtang Khola on suspension bridges to follow the Langtang Khola upstream on the south side (true left bank) of the Langtang Khola. Do not take the trail branching to the right to Syabru after 20-30 minutes. In **1½-1¾ hours** from the bridge, cross the Ghopche Khola to the few tea houses of **Domin** (aka, Dhoban) 5380 feet, 1640 m). A trail from Syabru joins in after 15 minutes. Pass a landslide area to suitably named **Landslide or "Pairo"**, (5500 feet, 1676 m), with lodges in **20-30 minutes**.

LANDSLIDE TO LANGTANG VILLAGE

Continue upstream in a lush oak forest to **Bambu** (6480 feet, 1975 m), a collection of lodges in a bamboo jungle with an area for tents, in **1 hour.** After another ¾-1 hour take a bridge across the Langtang Khola to a simple lodge on the north bank that receives little sunshine in the narrow gorge. Reach the first lodges of **Rimche** (7881 feet, 2402 m) in another ¾-1 hour. A further **20-30 minute** climb brings you to another lodge (8169 feet, 2490 m) or Rimche, where the valley-bottom trail meets the high north-side trail, described below for variation on the return to Syabrubesi. A few minutes beyond is another Rimche lodge.

Descend slightly to reach **Changdam** (8140 feet, 2481 m) in **15 minutes**, a cluster of lodges in a clearing. This location is also referred to as **Lama Hotel** for the first structure in 1973 that has since been replaced. Continue into more lush forest with hanging moss, bamboo, birch, and oak to two lodges 10 minutes apart, known as **Gumnachowk**, aka, Riverside and Chunama, (9101 feet, 2774 m), in **1–1¼ hours**.

Reach two more lodges at **Ghora Tabela** (9860 feet, 3005 m) in **¾–1 more hour** as the valley opens out. This was once a settlement of Tibetan Khampas but now hosts an army post where your park permit will be registered at a checkpost **10 minutes** beyond the lodges. Altitude gains should make you cautious for signs of acute mountain sickness.

Climb through pasture area and ascend to lodges at **Thang Shyap** (10,460 feet, 3188 m), in **¾-1 hour** and leave the forest behind to reach **Tchamki** (10673 feet, 3253 m), with a tea shop and lodge, in **15 more minutes**. The village of Langtang is visible up the valley. A long suspension bridge crosses a tributary to more shops. As of July 2009, lodge owners from Tchamki and above have reduced competition by allowing only selected lodges to open for business, depending on the season, and fixing prices at higher rates.

In another **30–45 minutes** reach lodges below **Kangtangsa**, a village also known as **Gomba**, for the monastery nearest to Langtang village. This *gomba* and the one at Kyangjin operate with villagers performing the rites, and monks visiting occasionally to officiate following the Nyingma tradition. To visit, ask a villager or lodge owner for the whereabouts of the *konyer* or key custodian. There is a smaller temple next to the main temple and *lama's* quarters adjacent to it. Continue climbing in the widening valley, to **Langtang** village (11,220 feet, 3420 m), **30 minutes** from Kangtangsa. Lodges are concentrated in the newer, lower part of town. A small hydroelectric plant powers a community-run bakery where fresh cookies and more are available! Except for joint operations, electricity for villagers is limited from early evening to early morning. Kangtangsa and Langtang provide opportunities to stay in a village while other locations up to here have been built for tourists. Try to arrange a home stay in the traditional upper part of Langtang to get a better sense of life in this valley.

LANGTANG VILLAGE TO KYANGJIN GOMBA

Continue to climb and pass *mani* prayer walls; the beautiful peak at the head of the valley is Gangchenpo. Pass tea shops and lodges as you pass below **Mundu** in **30-45 minutes**, a picturesque village off the trail where home stay might be arranged, and **10 minutes** beyond is **Simdum**. In **30 minutes**, pass a lodge sheltered behind a large boulder and **30 minutes** beyond, reach more tea shops in a grazing area known as **Yamphu** (12,160 feet, 3706 m), passing otherworldly landscape along the way, starkly different from the luxuriant vegetation on the way up the narrow valley.

Ahead is the moraine of Ledrup Lirung Glacier; cross its outflow on a cement bridge. Just before this bridge, stone stairs leads a few minutes up to a hermitage. Beyond the bridge, climb over boulders of the moraine to drop into **Kyangjin Gomba**, a collection of lodges below the eponymous *gomba* (monastery) (12,795 feet, 3900 m), in **30 minutes**, or **2¼-2½** from Langtang village.

ALTERNATE ROUTE, DHUNCHE TO LANDSLIDE (ALSO KNOWN AS PAIRO) VIA SYABRU

If you disembark from the bus in **Dhunche** (6594 feet, 2010 m), the administrative center for the Rasuwaa District, you will find shops, comfortable lodges, and an army check post. Register and pay the park entrance fee at the Langtang National Park headquarters and information center just over half a mile (1 km) before reaching the town (a 10-minute walk), if you didn't in Kathmandu, and keep the receipt for proof. Most of the newer part of the settlement serves district government functions as well as tourists. The older, charming Tamang area is below with a Tamang Heritage Museum as well. The route is described to Landslide (Pairo), at the junction with valley-bottom trail from Syabrubesi.

From **Dhunche,** there are shortcuts along the way to avoid long road switchbacks. Walk or ride the road 3½–4 miles (6 km) to **Thulo Bharku,** with tea shops and a restaurant, in **1½ hours** or less.

A road linking Thulo Bharku with Thulo Syabru is under construction and might make the following redundant, at least in places where the road and trail coincide. From Thulo Bharku, the trail branches up the hill to the right after crossing a stream and passes behind a school. Ascend through pleasant chir pine and rhododendron to a lodge in **25 minutes.** Pass above terraced fields to another simple lodge with a camping area above it and then cross several tributaries to the few houses of **Brabal** (7560 feet, 2304 m), **1¾-2 hours** from Thulo Bharku. Shedup Cheling Gomba (monastery), sits majestically on a spur splitting the two parts of this village, and a school lies below. If the weather complies, you will have great views of Ganesh Himal and peaks to the north in Tibet. Continue around a bend to a rest area with views up the Langtang valley in **20-30 minutes.** Contour and descend for another ¾-1 hour to **Thulo Syabru (aka, Syabru)** (7350 feet, 2240 m), a village strung out along the ridge with many lodges.

Toward the bottom of the village, pick up a trail that traverses through fields to the east, pass a few more lodges, and cross the Gopche Khola on a suspension bridge in **45 minutes.** Climb to a tea shop (6519 feet, 1987 m), and descend into a lush bamboo jungle to reach the trail junction (5670 feet, 1728 m), near the Langtang Khola in another **1 hour.** The trail meets the trail from Syabrubesi. Continue right to the east to cross a landslide near its terminus, and reach **Landslide**, aka **Pairo,** in **20 minutes.** The trail up the valley beyond this point has been described above, see **LANDSLIDE TO KYANGJIN GOMPA.**

KYANGJIN GOMBA

There are twenty-three lodges (Langtang village has eighteen) as well as a saloon and pool hall (the pool table was hauled in by helicopter). Additionally, a small medical shop at Yeti Guest House has an altitude chamber and stretcher. The large fenced-in area southeast of the lodges is an agricultural experimental plot for high-elevation growing.There is no longer an army post here. Remains of the former post can be seen in the pasture below, look for two large mounds of stones. The amount of wood used for fuel to support twenty-five to thirty soldiers alarmed local requests. Lodge owners prefer to use deadfall for fuel from the hillside across the valley and the army heeded their request to depart the ecologically sensitive area. Details for side trips around Kyangjin Gomba are given below the next section which describes starting from **Dhunche**.

ACTIVITIES IN THE UPPER LANGTANG VALLEY

Kyangjin Gomba (12,795 feet, 3900 m) is an idyllic base for exploring the upper valley. Visit the monastery, which has recently been expanded. The newer building across from the main entrance was completed in 2009. The cheese factory was started as a Swiss project in 1955, and at that time, products were carried to Kathmandu over the Ganja La high pass (but are now carried along the valley bottom to Syabrubesi and then transported to Kathmandu.) The original simple technology can be observed from May to October, when up to 5000 to 7000 kg of *nak* (female yak) and *chaumri* (yak crossbreed) cheese are produced. A weeklong festival at Kyangjin Gomba, **Dukpa Chesyi**, is celebrated toward the **end of July or early August** (the sixth month and fourth day according to the Tibetan calendar). This festival commemorates Buddha's first teaching and includes singing, dancing, drinking and archery, among other merrymaking activities.Horses can be hired for more leisurely sightseeing, but don not go higher if you could not walk yourself—or if you have a headache or other signs of AMS.

Side Trip to Lirung Glacier and Icefall.

*A half day trip from **Kyangjin Gomba** to the north reaches Lirung Glacier and icefall. The trail is found from the large boulder to the east of the gomba and passes a sleek white chorten (containing the relics of a lama). Head north, skirting the western flank of Kyangjin Ri. After **20-30 minutes**, the trail divides before crossing an extensive rockslide. (The lower (left) path descends to cross an outflow stream on a makeshift wooden bridge. This path can be difficult to follow due to crisscrossing grazing trails. The route contours up the gully to cross the same stream again and continues up to the lateral moraine to the east of the glacier.) The upper path crosses the rockslide area and continues up the gully to the right (east) of the stream before ascending sharply to a summer pasture area known as **Lado** (13, 661 feet, 4164 m) in another **30-40***

125

minutes. *Follow a faint trail north to the glacier, and climb the lateral moraine to the east for the best views in another* **20-30 minutes***.*

Side Trip to Glacial Lake. *This often frozen lake lies up a trough to the northwest of the gomba. Find the trail behind the gomba and head north through stone-built huts of a seasonal settlement. Just beyond, a stream is visible tumbling down from the lake. The trail up will be to the left (west) of it. Descend to cross a stream on a wooden bridge. The lake is above, just beyond the embankment to the north. Follow the trail west and after 10 minutes from the bridge, it ascends to the north along a ridge (the trail might be faint). Round a crest and contour down to the waters (13,212 feet, 4027 m) in* **45 minutes** *from the gomba. Langtang Lirung and Kimshung peaks tower above.*

Side Trip to Kyangjin Ri and Menchamsu *A* **1-1¼ hour** *climb up the hill behind Kyangjin Gomba known as Kyangjin Ri offers a breathtaking vantage point. Find the trail near the cheese factory, or, meet it above the middle area of the lodge cluster and ascend. Climb through boulders and zigzag across the hillside before reaching the rocky crest of Kyangjin Ri, locally known as Brana Chumbo (14,209 feet, 4331 m), festooned with prayer flags. From Kyangjin Ri, follow the ridge higher to* **Menchamsu** *(15,095 feet, 4601 m), a superlative viewpoint with more prayer flags in another* **hour***. Take care of footing on the trail as erosion has caused steep drop-offs.*

A slightly more gradual ascent to Menchamsu is to head up the gully to the east of Kyangjin Ri and follow it to a saddle (14936 feet, 4553 m) in **1¾-2 hours***. From the saddle traverse the ridgeline to the southwest to Menchamsu in another* **20 minutes***. This trail might be difficult to follow due to erosion and an abundance of grazing paths.*

Side Trip to Tsergo Ri Viewpoint. *The trail to Tsergo Ri can be seen from the lodges of Kyangjin Gomba as it zigzags up a ridge to the northeast. To reach this trail, head east out of town through grassland and over a boulder field to cross an* **alluvial fan** *(no bridge) in* **20-30 minutes***. Beyond the trail to Tsergo Ri branches north and ascends steeply up a ridgeline (while the trail to Langsisa Kharka continues east).*

After another **45 minutes** it divides. Take the upper path for a direct route to Tsergo Ri, which continues along the ridgeline. (The lower path (right) is a circuitous route that contours around the mountain to Digyabsa Kharka and Yala Kharka and gains Tsergo Ri from the southeast. It is not recommended and not in wide use and overrun with pasturing trails.) Reach the seasonal huts of **Dacha Pesa** (13,763 feet, 4195 m) in under **1-1¼ hours** from the alluvial fan.

Continue ascending along the ridgeline. Tsergo Ri, soaring above, is marked by prayer flags. This section from Dacha Pesa to the summer pasturing area of Thang Demo is exceptionally steep. Continue along the ridgeline and a little over **1-1¼ hours** from Dacha Pesa, the trail diverges again. Take the left (north) trail to continue on the direct route and reach the seasonal huts of **Thang Demo** (15,019 feet, 4578 m) **5 minutes** beyond. The Ganja La, a pass leading to Helambu, is south across the valley and flanked between Naya Kanga, the trekking peak summit to its west side, and Pangen Dopku to its east. From the huts of Thang Demo, water can be found with a nearby camping area about 650 feet (200 meters) to the northeast through a patch of boulders, GPS coordinates, N 28° 13.047', E 085° 35.630'.

Catch the trail continuing to Tsergo Ri above the huts and ascend between boulder fields, heading east, and then directly through the boulders and up to a ridge (15,869 feet, 4837 m) where there might be water in **1 hour** from Thang Demo. **Tsergo Ri** is due south along the ridge and up through more boulders. Reach the summit (16,368 feet, 4989 m), N 28° 12.788', E 085° 36.022' in less **30 minutes** (**1½ hours** from **Thang Demo** or **3½–4½ hours** from **Kyangjin Gomba**). Enjoy unsurpassed views in every direction!

Side Trip, Kyangjin Gomba to Langsisa Kharka
A long, unspoiled hike up the valley. Returning to Kyangjin makes for an arduous, full day, and food and headlamps should be carried in the event that darkness falls getting back. It would be best to bring shelter and supplies to camp at Langsisa.From **Kyangjim Gomba**, head east from the lodges to cross an alluvial fan (12,723 feet, 3878 m) **20-30 minutes** beyond. Pass an abandoned airfield (12,569 feet, 3831 m) to reach the

*north (right) bank of the Langtang Khola in **30-45 minutes**. Continue upstream to seasonal settlements of **Chadung** (12,950 feet, 3947 m) ¾-1 hour and **Numthang** (13,081 feet, 3987 m) in another **1-1¼ hours** where cheese is produced during the summer months.*

*Lateral and terminal moraines of the West Langtang Glacier loom ahead. Contour around the south terminus and climb to 13,556 feet (4132 m) with a view of the huts of Langsisa Kharka. Descend slightly to reach these herder shelters at **Langsisa Kharka** (13,484 feet, 4110 m) in **1-1½ hours**. Ahead are more huts and the main Langtang Glacier and the Tibetan border, a hard day's climb away. To the south across the valley lies beautiful Ganchenpo Peak and the terminus of the East Langtang Glacier and a difficult pass leading to a region east of Helambu. The first recorded crossing was by H. W. Tilman in 1949, however, there is no bridge across the river here.*

GANJA LA PASS

For experienced parties, the high pass known as Ganja La (16,805 feet, 5122 m) leads to Helambu. Mountaineering skills and the ability to use a rope and ice ax might be necessary. The route over **Ganja La**, usually a **3-day trip**, is normally possible from May to November, sometimes longer in dry years. Parties should be prepared for cold at any time of year. A guide would be useful and parties need to be self-sufficient for at least three days as there are no facilities until Tarke Ghyang in Helambu (a village described below).

RETURNING FROM LANGTANG TO SYABRUBESI VIA THE HIGH ROUTE

This linkup avoids backtracking along a high route from Rimche to Syabrubesi. Descend to reach the trail junction at **Rimche** (8202 feet, 2500 m), by the lodge named Ganesh View. The left branch descends to the valley bottom and is the quickest route to Syabrubesi, already described above in reverse. The path to the right ascends through open, steep country to **Sherpagaon** (8225 feet, 2507 m) an **hour** away with lodges.

Continue contouring and climbing along the steep valley wall for **1½-1¾ hours** to round a ridge to the Bhote Kosi Valley. A **45-minute** descent brings you to **Khangjim** (7480 feet, 2280 m), previously a Tibetan refugee settlement. **The Tamang Heritage Trail** connects with the Langtang trail at Khangjim.

The trail from Khangjim directly to Syabrubesi leaves below the middle of the hamlet. Avoid a branch heading to the right through fields and the trail diverges again in less than 5 minutes. The lower trail leads to Syabrubesi. Descend steeply for **¾-1 hour** to a junction. Stay left and contour above the river to reach the older part of Syabrubesi on the east side of the Bhote Kosi, just north of the Langtang Khola, in **1½ hours** from Khangjim. Cross the Bhote Kosi on a suspension bridge to continue to the newer part of Syabrubesi on the western side of the Trishuli River. Buses to Kathmandu depart three times daily at 7 am, 7:30 am, and the last bus departs around 9 am after first arriving from Thaambuchet (times are subject to change depending on season, demand and road condition).

GOSAINKUNDA LAKE

The Gosainkunda area is the location of several sacred, alpine lakes and a pilgrimage destination between Helambu and the Langtang valley. This region is sparsely populated. Trekkers can visit from Dhunche or Syabrubesi, reached by road from Kathmandu, or from the Langtang valley trek via Syabru village. It is especially spectacular in the spring when flowers are in bloom. If conditions permit, cross the Laurebina La high pass to link-up with the Helambu region. However, the route from Gosainkunda to Helambu is not feasible when snowfall necessitates mountaineering skills. Two options to reach Sing Gomba en route to Gosainkunda Lake are outlined below.

1-SYABRUBESI TO SING GOMBA VIA SYABRU

This route is for people returning from the Tamang Heritage Trail or from a circuit of Langtang via **Syabrubesi** (if returning down the valley bottom from Langtang, then from Landslide, aka, Pairo, follow in reverse the route described above, **Syabru to Landslide**).From the older section of Syabrubesi cross the Langtang Khola on a suspension bridge to its south (left) bank. Follow the Langtang Khola upstream for **20 minutes** before taking a side trail to ascend steeply to the right following powerlines most of the way to **Syabru** (7350 feet, 2240 m), **2-2½ hours** from the bridge.

SYABRU TO SING GOMBA

From **Syabru** (7350 feet, 2240 m), climb past a school to a signposted junction at the upper end of the settlement. The right branch leads west to Brabal and on to Dhunche. Head left up the east side of the ridge by an army post and a *chorten* below a Health Clinic and Trekker's Aid Station sponsored by The Mountain Fund (www.mountainfund.org). The trail zigzags up through the forest, passing a national park building in 15 minutes. Continue on switchbacks, taking the upper trail at junctions and the wider trail where you have a choice, generally following the ridgeline. Pass through an open area with prayer flags and *chorten* and by a couple of seasonal tea shops to reach a lodge at **Dursakang** (8720 feet, 2658 m), **1¼-1½ hours** from Syabru.

Shortly beyond Dursakang, the trail divides; stay left to reach another lodge above. There is no water available between the lodges at Dursakang and Probang Danda. Continue past *chorten* along the way and climb through magnificent oak, hemlock, and spruce until, after **45 minutes** the trail diverges beyond the last *chorten*. Take the right branch and stay with the widest trail. Reach lodges at **Probang Danda** (10,459 feet, 3188 m), spectacularly perched on a ridge, in **1-1¼ hours**. Ascend along a ridge, and just up from the lodges, stay right (to the west side of the ridge) for Sing Gomba (the path to the left heads directly to Cholang Pati bypassing Sing Gomba). Continue on a wide trail through an enchanting forest of rhododendron and large fir trees draped with moss. Pass to the left of a fenced compound to head west the collection of year-round lodges, a little-used *gomba*, and an impressive cheese factory of **Sing Gomba,** aka, **Chandan Bari** (10,840 feet, 3304 m) in **1 hour**.

2-DHUNCHE TO SING GOMBA

Keep in mind that the first 3300 feet (1000 m) of this steady climb of 8530 feet (2600 m) is exceptionally steep, and water is scarce. Be on the lookout for acute mountain sickness (AMS)! From Dhunche, the route begins at the first hairpin turn near a small Shiva shrine at the east end of town. Continue straight on a feeder road to pass a mineral water bottling plant on the uphill side before descending to cross the Gattekhola on a suspension bridge. Continue up the bank of the stream to a tea shop and lodge in a few minutes. Proceed by climbing up a gully to a crest with more climbing to **Deurali** (8776 feet, 2675 m), where there is a lodge, **2½–3 hours** from Dhunche. The trail is found to the north of the lodge. Continue climbing steeply, avoiding a left branch that heads down to Bharku, before passing an army post to reach Dimsa, known in Tamang language as Thomje (10118 feet, 3084 m), with basic lodging in **1¼ hours** from Deurali. Pass through oak to reach an impressive fir and rhododendron forest to the lodges of **Sing Gomba, aka, Chandan Bari,** (10,840 feet, 3304 m) in **1 hour**.

SING GOMBA TO GOSAINKUNDA

Pass the monastery and ascend along a wide trail on the south side of a ridge before crossing to the north side to **Cholang Pati** (11,873 feet, 3619 m) in **1¼-1½ hours**. Lodges are open during the trekking season, and the view of Ganesh and Langtang ranges makes a stay worthwhile. Continue for **¾-1 hour,** to seasonal lodges perched on a windy ridge, called **Laurebina,** aka Laurebina Yak, (12,800 feet, 3901 m).

Climb on, reaching a notch in the ridge with prayer flags and a shrine in another **¾-1 hour.** Cross the ridge to the south side and be careful of precipitous drop-offs although the trail is wide. Turn back if snowfall has made trail conditions unfavorable. **Gosainkunda Lake** (14,374 feet, 4381 m) with several lodges is reached in **1-1¼ hours**. During the full moon between mid-July and mid-August, it is buzzing with festival goers for the occasion of *Janai Purnima* when thousands of pilgrims come to pay homage to Shiva. Many ascend too fast and experience symptoms of (AMS). According to legend, Shiva created the lake to cool and cure his throat after drinking a poison that was threatening the destruction of the cosmos. Devotees believe that bathing in the waters here helps cleanse misdeeds and purifys *karma*.

GOSAINKUNDA TO HELAMBU

To continue to Helambu, contour the north side of the lake and ascend on an trail marked with cairns, to **Laurebina La** (15,121 feet, 4609 m) in **1–1¼ hours**. Descend to **Ayethang (Bheragoth)**, a simple, seasonal lodge (13,848 feet, 4221 m) near a trail junction, in **¾–1 hour**. Continue descending to the upper, seasonal lodge of **Phedi** (12,356 feet, 3766 m) in **1-1¼ hours**, with another seasonal lodge a few minutes below. Next to the upper lodge is a memorial *chorten* for people who perished when an airliner crashed just south of here during the monsoon of 1992. From the *chorten*, the trail branches. Do not descend right which travels down to eventually meet a road to Trishuli Bazaar. Head left (east) and descend to the lower lodge of Phedi, and then follow to the southeast from here with repeated, laborious ups and downs passing lodges at Gopte in **2½ hours** and **Mele Kharka** in another **30-40 minutes**. The trail continues through beautiful moss-draped rhododendron and fir forest and then ascends through juniper to the first of several lodges of **Tharepati** (11,975 feet, 3650 m) in **1¼ hours** from Mera Kharka.

From Tharepati, either traverse south along the main ridge to Pati Bhanjyang and on to Sundarijal to reach Kathmandu via the high route, or descend east to Melamchighyang. The latter route is described in the **THAREPATI TO SHERMATHANG AND MELAMCHI PUL BAZAAR** section. The route out to Sundarijal is described as a route of ascent into Helambu and can be followed in reverse to leave, please see **SUNDARIJAL TO THAREPATI**.

HELAMBU

Helambu can be approached from the northeast rim of the Kathmandu valley and is inhabited mostly by Yolmo, also called Sherpa but different than the Solu-Khumbu area people of the same name. The hill scenery and culture make up for the lack of spectacular, up-close mountain views, and the serene trails are a refreshing change of pace, especially when combined with busier treks to Langtang and Gosainkunda. Helambu is a majestic gem that receives sparse trekker traffic and is well worth a visit.

The trek starts from **Sundarijal** (4560 feet, 1390 m), near drinking water and hydroelectric stations, in the northeast corner of the Kathmandu valley, and passes through Shivapuri National Park , named for Shivapuri Peak (8963 feet, 2732 m). The park encompasses 61 sq miles (159 sq km) and is a catchment area that supplies Kathmandu valley with 8 million gallons (300 million liters) drinking water per day.

Bus service to Sundarijal is available from the Old Bus Park (aka, City Bus Park) near Ratna Park in central Kathmandu and infrequent mini-van service from Shahid (Martyr's) Gate. The ride takes about 1½ hours if all goes well, and you might be levied a fee for baggage. A taxi can also be hired, or you could walk, which might be a necessary option should a transport-halting strike (*banda*) be called. Additionally, there is now daily jeep and possibly bus service from Sankhu, a Newar town farther east from Baudhnath, up to Pati Bhanjyang, which would save a day's climb out of the valley.

SUNDARIJAL TO PATI BHANJYANG

From the bus park at **Sundarijal**, head upstream on a wide trail alongside a large water pipe to reach the Shivapuri National Park office and entry counter with nearby army post (5194 feet, 1583 m) in 30 minutes. The fee to cross through the Shivapuri National Park is 250 NRS for foreigners, 10 NRS for Nepalis. The ticket is valid for 7 days, and might be needed at a check point in Chisapani, especially if you are considering the **Kathmandu Valley Cultural Trail** to Nagarkot and beyond. A few minutes beyond the entry point, proceed left at a signed junction to a curious-looking dam of a water reservoir. Cross over the dam itself and continue uphill to the first lodges of **Mulkharka** (5521 feet, 1683 m), an **hour** from Sundarijal.

Mulkharka is widely spread out over the hillside. It takes an **hour** to ascend from the first lodges to the top end of the settlement at 6562 feet (2000 m). The next section passes through an isolated area uninhabited until Chisapani, and water can be sparse to nonexistent. Don't walk this area alone, as there have been instances of assaults north of Mulkharka. The trail continues up to **Burlang Bhanjyang** (7972 feet, 2430 m), in **1¼-1½ hours**. This pass marks the Shivapuri ridge, the Kathmandu valley's northern rim. Descend through a pleasant oak and rhododendron forest, and in **35–45 minutes**, reach a junction and continue right to gently climb to several lodges at **Chisapani** (7110 feet, 2167 m), in another **5 minutes**. Descend north to **Pati Bhanjyang** (5722 feet, 1744 m), in a saddle **1 hour** from Chisapani.

PATI BHANJYANG TO THAREPATI

The route continues along the general ridge system heading north with excellent vistas of the Himalaya. Begin by climbing to the left (north) of the hill forming the northeast side of the saddle. In less than 5 minutes, reach a road. Stay left and contour, avoiding a branch to the right after 25 minutes, to reach another saddle, **Thana Bhanjyang** (6027 feet, 1837 m), with a lodge and tea shops, in **30 minutes**. Climb steeply along the ridge to the north to the first lodge of **Chipling** (7169 feet, 2185 m), a hamlet scattered along the hillside, in **1 hour**. Take the uppermost trail at junctions for another **45 minutes** to the crest of **Joghin Danda, aka, Lapcho Danda**, (8047 feet, 2453 m), with several lodges located before and at the crest itself. Descend through oak forest on a trail lined with fern to the dispersed village of **Thodhang Betini** (7480 feet, 2280 m), in **45 more minutes**. Just outside of Thodhang, the trail diverges. Both branches lead to **Gulphu Bhanjyang** (6972 feet, 2125 m), a half-deserted village that lies in a saddle, in **30 more minutes**, **2-2¼ hours** from Chipling.

A **few minutes** north, reach a clearing and a trail junction, stay right to climb for **30 minutes** to a seasonal **lodge** and continue to another lodge

(8169 feet, 2490 m) in 30 more minutes. A **tea shop** is **5 minutes** farther up; keep left and ascend to 8432 feet (2570 m), just west of the summit before descending to homes and trekker lodges at **Khutumsang** (8100 feet, 2469 m), situated in a pass, **30 minutes** from the tea shop and **2 hours** from Gulphu Bhanjyang. Khutumsang has several lodges and a Langtang National Park checkpost.

The trail ascends the hill to the north. Stay with the widest path and climb through prickly-leaved oak along a ridge to the north to a simple lodge (9760 feet, 2975 m) in **1½ hours**. Continue to climb to the first lodge of Mangegoth (10,908 feet, 3325 m) in another **1½ hours, 3 hours** from Khutumsang. A clearing with more lodges (10,604 feet, 3232 m) is reached in **20-30 minutes.** Contour on the west side of the ridge to a notch with seasonal herders shelters (11,089 feet, 3380 m) in **30 minutes.** Cross over to the east side of the ridge and climb to reach more huts (11,450 feet, 3490 m) in another **30 minutes.** Continue for an **hour** to **Tharepati** (11,975 feet, 3650 m), with lodges along a ridge crest.

THAREPATI TO SHERMATHANG AND MELAMCHI PUL BAZAAR

Melamchighyang, lies below to the east. The trail decends from Tharepati's northern notch to a **cairn** near **1½ hours** a streambed (9698 feet, 2956 m). Head left (east) and cross a stream then pass above herders' huts in a clearingbefore crossing a tributary on a suspension bridge to **Melamchighyang,** aka Malemchigaon, 8400 feet, 2560 m), in **1½ hours** from the cairn. Melamchighyang is a serene, otherworldly place. Try to arrange a stay in a home rather than a lodge. At the west end is a hermitage made of boulders and claimed by locals to have built and used by Guru Rimpoche (aka, Padmasambava). To the north, past several *stupa*, is a well-regarded school and hostel. 5 minutes up the valley is a small, sacred cave with a persistent trickle of water. Purportedly, a consort of Guru Rimpoche named Kondoma bathed here during her monthly moon cycle. There are no more settlements up this valley.

To continue to Tarke Ghyang, descend below the *gomba* (monastery) along a small spur. Pass a few *chorten* to reach a crest with a tea shop, *chorten*, and prayer flags in 35 minutes (7162 feet, 2183 m). You can just make out the bridge below here, north of where the powerline crosses the river. In less than 15 more minutes reach another *chorten* and stay left to generally follow the powerlines. From here to the bridge, many trails intersect the route. Follow the widest and reach a bridge over the **Melamchi, aka Yolmo, Khola,** (6200 feet, 1890 m) **1½ hours** from Melamchighyang. There is a simple lodge on the (west) side of the river. Legend has it that a fierce dragon once guarded this crossing and Guru Rimpoche subdued the beast, transforming it into the large boulder near the lodge.

Cross to the east (true left) bank and head downstream to reach a *gomba* (Palma Chholing Monastery) among the houses of **Nakote** village in **30 minutes**. From the *gomba*, the more direct route to meet the motor road branches right to follow along the river, but this route may be impassable in the rainy season. The usual route stays high to Tarke Ghyang and leads gently up to the south of the *gomba* to around a small spur before crossing a tributary with a pair of mills in **10 minutes**. In another **10 minutes**, stay left. The right branch heads to a cave once used by the renowned, eleventh-century ascetic **Jetsun Milarepa**, revered by Vajrayana Buddhists, especially of the Kagyu lineage. The side trip from here to this cave and *gomba* is outlined below.

Side Trip to Milarepa Cave. Contour to the right (south) at the last branch mentioned above and contour south across several streams to pass a mani wall with two chorten in 20-30 minutes. Just beyond, stay right and cross more streams to reach a trail junction in 10-15 minutes. (The upper path here ascends to Tarke Ghyang in 2½ hours. It is a difficult route to follow, and asking locals for the way would be necessary.) Descend right to a stupa just below the junction and stay on the right (north) side of a stream heading down to the west. Stay right at another junction below to descend steeply to the gomba (5896 feet, 1797 m, N 27°59.424' E085°32.099') in 30 minutes from the stupa. Milarepa's cave lies behind the gomba. Both it and the gomba are kept locked and the 'konyer', or key custodian, may be difficult to find. Below is another cave as well as a retreat center that requests privacy. The lower route from Nakote to Thimbu passes below the compound and is a more direct route in from Nakote, depending but not traversable in the rainy season.

To continue onward to Tarke Ghyang (from the branch 10 minutes beyond the tributary crossing with a pair of mills above Nakote, mentioned above the previous Side Trip description), take the trail to the left and proceed steeply up a spur along a ridgeline to a *stupa* (7546 feet, 2300 m) with nearby simple lodging in **¾-1 hour**. Continue ascending to another *stupa* (8136 feet, 2480 m) just south of a *gomba* in **30 more minutes**. Enter a gulley and climb out to the closely built homes of **Tarke Ghyang,** a Yolmo village (8400 feet, 2560 m), in another **30 minutes (2-2½ hours** from Nakote). A trail arrives here from the Ganja La (16,805 feet, 5122 m) and the Langtang valley several days away. To cross the high pass, food, shelter, and fuel must be carried, and the party should be experienced and equipped for snow climbing. The Bhutanese style *gomba* has a curious sign prohibiting weapons, drunkeness, fighting, and destruction inside the main hall on punishment of fine.

Tarke Ghyang to Melamchi Bazaar via Thimbu or Kiul

The direct option from Tarke Ghyang to the road is to descend south to the hamlet of **Thimbu** (5184 feet, 1580 m) in **2½ hours**. If the road is in disrepair, continue to **Kiul** (4200 feet, 1280 m) in another **1¼ hours**. To follow this route, head right and descend just after the large Hotel Tarke Ghyang at the lower end of the settlement.

Tarke Ghyang to Melamchi Bazaar via Shermathang

The longer, more scenic route from **Tarke Ghyang** contours to Shermathang before following along the ridge to meet the road at Melamchi Pul Bazaar. Head left just after a stream at the lower end of Tarke Ghyang, near a *stupa* and above the large Hotel Tarke Ghyang, to follow the powerlines as you contour along the hillside. Pass below Shettigang (8580 feet, 2615 m), a few houses with a *gomba*, in 30 minutes. The trail contours in prickly-leaved oak forest to cross several tributaries to **Gangal** (8218 feet, 2505 m), with *gomba* and lodge, on the crest of the ridge, **1¾ hours** from Tarke Ghyang. There is a nunnery on a prominent spur below the village. Continue contouring, taking the uphill trail at junctions to **Shermathang** (8491 feet, 2588 m), in another **1¾ hours**. The village is spread out along a notch in the ridge and has a Langtang National Park check post. A motor road reaches Shermathang, but the monsoon rains regularly wash it out, and bus service is not yet available.

To continue to the bus service at Melamchi Pul Bazaar, head south following the road for 45 minutes, to a shrine with a massive golden figure of a seated Guru Rimpoche (8215 feet, 2504 m). Shortly beyond, reach a *stupa* and two tea shops, where the route diverges. To the right is the road, and left is the footpath. Following the footpath reach a *stupa* (7946 feet, 2422 m) in less than 30 minutes with a pleasant vista to the south. Descend to another *stupa* in 15 minutes near the village of **Raitanyang** (7300 feet, 2225 m), in **1½ hours** from Shermathang.

Continue with trails that make a shortcut of the road to **Kakani** (6398 feet, 1950 m) in **30-45 minutes**. Kakani has lodges and lies in a notch in the ridge south of a school. The next section might be a bit unclear; the goal is a prow at the bottom of the ridge to the south. Follow the widest trail passing *chorten* and follow the road with occasional shortcut trails. **Dubhachaur, aka Pokhari Bhanjyang** (5138 feet, 1566 m) is a Tamang village strung out on the ridge **1¼-1½ hours** from Kakani. Continue descending. The steep trail follows the ridge and intersects the road several times to eventually reach a long suspension bridge over the Melamchi Khola (2677 feet, 816 m), **1¾ hours** from Dubhachaur. Cross to the south bank, and head left to Melamchi Pul Bazaar (2690 feet, 820 m) with lodging if you miss the last bus at 3 pm (times subject to change according to season and demand).

MELAMCHI PUL BAZAAR TO SUNDARIJAL

Alternatively, if you would like to walk out to Sundarijal, head right after crossing the bridge over the Melamchi Khola from Kakani and follow the road 3½–4 miles (6 km) to **Talamarang** (3058 feet, 932 m) with simple lodging, shops, and tea houses, in **1–1¼ hours**. From Talamarang there are two routes to Pati Bhajyang. The lower begins along the river bottom but is unsuitable in the rainy season. The high route offers better views and ascends steeply to the south and follows a dirt road much of the way with trail shortcuts. Both trails are currently little used by trekkers and it would be wise to have a travel companion for safety.

Ascend steeply the hill to the south, following the the road with occasional trail shortcuts. Reach **Terse** (4428 feet, 1350 m) in **¾-1 hour** and then **Majagaon** (or Tarambra, the Tamang name) (4944 feet, 1507 m) **30 minutes** later. The route diverges from the upper end of the village. Take the right (west) branch to contour around the valley to cross a **tributary** in **30 minutes** before ascending to **Batase** (5489 feet, 1673 m) in **25 more minutes**, about **2¼ hours** from Talamarang.

Batase is a sprawling village where home stay might be arranged. It has a hostel for students and sees occasional foreign volunteers. From **Batase** onward, there are many junctions and the trail can be difficult to follow. Ascend gradually and contour, keeping to the north side of the ridge, to reach the ridge crest village of **Thakani** (6004 feet, 1830 m) in **¾-1 hour**. Continue to a **saddle** in **15 minutes** and keep north of the ridge to a **junction** in **15 more minutes**. Take the left (upper) trail and pass above the village of Kabre on a fern-lined trail to the hamlet of **Palchen** (6243 feet, 1903 m) at a crest in **20-30 more minutes**, **¾-1 hour** from Thakani. Stay left to cross to the south side of the ridge and contour west before descending to **Pati Bhanjyang** in **¾-1 hour.** From here, follow in reverse the section above **SUNDARIJAL TO PATI BHANJYANG.**

NEPALI LANGUAGE AND GLOSSARY

INTRODUCTION

Nepal has over 90 distinct languages. Nepali is the national language and used as the second tongue by half of the population. There are many variations in how it is spoken and efforts to speak Nepali will set you apart and be appreciated by your hosts.

Nepali is an Indo-European language derived from Sanskrit and became one of India's official languages in 1992. It is written in Devanagari script (as are Hindi and Sanskrit), and transliteration to the Roman script is used throughout the book. There are several sounds in Nepali that are not common in English and transliteration will not be precise. In these instances, pronunciation might be challenging.

GLOSSARY

Transliteration of the Nepali as well as the actual Devanagari script is provided to facilitate understanding. If pronunciation proves difficult, show the script with the Nepali word or phrase in Devanagari to the person with whom you are communicating.

Transliteration pronunciation guidelines:

a as the *a* in about or the *u* in cup, hut (å is nasalization of the **a** sound)
aa as the *a* in far or *o* in top, dot (åå is nasalization of the **aa** sound)
e as the *e* in latte or *ey* in whey or the *ay* in day
i as the *i* in miss, tip, hit
o as the *o* in more, grow, snow, crow
u as the *ue* in true or *oo* in roof, moo (ů is nasalization of the **u** sound)
D , T and N (capitalized letters): curl the tongue back so that the tip of it touches the roof of the mouth while producing the sound. Otherwise, the lower case **d, t** and **n** sounds are made with the tip of the tongue toward the front teeth
The letter **h** after a consonant indicates aspiration or a breathing out with the accompanying sound with the exception of *ch*, which is not aspirated (breath is not expelled with the sound) while *chh*, is aspirated.

FAMILY

ENGLISH	TRANSLITERATION	DEVANAGARI
mother	aamaa	आमा
father	buwaa, baabu	बुवा or बाबु
older sister	didi	दिदी
younger sister	bahini	बहिनी
older brother	daai, daaju	दाइ or दाजु
younger brother	bhaai	भाइ
daughter	chori	छोरी
son	choraa	छोरा
you (familiar)	timi	तिमी
you (formal)	tapaai	तपाई
she/he (familiar)	u	उ
she/he (formal)	wahåå	वहाँ
I	ma	म
me	malaai	मलाई
my	mero	मेरो

FOOD AND DRINK

ENGLISH	TRANSLITERATION	DEVANAGARI
appetizing,	miTho or swaadishT	मीठो, स्वादिष्ट

delicious, tasty		
apple	syaau	स्याउ
banana	keraa	केरा
basil	tulsi	तुल्सी
black tea	kaalo chiyaa	कालो चिया
chickpeas (garbanzo beans)	chanaa	चना
chutney (pickled salsa)	achaar	अचार
coriander	dhaniyåå	धिनयाँ
diarrhea	pakhaalaa, disaa	पखाला or दिसा
distilled, local alcoholic drink	raksi	रक्सी
egg	ful, aNDaa	फुल or अण्डा
enough	pugyo, bhayo	पुग्यो or भयो
fermented, locally made alcoholic beverage	jååD, chhyaang	जाँड or छ्याङ्
fermented millet alcoholic beverage	tongbaa, tumbaa	तोङ्बा or तुम्बा
flatbread (unleavened bread)	roTi , chapaati	रोटी or चपाती
food/meal (rice, lentils vegetables, ie, daal-bhaat-tarakaari)	khaanaa	खाना

ginger	aduwaa	अदुवा
green leafy vegetables (eg, spinach, mustard greens)	saag	साग
lemon	kaagati	कागती
lentils	daal	दाल
less sugar	chini kam	चिनी कम
maize (corn)	makai	मकै
meat, flesh, muscles	maasu	मासु
milk	dudh	दूध
mixed vegetable dish	tarakaari or sabji	तरकारी or सब्जी
potato	aalu	आलु
monosodium glutamate (MSG)	ajinomoTo	अजीनोमोटो
rice (cooked)	bhaat	भात
salt	nun	नून
salty	nunilo	नुनिलो
sour	amilo	अमिलो
soybeans	bhaTmaas	भटमास
spicy	piro	पिरो
sugar	chini	चिनी
sweet	guliyo	गुलियो

sweet milk tea	chiyaa (or, more precisely, dudhko chiyaa)	चिया (दूधको चिया)
to boil	umaalnu, usinnu	उमाल्नु or उसिन्नु
to cook	pakaaunu	पकाउनु
to eat	khaanu	खानु
to heat up/make warm	tataaunu	तताउनु
water	paani	पानी
yogurt (aka, curd)	dahi	दही

ADDITIONAL VOCABULARY

ENGLISH	TRANSLITERATION	DEVANAGARI
animal	janaawar	जनावर
bag	jholaa	झोला
big	Thulo	ठूलो
bird	charaa	चरा
blanket	sirak, kammal, kambal	सिरक or कम्मल or कम्बल
bridge	pul	पुल
Buddhist monastery	gombaa, gumbaa	गोम्बा or गुम्बा
Buddhist scroll painting	thaankaa	थान्का
Buddhist structure/memorial	stupaa, chorTen	स्तुपा or चोर्टेन
butterfly	putali	पुतली

cheap	sasto	सस्तो
cicada	jhaaukiri	झाउकिरी
clean	safaa	सफा
cold (adj)	chiso	चिसो
cold (weather)	jaaDo	जाडो
correct, good	Thik , raamro	ठीक or राम्रो
danger	khataraa	खतरा
diarrhea	pakhaalaa,disaa	पखाला or दिसा
dirty	fohor	फोहोर
donation	daan	दान
down (adv)	tala	तल
evening, dusk	belukaa, såååjha	बेलुका or साँझ
expensive	mahågo	महँगो
flower	phul	फूल
forest	ban, juNgal	बन or जङ्गल
gateway, village archway	kaaNi	काणी
hat or cap made of cloth fabric	Topi	टोपी
help, assistance	maddat	मद्दत
here	yahåå	यहाँ
hills	pahaaD	पहाड
Himalayan range	himaalaya	हिमालय
Hindu temple	mandir	मन्दिर

hour	ghanTaa	घन्टा
injured	ghaaite	घाइते
kerosene	maTTitel	मट्टितेल
key	chaabi	चाबी
lake	taal	ताल
landslip	pahiro	पहिरो
leech	jukaa	जुका
left (direction)	baayåå	बायाँ
long	laamo	लामो
love	maayaa, prem	माया or प्रेम
lowland plains	tarai	तराई
map	naksaa	नक्सा
maybe	holaa	होला
medicinal herbs	jaDibuTi	जडीबूटी
money	paisaa, rupaiyåå	पैसा or रुपैयाँ
monkey	båådar	बाँदर
morning	bihaana	बिहान
Mount Everest	sagarmaathaa	सगरमाथा
mountains, range	himaal, parbat	हिमाल or पर्वत
new	nayåå	नयाँ
night	raat	रात
no, is not	hoina , åha, chhaina	होइन or अँह or छैन

not good	naraamro	नराम्रो
oil, can also mean fuel, gasoline	tel	तेल
old	puraano	पुरानो
orphan	anaatha	अनाथ
party	bhoj	भोज
fast, quick	chhiTo	छिटो
prayer inscribed stone or wall of such prayer stones (also means 'jewel')	maaNe	माणी
rain	paani parnu	पानी पर्नु
ready, prepared	tayaar	तयार
religion, religious practice, duty	dharma	धर्म
rest area, usually with a platform and shade tree	chautaaraa	चौतारा
rhododendron (red rhododendron)	guråås (laaliguråås)	गुराँस (लालीगुराँस)
ridge	DååDaa	डाँडा
right (direction)	daayåå	दायाँ
river	nadi, kholaa	नदी or खोला
room	koTaa	कोठा
room for sleeping	sutne koTaa	सुत्ने कोठा
route, path, trail, road	baaTo	बाटो

service	sewaa	सेवा
shepards' shelter	goTh	गोठ
short	chhoTo	छोटो
sick, ill	biraami	बिरामी
slow	Dhilo	ढिलो
small	saano	सानो
snow	hiŭ	हिउँ
shop (n.)	pasal	पसल
straight	sidhaa	सीधा
strike (closure)	banda	बन्द
suffering, hardship	du-kha	दुःख
sunlight	ghaam	घाम
tall, high	aglo	अग्लो
thanks	dhanyabaad	धन्यबाद
that	tyo	त्यो
there	tyahåå	त्यहाँ
this	yo	यो
to be tired	thakaai laagnu	थकाइ लाग्नु
to do	garnu	गर्नु
to go	jaanu	जानु
to walk	hiDnu	हिंड्नु
today	aaja	आज
toilet	charpi	चर्पी

tomorrow	bholi	भोलि
tree	rukh	रूख
up (adv)	maathi	माथि
very, much	ekdam, dherai	एकदम , धेरै
village	gaaů	गाउँ
vipassana	vipashyanaa	विपश्यना
walking stick	lauro	लौरो
What?	ke	के ?
When?	kahile	कहिले ?
Where?	kataa, kahåå	कता or कहाँ ?
Which?	kun	कुन ?
Who?	ko ho	को हो ?
Why?	kina	किन ?
worship/prayer/ritual	pujaa	पूजा
yes, is	ho, hunchha, hajur (polite form)	हो or हुन्छ or हजुर
yesterday	hijo	हिजो

USEFUL WORDS AND PHRASES

ENGLISH	TRANSLITERATION	DEVANAGARI
Hello (and goodbye)	namaste (or, more formally, namaskaar)	नमस्ते (or नमस्कार)
How are you?	tapaailaai kasto chha?	तपाईलाई कस्तो छ ?
What is (happening/going on)?	ke chha?	के छ ?
See you again (goodbye)!	pheri bheTaulaa	फेरी भेटौला
How much?	kati ho, kati parchha	कति हो or कति पर्छ?

Thank you	dhanyabaad	धन्यवाद
I am sorry/I beg your pardon	malaai maaph garnus	मलाई माफ गर्नुस्
I have diarrhea	malaai pakhaalaa (or disaa) laageko chha	मलाई पखाला (दिसा) लागेको छ
I have a fever	malaai jwaro aayeko chha	मलाई ज्वरो आएको छ
This tastes good!	yo miTho chha	यो मिठो छ
I am thirsty	malaai pyaas (or, tirkhaa) laageko chha	मलाई प्यास (तिर्खा) लागेको छ
I am hungry	malaai bhok laageko chha	मलाई भोक लागेको छ
Is there a shop here?	yahåå pasal chha holaa?	यहाँ पसल छ होला ?
Please don't add tasty powder (MSG/ajinomoto)	kripyaa khaanaamaa ajinomoTo naraakhnu holaa	कृपया खानामा अजिनोमोटो नराख्नुहोला
I am a vegetarian	ma shaakaahaari hů	म शाकाहारी हुँ
I do not eat meat	ma maasu nakhaane	म मासु नखाने
Is food available here?	yahåå khaanaa paainchha?	यहाँ खाना पाइन्छ ?
May I stay at your house?	ma tapaaiko gharmaa basna sakchhu?	म तपाईको घरमा बस्न सक्छु ?
Where can I stay?	ma kahåå basna sakchhu holaa?	म कहाँ बस्न सक्छु होला ?
Is there a place to stay here?	yahåå basne suvidhaa chha holaa?	यहाँ बस्ने सुविधा छ होला ?

Is there a lodge here?	yahåå laj chha holaa? (or, yahåå sutna paaincha holaa)	यहाँ लज छ होला ? (यहाँ सुत्न पाइन्छ होला ?)
What is the name of this village?	yo gaaůko naam ke ho?	या गाउँको नाम के हो ?
What time is it?	ahile kati bajyo? (or, samaya kati bhayo holaa?)	अहिले कति बज्यो ? (समय कति भयोहोला?)
I don't know	malaai thaahaa chhaina	मलाई थाहा छैन
How much is it?	yo kati ho? (or, yasko kati ho?)	यो कति हो ? (यसको कति हो ?)
How many?	kati waTaa? (or, kati?)	कति वटा ? (कति ?)
Do you have children?	tapaaikaa bacchaa (chhoraa chhori) chhan?	तपाईंका बच्चा (छोराछोरी) छन् ?
Are you married?	tapaaiko bibaaha bhayo?	तपाईंको विवाह भयो ?
How old are you?	tapaaiko umer kati bhayo?	तपाईंको उमेर कति भयो ?
Have you eaten?	tapaaile khaanaa khaanu bhayo?	तपाईंले खाना खानुभयो ?
I have eaten	maile khaaisake	मैले खाइसकें
Where are you going?	tapaai kahåå jåådai hunuhunchha?	तपाईं कहाँ जाँदै हुनुहुन्छ ?
I am going to…	ma ….. Thaaůmaa jåådai chhu	म …. ठाउँमा जाँदैछु
What is this?	yo ke ho?	यो के हो ?

Where are you from?	tapaai kahåå baaTa aaunu bhayeko ho?	तपाईं कहाँबाट आउनुभएको हो ?
I am from...	ma ..... baaTa aayeko hů	म .... बाट आएको हुँ
Which country?	kun desh?	कुन देश ?
What is your name?	tapaaiko naam ke ho?	तपाईंको नाम के हो ?
My name is	mero naam ... ho	मेरो नाम ... हो
I am fine	malaai Thik chha (or, ma sanchai chhu)	मलाई ठिक छ (म सञ्चै छु)
How are you?	tapaailaai kasto chha? (or, tapaailaai sanchai chha?)	तपाईंलाई कस्तो छ? (तपाईंलाई सञ्चै छ ?)
I like	malaai manparchha	मलाई मनपर्छ
I do not like?	malaai manpardaina	मलाई मनपर्दैन

NUMERALS

ROMAN NUMERAL	NEPALI NUMERAL	TRANSLITERATION	DEVANAGARI
0	०	shunya	शून्य
1	१	ek	एक
2	२	dui	दुई
3	३	tin	तीन
4	४	chaar	चार
5	५	pååch	पाँच
6	६	chha	छ
7	७	saat	सात
8	८	aaTh	आठ
9	९	nau	नौ
10	१०	das	दस
20	२०	bis	बीस
30	३०	tis	तीस
40	४०	chaalis	चालीस
50	५०	pachaas	पचास
60	६०	saaThi	साठी
70	७०	sattari	सत्तरी
80	८०	asi	असी
90	९०	nabbe	नब्बे
100	१००	say, ek say	सय or एक सय
500	५००	pååch say	पाँच सय
1000	१०००	hajaar, ek hajaar	हजार or एक हजार

KATHMANDU AND POKHARA TIPS

KATHMANDU:

A. Don't miss **the full moon revelry at *Baudhnath Stupa*** when the area is filled with Buddhist devotees (Siddhartha Gautama, later known by the title **Buddha**, was born in Lum bini, Nepal, during a full moon and is said to have gained spiritual liberation and died on full moon days). Climb to the highest plinth admissible and circumambulate the *stupa* in a clockwise direction for an unforgettable experience. The *stupa* itself is enchantingly lit up as dusk falls. Rooftop restaurants in the area offer the best vantage.

B. Enjoy a lip-smacking plate of steamed *momo*, one of the most satisfying and popular dishes in Nepal. These round or crescent-shaped dumplings are accompanied by homemade dipping sauce and found in nearly every restaurant and food stall in the Valley and the best value on the menu.

C. Hike to Shivapuri peak through a luxuriant jungle. The summit offers sensational vistas of the snowy titans to the north, especially the Ganesh and Langtang ranges. Bring along an offering (eg, dry goods, sweets or other donation) for the yogi hermits who live near the top and keep a lookout for the **Spiny Babbler**, a bird found only in Nepal.

D. Take in the resplendent, broad panorama of the densely populated Kathmandu Valley from ***Swayambhunath Stupa***. Also known as **The Monkey Temple** for its furry (but ferocious) inhabitants. This shrine is especially favored by Newari Buddhists who circumambulate it in the morning and evening.

E. Explore ancient hamlets on the southern fringes of the Valley, including Kirtipur, Chobar, Bungamati, Khokhana, Godawari and beyond for an inkling of a timeless way of life unchanged for centuries.

F. Bicycle to Panauti, 30 kms (19 mi) to the southeast of Kathmandu Valley, on a serene back road. Return along the Arniko Highway by way of Sanga Pass where you can pay homage to a **colossal statue of Shiva overlooking the Valley**.

G. Search for souvenirs between **Asan Chowk and Indra Chowk**. The pulsating bazaar 10 minutes south of Thamel is packed two stories high with merchandise and swarming with vendors, shoppers, onlookers, general pedestrian commuters, and honking motorcyclists. Additionally, after you get your trekking permits at Bhrikutimandap, visit nearby **Hong Kong Bazaar**, a tarp covered tunnel made with bamboo struts. Although 1.25 mi (2 km) long, the merchandise is as temporary as the daily rise and fall of the sun. Goods are hauled in each morning and lugged away every evening.

H. Don't miss an otherworldly **prayer session at a Vajrayana monastery** (usually early morning and evening). Drift into contemplative reverie with the singsong chanting accompanied by drums, bells, horns and conch shell blasts.
I. The captivating **Durbar Squares of Kathmandu, Patan and Bhaktapur** reveal a medieval era when royalty reigned. Be sure to have ample disc space for many memorable photos.

J. **Visit Pharping to the southwest of Kathmandu Valley** and pay honor to holy **Asura Cave**, favored by wandering yogi **Gorakhnath** and Tibetan Buddhist patron saint **Padmasambhava**. For those not troubled by the sight of blood and slaughter, Dakshinkali Temple lies below in a gorge. Animal sacrifices take place daily to appease the bloodthirsty Hindu Goddess **Kali**.

K. Drop by a cozy drinking establishment (suggested: Baudhnath, Patan and Jyatha) for *tongbaa,* a fermented millet drink, and finger foods. If you find a genuine one, usually run by Sherpa, Rai or Limbu owners, it will be elbow to elbow with locals. Best of luck finding a seat in the cold season when *tongbaa* drinking reaches a zenith.

L. Savor Nepal's national dish, *Dal Bhat*, for a completely satsifying, well-rounded meal.

POKHARA:

M. **PARAGLIDE**...float down to Pokhara from the aerie perch of Sarangkot and enjoy a bird's eye vista of the Himalaya on the descent; bring a raptor along (Parahawking) for the glide of your life. Sarankot also has a newly built 1.1 mile (1.8 km) **zipline** that drops over 600 m in less than two minutes.

N. **Bicycle from Pokhara to Begnas Lake** and reward yourself with a dip in its refreshing waters. Roadbuilding along the Annapurna Circuit is a boon for bicyclists. You can porter the cycle over steep sections including the Thorung La!

O. **Hike up to Peace Pagoda (aka, Shanti Stupa) or Sarangkot**, jumping off point for paragliders and parahawkers and be rewarded with staggering vistas of the mighty Himalaya. Unclimbed Macchapuchhre ("Fishtail") steals the show.

P. Spend a half day or more at the **Mountaineering Museum**, dedicated to the Himalaya and people living among and climbing them. Displays feature historical information on ascent history and include mountaineering gear and personal accounts. Other exhibitions cover culture, plant and wildlife as well as environmental issues in the Himalaya.

Q. Wander along the placid shores of **Phewa Tal**, and rent a boat for a more rejuvenating experience on its waters. Take in a meal at a shoreline restaurant with nightly song and dance performances.

Scale 1:5000000

0   50   100   150   200

N

TIBET
(CHINA)

INDIA

Protected Areas

1. Api-Nampaa Conservation Area
2. Sulkla Phant Wildlife Reserve
3. Khaptad National Park
4. Rara National Park
5. Bardiya National Park
6. Banke National Park
7. Shey-Phoksundo National Park
8. Dhorpatan National Park
9. Annapurna Conservation Area
10. Manaslu Conservation Area

11. Chitwan National Park
12. Parsa Wildlife Reserve
13. Langtang National Park
14. Shivapuri National Park
15. Gauri-Shankar Conservation Area
16. Sagarmatha National Park

17. Makalu-Barun National Park
18. Makalu-Barun Buffer Zone
19. Kangchenjunga Conservation Area
20. Koshi Tappu Wildlife Reserve

Sagarmatha
(Mt. Everest)

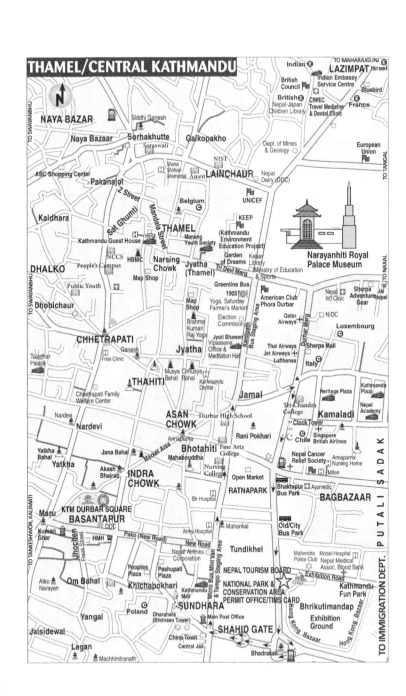

THAMEL/CENTRAL KATHMANDU

N

TO SWAYANBHU

TO MAHARAJGUNJ

LAZIMPAT Israel

Indian

British Council

Indian Embassy Service Centre

Bluebird

British
Nepal-Japan
Children Library

CIWEC
Travel Medicine
& Dental Clinic

France

NAYA BAZAR

Siddhi Ganesh

Naya Bazaar

Sorhakhutte

Galkopakho

Saraswati

Dept. of Mines
& Geology

European Union

ABC Shopping Center

Pakanajol

Z Street

Mana
Mohan
Memorial

NIST

Amrit

LAINCHAUR

Nepal
Dairy (DDC)

TO TANGAL

Kaldhara

Sat Ghumti

Mandala Street

Belgium

THAMEL

Kathmandu Guest House

Manang
Youth Society

UNICEF

KEEP

(Kathmandu
Environment
Education Project)

DHALKO

NCCS

People's Campus

HBMC

**Narsing
Chowk**

Map Shop

**Jyatha
(Thamel)**

Garden
of Dreams

Tri Devi Marg

Kaiser
Library

Ministry of Education
& Sports

Narayanhiti Royal
Palace Museum

Public Youth

Dhobichaur

Map
Shop

Greenline Bus
1905

Yoga, Saturday
Farmer's Market

American Club
Phora Durbar

Qatar
Airways

NIDC

Nepal
Int'l Clinic

Sherpa
Adventure
Gear

Jai
Nepal

Luxembourg

TO NAXAL

CHHETRAPATI

Brahma
Kumari
Raj Yoga

Ganesh

Free Clinic

Jyatha

Election
Commission

Jyoti Bhawan
Vipassana
Office &
Meditation Hall

Thai Airways
Jet Airways
Lufthansa

Sherpa Mall

Italy

Kanti path
Bus Staging Area

Tuladhar
Palace

THAHITI

Musya
Bahal

Chhusya
Bahal

Kathmandu
Dental

Jamal

Heritage Plaza

Kathmandu
Plaza

Nepal
Academy

Chhetrapati Family
Welfare Center

Tri-Chandra
College

Kamaladi

Nardevi

Nardevi

**ASAN
CHOWK**

Durbar High School

Rani Pokhari

Clock Tower

Chile

Singapore
British Airlines

Yatkha
Bahal

Jana Bahal

Annapurna

Bhotahiti

Fine Arts
College

Nepal Cancer
Relief Society

Annapurna
Nursing Home

Yatkha

Akash
Bhairab

Market Area

Mahabouddha

Nursing
College

Open Market

Miteri

**INDRA
CHOWK**

RATNAPARK

Bhaktapur
Bus Park

Ayurvedic

BAGBAZAAR

Bir Hospital

KTM DURBAR SQUARE

Maru

BASANTAPUR

DDC

Mahankal

Old/City
Bus Park

Kumari
Ghar

Jhochhen

HMH

Freak Street

Pako (New Road)

Army Hospital

Tundikhel

Mahendra
Police Club

Model Hospital

Nepal Medical
Assoc. Blood Bank

TO TANKESHWOR, KALIMATI

Atko
Narayan

Om Bahal

Peoples
Plaza

Pashupati
Plaza

New Road

Nepal Airlines
Corporation

NEPAL TOURISM BOARD

Exhibition Road

**Kathmandu
Fun Park**

Khichapokhari

Kathmandu
Mall

Micro Bus, Mini Van
& Tempo Staging Area

★ **NATIONAL PARK &
CONSERVATION AREA
PERMIT OFFICE/TIMS CARD**

Bhrikutimandap

Yangal

Poland

Dharahara
(Bhimsen Tower)

SUNDHARA

Main Post Office

Exhibition
Ground

Jalsidewal

China Town

SHAHID GATE

Lagan

Central Jail

Bhadrakali

Hong Kong Bazaar

Machhindranath

TO IMMIGRATION DEPT.

PUTALI SADAK

CENTRAL KATHMANDU

YAK & YETI
Luxemburg
Portugal
Sita Air
China, Gorkha & Buddha
Kamal Pokhari

Vipassana Office & Meditation Hall
ANNAPURNA
Sherpa Mall
Indian Air
Thai
Italy
KTM Model
Russian Culture

Bishwo Jyoti Cinema Hall
Kamaladi

Heritage Plaza
Kuwait Saudi Arabian Nepal Airlines
Kumari

Jamal
REIYUKAI

Malaysia, Air Nepal Int'l
Ghantaghar (Clock Tower)
Kamaladi Ganesh

Rani Pokhari
Chile
Singapore Air, Delta Airlines, Silk Air, Air Nepal, Australian Air, Cathay Air, Pacific, Uzbekistan, Philipines
Bhojan Griha

RATNAPARK
Open Market
JIIP, Nepal Cancer Relief Centre
New Zealand
Khett Bazaar (organic)

Bir Hospital
Bhaktapur Bus Park
Ayurvedic
BAGBAZAR
DILLI BAZAAR

Mahankal
Old City Bus Park
Tukucha Khola

PUTALISADAK
KALIKASTHAN

Nepal Airlines Building
Mahendra Police Club
Model
Nepal China Society

Tundikhel
Blood Bank
Iceland

Exhibition Road
Laxmi Plaza

Kathmandu Mall
Nepal Tourism Board, National Park & Conservation Area Permit Office/ TIMS Card
Kathmandu Fun Park
Exhibition Ground
Ichhamati
IMMIGRATION DEPARTMENT

SUNDHARA
Bhrikutimandap
Buddha Ratna Vihar

Hong Kong Market

SHAHID GATE
Bhadrakali
SINGHA DURBAR

China Town
Nepal Telecom
Rastriya Banijya Bank (Head Office)
Office of Attorney General

Central Jail
NEPAL ARMY HEADQUARTER
Supreme Court

Nepal Bar Association

Dasharath Rangsala (National Stadium)
Tukucha Khola
Department of Archaeology

Swimming Pool

United World Trade Center
TRIPURESWOR
Maiti Ghar
Babar Mahal

Ram Shah Path

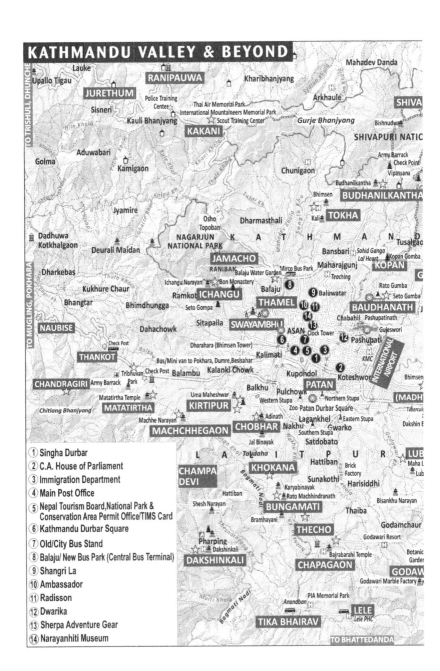

KATHMANDU VALLEY & BEYOND

TO TRISHULI, DHUNCHE

Lauke
Upallo Tigau
RANIPAUWA
Kharibhanjyang
Mahadev Danda

JURETHUM
Sisneri
Police Training Center
Thai Air Memorial Park
International Mountaineers Memorial Park
Scout Training Center
Arkhaule
SHIVA

Kauli Bhanjyang
Gurje Bhanjyang
Bishnudwa
KAKANI
SHIVAPURI NATIC

Golma
Aduwabari
Kamigaon
Chunigaon
Army Barrack
Check Point
Vipassana

Budhanilkantha
Bhimsen
BUDHANILKANTHA

Jyamire
Osho Topoban
Dharmasthali
Kali
TOKHA

Dadhuwa
Kotkhalgaon
Deurali Maidan
NAGARJUN NATIONAL PARK
K A T H M A N
Bansbari
Sahid Ganga Lal Heart
Kopan Gomba
Tusalgao
KOPAN

Dharkebas
JAMACHO
RANIBAN
Balaju Water Garden
Mirco Bus Park
Maharajgunj
Teaching
G

Kukhure Chaur
Ichangu Narayan
Bon Monastery
Balaju
Rato Gumba
Seto Gumba

Bhangtar
Bhimdhungga
Seto Gompa
ICHANGU
THAMEL
Baluwatar
BAUDHANATH

NAUBISE
Dahachowk
Sitapaila
SWAYAMBHU
ASAN Clock Tower
Chabahil
Pashupatinath
Gujeswori
Seto Gumba

Ramkot
Dharahara (Bhimsen Tower)
Pashupati
KMC

THANKOT
Bus/Mini van to Pokhara, Dumre, Besisahar
Kalimati

CHANDRAGIRI
Army Barrack
Tribhuvan Check Post
Park
Balambu
Kalanki Chowk
Kupondol
Koteshwor
Bhimsen

Matatirtha Temple
Uma Maheshwar
Balkhu
Pulchowk
PATAN
(MADH

Chitlang Bhanjyang
MATATIRTHA
Western Stupa
Northern Stupa
Tuberculi

Machhe Narayan
KIRTIPUR
Zoo Patan Durbar Square
Dakshin B

MACHCHHEGAON
CHOBHAR
Nakhu
Adinath
Eastern Stupa
Gwarko

Jal Binayak
Southern Stupa
Satdobato

L A
Taladaha
I T
P U R
LUB

CHAMPA DEVI
KHOKANA
Hattiban
Brick Factory
Maha L
Lub

Hattiban
Karyabinayak
Sunakothi
Harisiddhi
Bisankhu Narayan

Shesh Narayan
Rato Machhindranath
BUNGAMATI
Thaiba
Godamchaur

Bramhayani
THECHO
Godawari Resort

Pharping
Dakshinkali
Bajrabarahi Temple
Botanic Garder

DAKSHINKALI
CHAPAGAON
GODAW

Godawari Marble Factory
GODAW

PIA Memorial Park
Anandban
LELE
Lele PHC

TIKA BHAIRAV
TO BHATTEDANDA

TO MUGLING, POKHARA

① Singha Durbar
② C.A. House of Parliament
③ Immigration Department
④ Main Post Office
⑤ Nepal Tourism Board,National Park & Conservation Area Permit Office/TIMS Card
⑥ Kathmandu Durbar Square
⑦ Old/City Bus Stand
⑧ Balaju/ New Bus Park (Central Bus Terminal)
⑨ Shangri La
⑩ Ambassador
⑪ Radisson
⑫ Dwarika
⑬ Sherpa Adventure Gear
⑭ Narayanhiti Museum

Chagaon

Pati Bhanjyang

Thakani

Niglen

MELAMCHI

Shobare Khola

Telephone Facilities
Maiti Nepal
9 Lodges
Cheese Factory
CHISAPANI
Park Check Point

Sulikot Ghyang

PURI PEAK

Shivapuri Lek

NETIF Tourist Shelter

Thulo Daap

Baghdwar

Burlang   View Point   Sano Daap
NAL PARK   Bhanjyang

Jaisigaon

Rokatol

BAHUNEPATI

Jarke Khola

Sindhu Khola

View Point

NAGI GOMBA   Bhotechaur

MANICHUR

Mulkharka

Army Barrack, Reservoir
National Park Entrance NETIF Community House
Scout Training Centre Water Fall, Check Point

Fair in Janai   Jhule
Purnima

Nanggle Bhare

Majhitar

Chauki
Bhanjyang

Nanggle

CHAPABOT

SUNDARIJAL

Dhand Khola

Telephone Facilities

Jarsingpauwa

SIPAGHAT

B.P. Museum

Gokarna Mahadev

BAJRAYOGINI

JARSINGPAUWA
COMMUNITY
FOREST

Raniban

OKARNA

Indrayani

Kattike Bhanjyang

Gairibisauna

GOKARNA
RESERVED
FOREST

Changu Narayan

Manahara Kh.

"Jungle Walk" Mahankal

SANKHU

Ghatte Khola

NETIF/NNTDC Office

NAGARKOT

Hiuwapati

orpati

Mulpani

TILKOT
RESERVED
FOREST

Public Toilet Tea House, Telephone

Cha Khola

Manahara Kh.

**CHANGU
NARAYAN**

Deurali
Bhanjyang

BAGESHWARI
RESERVED
FOREST

View of Langtang Range

Nayagaon

Nil Barahi

Jhaukhel

Fair in Janai
Purnima

Rohini Bhanjyang

Bode

Army Barrack

Radha Krishna Temple

Maha Laxmi

Ghimiregaon

Pati Vihar

Nagarkot View Tower

B   H   A   K   T   A   P   U   R

YAPUR) THIMI

Kamalbinayak

Nytapol

BHAKTAPUR

Anaikot

Kaasi Bhanjyang

Devitar

Bhaktapur Durbar
Square   Jagati   Brick Factory

Chokhu Khola

Pemaa Chholing Gomba

larahi

Army Barrack

Bhagwati Temple

Tanchowk

Gamcha

Suryabinayak

NALA

Rabi

SURYABINAYAK

Nangkhel

Opi

HU

axmi Temple

SANGA

Narayan

Rabi Bhanjyang

hu Bus Stop

Sanga Bhanjyang

Chandeshwari

Lamatar

BANEPA

Dhungeni Bus Stop

Ghyampedanda

Kankrabari

Banepa Bus Park

Thakurigaon

Ranikot Bhanjyang

Army Barrack

Dhulikhel Lodge Resort

Lakuri Bhanjyang

Dhulikhel Bus Park

Gaukuleshwar

Phuldi Khola

DHULIKHEL

al

Godawari Kunda

Manedobhan

Thumki

Chamkhar

CDO Offife, NETIF Office Kalika Temple
Chamber of Commerce Kabre
Red Cross Training Centre Bhanjyang

ARI

Sipilethok

audhara Mandir

Chapakharka

Taukhal

Dalinchowk

Faskot

Phulbari

Army Barrack

Bramhayani

PANAUTI

Shangkheshwari

PHULCHOKI PEAK

N

KHOPASI   Pasthali   **NAMO BUDDHA**

1   2   3 klms

Scale 1:200.000

BALTHALI

Naudhara Mandir

Phulchowki Khola

Puntanchha Khola

Rosi Khola

Gandi Khola

Anai Khola

Chhether Khola

Sunkoshi Khola

TO BARHABISE, KODARI

TO SINDHULI

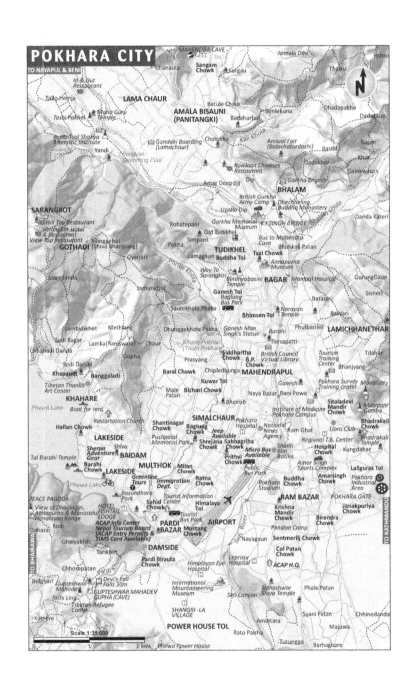

POKHARA CITY

TO NAYAPUL & BENI

MAHENDRA CAVE
Chanaute Sangam Chowk Kargau Armala Dihi Pabro
Thaiku

In & Out Restaurant
Tallo Hemja
Tashi Pakhet
Mahu Guru Temple
Benfial Sal Shakya Monastic Institute
Yandi
Penghan Swimming Pool

LAMA CHAUR
Batule Chaur
AMALA BISAUNI (PANITANGKI)
Badaharbot
Simlekuna
Dhadapakha
Dadagaun

Gandaki Boarding (Lamachaur) Chandika
Kali Khola
Annual Fair (Balachaturdashi)
Bastal
Najim
Khor

Kowloon Chineses Restaurant
Dadakhor
Gairiswara x

Amar Deep Dip Gorkha English
BHALAM

British Gurkha Army Camp
Upallo Dip
Dhechhiling Buddha Monastery
Seti Khola
Danda Kateri

SARANGKOT
Hill Top Restaurant
Sarangkot Hotel & Restaurant
View Top Restaurant
GOTHADI Silingeebot (Shiva Bhanjyang)
Gyarjati

Rohatepani
Gorkha Memorial Museum
Old Tudikhel
Simpani
Pakha
Lamagaun Buddha Tol

K.I SINGH BRIDGE
Bus to Mahendra Cave
Bhimkali Patan
Taxi Chowk
Annapurna Museum

Haredanda
Jamunghot
Pokha
Way To Sarangkot
Bindhyabasini Temple
Ganesh Tol
Baglung Bus Park

BAGAR Manipal Hospital
GurungGaun
Sisneri

Phirke Khola
Saurekhola Phaka
Bhimsen Tol
Narayan Temple
Batase
Baiyari

Lambidikhet Methlang
Sedi Bagar
Lamka(Raniswara) Chaur
Chhadi Danda
Gupha

Dhunggekhola Pakha Ganesh Man Singh's Statue
Khudi Pokhari (Thulo Pokhari)
Barahi
Tersapatti
Phulbarika
LAMICHHANETHAR
Tilahar

Sedi Danda
Khapaudi Banggaladi
Tibetan Thanka Art Center
KHAHARE
Phewa Lake Boat for rent

Prasyang
Baral Chowk Chipledhunga
Male Patan
Bichari Chowk

Siddhartha Chowk
B.P. Chowk
Kuwar Tol
Naya Bazar
Bhairav

British Council Virtual Library
MAHENDRAPUL
Ganesh
Rani Powa

Tourism Training Center
Bhanjyang
Pokhara Survey Training center Monastery
Sitaladevi Mandir Chowk
Matepani Gumba

Restoration Church
Hallan Chowk
LAKESIDE
Sherpa Adventure Gear
Shiva
BAIDAM
Barahi Chowk
Tal Barahi Temple
LAKESIDE

Shantinagar Chowk
Pushpalal Memorial Park
SIMALCHAUR
Baglung Chowk
Jeep Available
Shrejana Chowk
Pokhara Hospital
Sabhagriha Chowk
Prithvi Chowk
Micro Bus Available

National News Agency
Ram Ghat
Shanti Ban Batika

Institute of Medicine Pokhara Campus
Lions Club
Regional T.B. Center
Hospital Chowk
Bhadrakali Chowk
Bhadrakali Temple
Kungdahar

Amar Singh Sports Complex
Laliguras Tol

MULTHOK Milan Chowk
Greenline Tours
Immigration Dept.
Basundhara Park
Ratna Chowk
Public Bus Park
Buddha Chowk
Pokhara Stadium
Amarsingh Chowk
Pokhara Industrial Area

Phewa Lake

PEACE PAGODA
View of Dhaulagiri, Annapurna & Manasalu Himalayan Range
Dahara
Kodi
Ghaiyakhet
HOTEL FISHTAIL LODGE
ACAP Info Center
Nepal Tourism Board (ACAP Entry Permits & TIMS Card Available)

Sahid Chowk
Tourist Information Center
Himalaya Tol
Tourist Bus Park
PARDI BAZAR
Mustang Chowk
AIRPORT

Krishna Mandir Chowk
RAM BAZAR POKHARA GATE
Janakpuriya Chowk
Birendra Chowk
Pension Camp

Tarikket
DAMSIDE
Pardi Birauta Chowk
Nayagaun
Sentmerij Chowk

Chhoepatan
Belghari Gupteshwar Mahadev
Devi's Fall
Falls 30m
GUPTESHWAR MAHADEV GUPHA (CAVE)
Tashi Ling
Tibetan Refugee Camp
Kampre

Himalayan Eye Hospital
Leprosy Hospital
ACAP H.Q.
Col Patan Chowk

International Mountaineering Museum
Sidheshwor Shiva Temple
Phale Patan

SHANGRI-LA VILLAGE
Seti Canyon
Amintara
Syani Patan
Chhinedanda

Scale 1:35 000
0 2 kms Phewa Power House
POWER HOUSE TOL
Rato Pairha
Tutungga
Majuwa
Barhaghare

TO BHAIRAWA

TO KATHMANDU

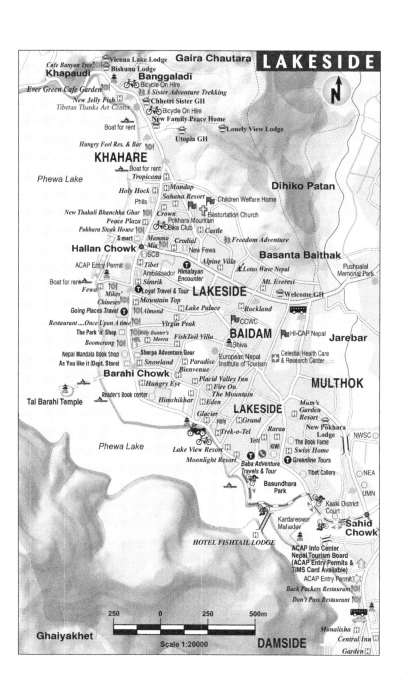

LAKESIDE

Cafe Banyan Tree
Vienna Lake Lodge
Gaira Chautara
Khapaudi
Bishunu Lodge
Banggaladi
Ever Green Cafe Garden
Bicycle On Hire
3 Sister Adventure Trekking
New Jelly Fish
Chhetri Sister GH
Tibetan Thanka Art Center
Bicycle On Hire
New Family Peace Home
Boat for rent
Lonely View Lodge
Utopia GH
Hungry Feel Res. & Bar
KHAHARE
Boat for rent
Tropicana
Phewa Lake
Holy Hock
Mandap
Dihiko Patan
Sahana Resort
Phils
Children Welfare Home
New Thakali Bhanchha Ghar
Crown
Restoration Church
Peace Plaza
Pokhara Mountain
Pokhara Steak House
Bike Club
Castle
S-mart
Mamma
Crodial
Freedom Adventure
Hallan Chowk
Mia
New Fewa
Basanta Baithak
Tibet
Alpine Villa
ACAP Entry Permit
Lotus Wave Nepal
Pushpalal
Ambassador
Himalayan
Memorial Park
Boat for rent
Simrik
Encounter
Mt. Everest
Fewa
Loyal Travel & Tour
LAKESIDE
Welcome GH
Mikes'
Mountain Top
Chineses
Almond
Lake Palace
Rockland
Going Places Travel
Virgin Peak
CCWC
Restaurant ....Once Upon A time
Billy Bunter's
BAIDAM
HI-CAP Nepal
Jarebar
The Park 'n' Shop
HBL
Meera
FishTail Villa
Shiva
Boomerang
Sherpa Adventure Gear
Nepal Mandala Book Shop
Snowland
Paradise
European Nepal
Celestial Health Care
As You like it (Dept. Store)
Bienvenue
Institute of Tourism
& Research Center
Barahi Chowk
Placid Valley Inn
Fire On
MULTHOK
Hungry Eye
The Mountain
Mum's
Tal Barahi Temple
Reader's Book center
Himshikhar
Eden
Garden
Resort
Glacier
LAKESIDE
New Pokhara
Holy
Grand
Lodge
Phewa Lake
Trek-o-Tel
Raraa
Yeti
The Book Fame
NWSC
Lake View Resort
KIWI
Swiss Home
Moonlight Resort
Baba Adventure
Greenline Tours
Travels & Tour
Tibet Gallery
NEA
Basundhara
Park
UMN
Kaski District
Court
Kardareswor
Mahadev
Sahid
Chowk
HOTEL FISHTAIL LODGE
ACAP Info Center
Nepal Tourism Board
(ACAP Entry Permits &
TIMS Card Available)
ACAP Entry Permit
Back Packers Restaurant
Ghaiyakhet
Don't Pass Restaurant

250   0   250   500m

Monalisha
Central Inn
DAMSIDE
Garden

Scale 1:20000

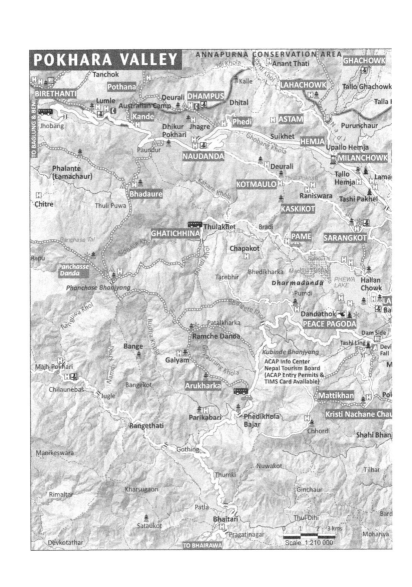

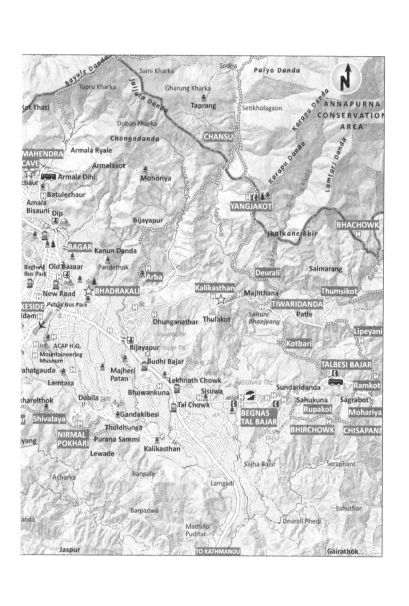

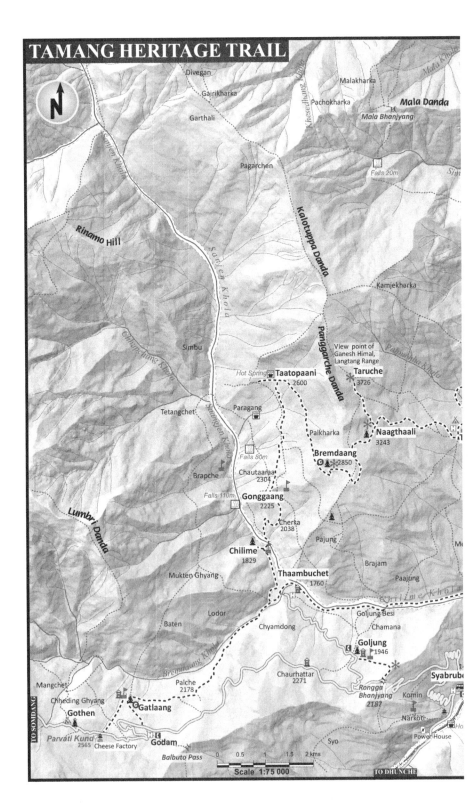

TAMANG HERITAGE TRAIL

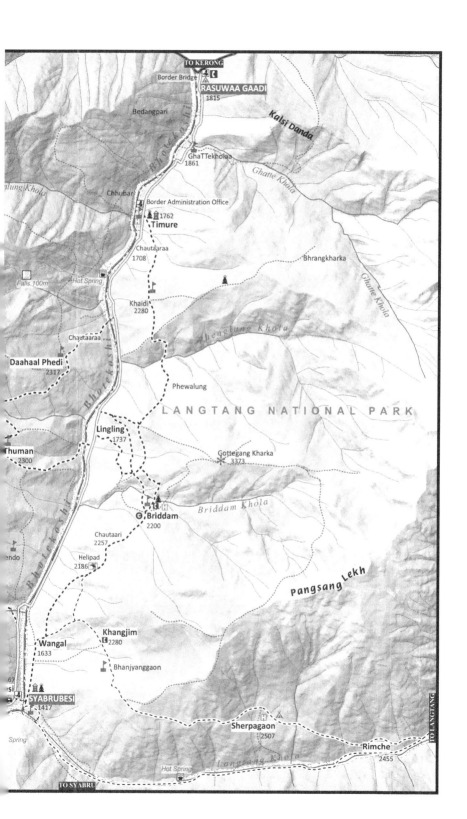

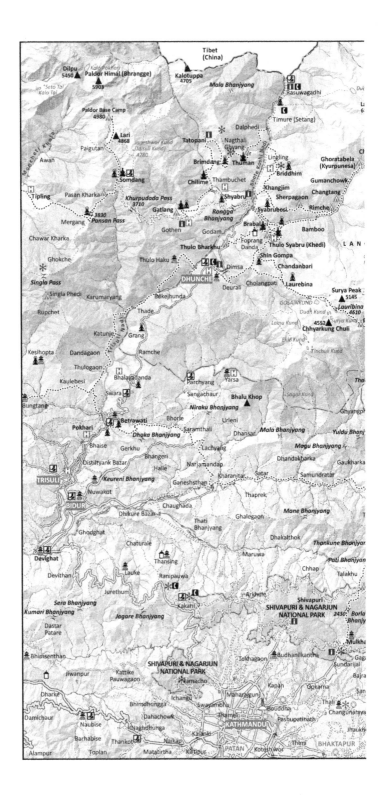

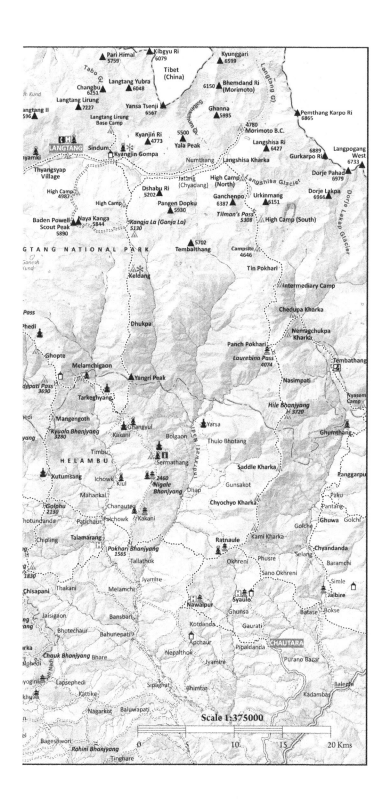

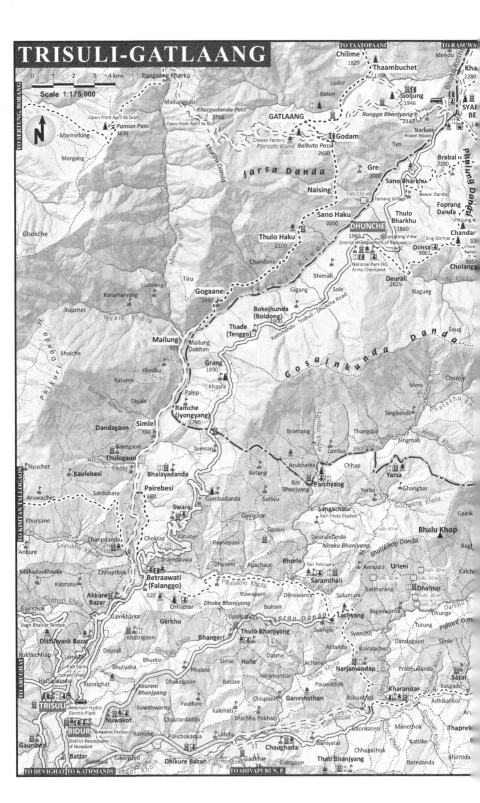

TRISULI-GATLAANG

about the author

Alonzo Lyons is co-author of Trekking Nepal (Mountaineers Books, 2011) and writes for magazines, newspapers and online editions, chiefly about Nepal and greater Asia.

He was born and raised in the developing world named planet earth and grew up in the northwest of North America, where potato fields extend as far as the imagination can dream. His work experience includes such non-lucrative positions as wildland firefighter, YMCA basketball referee, chemotherapeutics research technician and eventually a stint at an Idaho winery.

He first came to Nepal in the mid-1990s and returns every available chance. Lyons has spent many formative years in *Ajia*, a home away from home, where wages might be low but "Gross National Happiness" is relatively high (notwithstanding occasional pogroms). Although conversational in Nepali, Thai, and Japanese, he is skillful at mispronunciation, too.

He has an ornamental master's degree in epidemiology, the result of an injudicious decision to attend Stanford University and become heavily shackled to debt. Nowadays, Lyons is attracted to Iyengar style yoga, aroused during a visit to Rishikesh, India, where the Mother Ganga emerges from the Himalaya. He also "contemplates his navel" (meditates), mostly Mahasi Sayadaw style; the wandering mind typically has the best of it during internal liaisons. He is currently trying to get around being his own mightiest nemesis while drifting through the Milky Way nomad's land (on the far side of Nearer Vanna) and taking the long way home.

www.namasteguidebooks.com

Made in the USA
Coppell, TX
18 September 2022

83324415R00105